STUDIES IN
BEAUMONT, FLETCHER, AND MASSINGER

Studies in
BEAUMONT, FLETCHER, AND MASSINGER

By

BALDWIN MAXWELL

1966

OCTAGON BOOKS, INC.

New York

Reprinted 1966
by special arrangement with The University of North Carolina Press

OCTAGON BOOKS, INC.
175 FIFTH AVENUE
NEW YORK, N.Y. 10010

LIBRARY OF CONGRESS CATALOG CARD NUMBER: 66-18038

Printed in U.S.A. by
NOBLE OFFSET PRINTERS, INC.
NEW YORK 3, N. Y.

63710

Preface

OF THE SEVENTEEN studies which are printed in this volume, eight appear for the first time. The others, with a varying amount of change, are reprinted from periodicals. To the editors and publishers of these periodicals, I wish to express my thanks for their permission to reprint and for the opportunity to re-examine and, at times, revise my earlier views. "*The Knight of the Burning Pestle* and *Wily Beguiled*" is reprinted from *Modern Language Notes,* as are also the studies of *The Noble Gentleman* and *The Night-walker*—the former with a great many additions and the latter much as it originally appeared. "*Love's Pilgrimage* and Its Relation to *The New Inn*" appeared first in the number of *Studies in Philology* entitled *Royster Memorial Studies,* 1931. The first part of the discussion of *Henry VIII* is reprinted from *The Manly Anniversary Studies,* 1923, and the second part from *Modern Philology.* In *Modern Philology* also appeared, in shorter form, the paper on *The Woman's Prize.* Three of the studies are reprinted, with additions, from *The Philological Quarterly:* "The Hungry Knave in the Beaumont and Fletcher Plays," "*Wit without Money,*" and "The Date of *The Pilgrim.*"

I wish also to express my thanks to Dean George D. Stoddard of the Graduate College of the University of Iowa, a generous grant from whose budget made this volume possible.

Contents

STUDIES IN
BEAUMONT, FLETCHER,
AND MASSINGER

I

The Alternate Titles, Dramatis Personae, and Lists of Actors Appearing in the Second Folio

MANY WHO have discussed the Beaumont and Fletcher plays have drawn certain conclusions from assumptions which need to be checked. It has been assumed that the presence of subtitles or alternate titles is an indication of a play's having undergone revision; that omissions or confusion in the dramatis personae as given in the Second Folio likewise indicate revision; and that the lists of actors accompanying certain plays in the Second Folio are the lists of the original performers and hence indicate both the company by which a play was first performed and the date of this first performance.

I

THE ALTERNATE TITLES

In discussing the date of *Love's Cure*, Mr. Oliphant observes that "Another token of the play's having been rewritten is afforded by its double title. The plays to which double titles are given in either folio are *The Woman's Prize, Rollo, Love's Cure, Philaster, The Night-walker,* and *The Nice Valour;* and there is not one of these that is to be considered as wholly of one date."[1] Similarly in writing of *The Bloody Brother*, he notes that "Its alternative title ('Rollo') serves to show that there were two versions of it."[2] Without denying that any of the Beaumont and Fletcher plays having double titles underwent revision, one may certainly question the statement that the presence of a double title "serves to show that there were two versions" or even revision.

That the dramatic companies did at times seek to profit by deceiving the public with a new name for an old play is proved

[1] E. H. C. Oliphant, *The Plays of Beaumont and Fletcher* (New Haven and London, 1927), p. 420.   [2] *Ibid.*, p. 458.

by an entry in the records of Sir Henry Herbert: "Received of ould Cartwright for allowing the [Fortune] company to add scenes to an ould play, and to give it out for a new one, this 12th of May, 1636 – £1.0.0";[3] and by two passages with which Dr. Adams elucidates the entry, the opening line of the prologue to *The False One,* "New titles warrant not a play for new," and a sentence from Donald Lupton's *London and the Countrey Carbonadoed and Quartered* (1632), "The players are as crafty with an old play as bauds with old faces; the one puts on a fresh colour, the other a new face and name." But that not all double titles originated in such trickery and deceit is shown by the large number of academic Latin plays which have them, such as *Bellum Grammaticale sive Nominum Verborumque Discordia Civilis, Thibaldus sive Vindictae Ingenium, Tomumbeius sive Sultanici in Aegypto Imperii Everso,* etc., many of which were possibly never acted and few of which were probably ever revived or revised. Not viewed as substitutes, the alternate titles of these plays are rather intended as elaborations or explanations. With the same explanatory purpose Jonson uses alternate titles for *Volpone or The Fox, Epicoene or The Silent Woman.* Less explanatory are the alternate titles of *The Fountain of Self-Love, or Cynthia's Revels,* and *Poetaster, or The Arraignment;* yet, as both of these plays were published with double titles within a year of their first performance, it is most unlikely that there could have been much revision or any intention to deceive. Some poets, indeed, like William Percy, seem to have preferred a double title. It can hardly be doubted that Percy's four plays preserved in manuscript were never revived, and as he in his stage directions indicates certain things to be done if the plays be presented by "Actors" and suggests modification that may be made if they are presented by "Powles," the natural assumption is that at the time the texts were prepared the plays had never been acted. Yet all four plays have double titles.

Among the plays licensed by Herbert there are many, of course, with alternate titles, some of which he notes as old while

[3] *The Dramatic Records of Sir Henry Herbert,* ed. Joseph Quincy Adams (New Haven, 1917), p. 37.

others he labels new.   Finally, such a manuscript play as *The lanchinge of the Mary, Or the seamans honest wyfe*, "written by .W:M. gent. in his returne from East India. āo. 1632," and bearing the license of Sir Henry Herbert "27. June. 1633," indicates that a double title might be assumed before a play had ever been performed.

In addition to the six Beaumont and Fletcher plays which, as has been said, carry double titles in one of the folios, there were several others which seem at times to have passed under other names than those given them in the folios. *The Woman Hater* was in 1649 given the subtitle *The Hungry Courtier;* *Monsieur Thomas* was *c.* 1661 published as *Fathers own Son;* the manuscript of *The Humorous Lieutenant* is headed *Demetrius and Enanthe;* and late in the century the same play appeared with the subtitle *Generous Enemies.* Compared to the plays of other dramatists, however, the number of Beaumont and Fletcher plays with double titles is not large, and the frequent use of the double titles for new plays during the period renders unwarranted the assumption that such titles "serve to show that there were two versions" of all Beaumont and Fletcher plays having them.

2

THE DRAMATIS PERSONAE

The dramatis personae and the lists of actors appeared in most instances first in the Second Folio of 1679, and illustrate the desire for completeness to which the publishers refer in their address "To the Reader." After noting that this edition contains "several Prologues and Epilogues, with the songs appertaining to each Play, which were not in the former Edition," and "Seventeen Plays more than were in the former," the Booksellers ask the reader to observe that "whereas in several of the Plays [in the earlier folio] there were wanting the Names of the persons represented therein, in this Edition you have them all prefixed, with their Qualities; which will be a great ease to the Reader." As a matter of fact, however, the First Folio includes no list of persons represented, although every one of the plays which had appeared in the First Folio is in the Second accompanied by such a list. Before the omissions and the confusion of these lists may be viewed as evidence for revision of certain plays, inquiry should be made into the origin of the lists.

Although the title-page of the Second Folio states, as had that of the folio of 1647, that the plays have been "Published by the Author's Original Copies," there is every reason to believe that the printers in 1679 did not possess any manuscripts of the plays. The statement is simply reprinted verbatim from the earlier title-page. Had they had any manuscripts, they would hardly have failed to call attention to them in boasting the correctness of their text. Their corrections they attribute to another source:

And we were very opportunely informed of a Copy which an ingenious and worthy Gentleman had taken the pains (or rather the pleasure) to read over; wherein he had all along Corrected several faults (some very gross) which had crept in by the frequent imprinting of them. His Corrections were the more to be valued, because he had an intimacy with both our Authors, and had been a Spectator of most of them when they were Acted in their lifetime. This therefore we resolved to purchase at any Rate; and accordingly with no small cost obtain'd it. From the same hand also we received several Prologues and Epilogues, with the Songs appertaining to each Play, which were not in the former Edition, but are now inserted in their proper places.

Similarly the seventeen plays which had been omitted from the First Folio are, the Booksellers tell us, "Print[ed] out of 4to in this Volume."

But even if we accept the unlikely hypothesis that the publishers had indeed the theater manuscripts of the plays which they reprinted, it is not probable that they would have found in them either lists of actors or dramatis personae. Few of the manuscripts which have survived seem to contain lists of the persons represented, and when such a list does appear, the usual assumption would be that the manuscript had been prepared for the printer. Of the nineteen manuscript plays, reprints or descriptions of which I have at hand, only four contain a list of personae:[4] *The Welsh Embassador*, *The Faithful Friends*, the amateurish *The Lanchinge of the Mary*, and *Two Noble Ladies*. To the confused list of *The Faithful Friends*, I shall refer later. Of the fourth of these manuscripts, *Two Noble Ladies*, the editor of the Malone Society reprint writes:

The verso of this leaf [the title-page occupying the recto] was originally left blank, but was subsequently filled by a second title and a list of personae in another hand. This hand is considerably later in appearance than that of the text, though there need not in fact be much difference of date between them. . . . The form of this title, and the list of 'The Actors Names' that follows, very strongly suggest that they were added with a view to publication.[5]

In the list preceding the manuscript of *The Faithful Friends*, according to Dr. Tannenbaum, "Marius was first described as 'Brother' to Lelia, but 'Brother' was struck out, and 'Friend of Tullius and Lover of Leelia' substituted."[6] Dr. Tannenbaum correctly observes that this and other changes cannot be copyist's errors and corrections. His suggestion is, therefore, that the changes were the work of the author, to which Mr. Oliphant appends the query, "May they not, however, possibly be a reviser's?"[7] Both of these suggestions seem equally unacceptable. Unless the story of the earlier play was completely different from that of the play we have, the changes certainly could not have been introduced by a reviser. Neither would the author have been likely to confuse such relationships as brother and lover. His doing so could be understood only if he wrote Marius thinking he had written Tullius; but as Tullius is the principal figure in the play and the rôle of Lelia comparatively small, Tullius would hardly have been described by the author as Lelia's brother. The only logical explanation of the error and correction would seem to be that the list was constructed

[4] Those without dramatis personae: *Believe as you list*, *Sir Thomas More*, *Game at Chess* (4 MSS), *Parliament of Love*, *Second Maiden's Tragedy*, *John a Kent and John a Cumber*, *The Captives*, *The Elder Brother*, *Edmond Ironsides*, *Humorous Lieutenant*, *Richard II* (*Woodstock*), *Charlemagne* (*The Distracted Emperor*).

[5] Malone Society Reprint, edited by Rebecca G. Rhoads, 1930, p. vii.

[6] Quoted from private correspondence by Oliphant, *op. cit.*, p. 361.

[7] *Ibid.*

neither by the author nor by a reviser, but by one commissioned to prepare the manuscript, if not for the press, at least for the reader.

Neither is it likely that the origin of the dramatis personae in the Beaumont and Fletcher folio is to be traced to "plots" or other memoranda of the theater. The most frequent omissions are the mute characters and the crowds, which would of course be the very entries most essential in the theater. Clearly the printing of the names of the characters who were to appear was regarded merely as what the Booksellers termed an "ease to the Reader." Even so, comparatively few of the early quartos are equipped with them. Some of the Beaumont and Fletcher quartos have them; some do not. Although none was given for the thirty-three plays in the First Folio, when these plays were reprinted in the Second Folio every one of them was equipped with a list of dramatis personae. Moreover, it seems quite clear that all thirty-three[8] of these lists were prepared at the same time and according to a definite plan.

Of the fifty-one plays in the Second Folio, for only five are no dramatis personae given.[9] The lists before six other plays differ from the generally adopted form either in giving no identifications for the characters or in intermingling the feminine characters with the masculine;[10] while five others, though grouping the women together, do not set them apart under the heading "Women,"[11] two of the five placing the women ahead of the nameless extras. The lists before the remaining thirty-five are identically prepared. Under the caption "Persons Represented in the Play" are listed first the male characters, then the nameless, and then the female under the heading "Women." All thirty-three of the plays from the First Folio are among

---

[8] Although the Booksellers of the Second Folio claim to add only seventeen plays to those reprinted from the First Folio, they really add eighteen. No asterisk is placed beside *The Wild-Goose Chase* to designate that it, first published in 1652, was omitted from the folio of 1647.

[9] *Faithful Shepherdess, Rule a Wife, M. Thomas, Thierry and Theodoret,* and *The Woman Hater.*

[10] *Maid's Tragedy, The Scornful Lady, Knight of the Burning Pestle, The Nightwalker, The Coronation, Two Noble Kinsmen.*

[11] *Philaster, The Elder Brother, King and No King, Wit without Money, The Wild-Goose Chase.*

these thirty-five. Their uniformity renders it practically certain, therefore, that the lists did not originate in the theater but were later prepared from a copy of the folio of 1647, probably no earlier than 1679.

Finally, many of the inaccuracies in the dramatis personae are of a sort which cannot be explained by assuming that the plays have undergone revision, but only by recognizing that the lists were drawn up, sometimes with very little effort, by one only vaguely familiar with the plays, who at times, wearying of the task assigned him, constructed a list by merely glancing at the pages and without reading the play in its entirety. Dr. McKerrow has noted, for instance, that in the list of characters preceding *The Spanish Curate* Angelo Milanes is regarded as two persons, Angelo and Milanes.[12] Similar confusion marks the list before *The Noble Gentleman*, where Marine is listed both as Monsieur Marine and as Duke, and like errors occur in many of the lists.

Obviously, the omissions and confusion in the dramatis personae are of no value in questions of revision. The chances are that none of the lists (unless it be that of *The Wild-Goose Chase*, published for the actors in 1652) had its origin from the playwrights or from one connected with the theater. Certainly those for the thirty-three plays reprinted from the First Folio owe their existence only to the desire of their publishers in 1679 to make the folio complete and to furnish "ease to the Reader."

3

THE LISTS OF ACTORS

The lists of actors which appear before a number of plays in the Second Folio may not, however, be so easily dismissed as without authority. Unlike the dramatis personae, these lists could not without records have been compiled by a clerk from the plays themselves. Moreover, their inclusion could have added little contemporary interest to the volume of 1679, for most of the actors' names could have meant little or nothing

---

[12] *The Works of Beaumont and Fletcher*, Variorum Edition, ed. A. H. Bullen (London, 1904-12), II, 122.

to the readers of that time. The publishers, therefore, having no reason to deceive, may safely be assumed to have had some record of each cast published. Scholars have always so assumed, and in the belief that in most cases these lists represent the cast of the original performance, have from them determined the dates and stage history of many of the plays.

To what extent this view of the lists has entered into the history of the plays may be seen by examining an hypothesis of Mr. Oliphant. Of the fifty-one plays in the Second Folio, twenty-five are preceded by a list of actors, twenty-four of them being plays reprinted from the First Folio and the twenty-fifth being *The Wild-Goose Chase*, which the actors themselves had published in 1652 with the names of the twelve actors who had taken the principal parts in it. Of the thirty-eight plays in the Second Folio known to have belonged at one time or another to the King's Men, twenty-three have lists of actors. "As every play definitely known to have been first performed by the King's and not published in quarto prior to 1647 had a list of actors attached in the second folio," Mr. Oliphant thinks we are justified "in assuming that, if these seven plays without lists, previously unpublished, had also been originally King's plays, they too would have had lists attached."[13] It may be recalled, however, that several of the plays are known to have belonged to the King's Men solely because of the attached lists of actors and that, as I shall note later, four of the lists Mr. Oliphant recognizes as suitable not for the original productions but for later revivals. To accept Mr. Oliphant's thesis that none of the previously unpublished plays not a King's play has a list, and the reverse, that every King's play has a list, it is necessary to assume that the lists originated from someone within the theater. It is difficult to believe that a manager, a prompter, or anyone else, when preparing for production a revision of an old play, would, before listing the principal actors to take part, stop to ask himself whether the play had been first produced by his company.

[13] *Op. cit.*, p. 130. Cf. A. H. Thorndike: ". . . without an actors' list, therefore probably not acted by the King's men."—*Influence of Beaumont and Fletcher on Shakspere* (Worcester, Mass., 1901), p. 72.

Even though we were to accept such careful consideration by a manager as not impossible, it would remain to be explained how such notes would have come into the possession of the publishers of the folio of 1679. There is, as I believe I have shown, no justification for assuming that the publishers possessed either manuscripts or "plots." Indeed, had they possessed both, it is hardly likely that there could have been found in them the information from which the lists might be constructed, for, although actors' names not infrequently appear in the extant manuscripts and "plots," they are generally only those of the minor actors, while the names appearing in the Beaumont and Fletcher folio are those of only the principal actors.

What, then, can be the origin of these lists of actors? Although the evidence indicates that they were not prepared from theater manuscripts or notes, there can be no doubt that they are authoritative lists of those who acted in the plays. Fleay suggested that "The names had been probably supplied by Fletcher himself."[14] To whom and for what purpose he had "supplied" them, and where they had been during the fifty-four years since Fletcher's death, Fleay does not explain. If they had been prepared by Fletcher, why were they not included in the First Folio, for the folios of both Shakespeare and Jonson had listed the principal actors? Nor does Fleay explain why Fletcher or another during his lifetime should have prepared lists of actors for only certain plays which printers would not have published in quarto within twenty-two years of his death— for only plays which, with the exception of *The Wild-Goose Chase* (printed for the actors in 1652 with a list much longer than the others), were destined to be included in the folio of 1647. The fact that every list of actors appearing first in the Second Folio is appended to a play which had been included in the First Folio argues that the lists had been made upon the basis of and perhaps as marginal notes in the folio of 1647. This view is further supported by the general similarity in form with which the lists were prepared. As the only other list of actors

[14] F. G. Fleay, *Biographical Chronicle of the English Drama*, 2 vols. (London, 1891), I, 175.

appended to a Beaumont and Fletcher play is that of the 1652 edition of *The Wild-Goose Chase,* the most likely conclusion seems to be that that list, prepared by the actors themselves, suggested similar notations to a possessor of the First Folio. The lists, therefore, would date not only after 1647, but even after 1652, although the one making the notations may have had his information from a much earlier date.

That there was at least one gentleman of that time who would have been interested in compiling such facts and entering such notations, we are told by the publishers in 1679. He was, of course, the "ingenious and worthy Gentleman" who "had taken the pains (or rather the pleasure)" to correct the faults of the First Folio, and whose "Corrections were the more to be valued, because he had an intimacy with both our Authors, and had been a Spectator of most of them when they were Acted in their life-time." He it was, also, from whom the publishers claimed to have "received several Prologues and Epilogues, with the Songs appertaining to each Play, which were not in the former Edition."[15] It would seem obvious that the Ingenious Gentleman was not an actor, but one who because of friendship or because of his interest in the drama had both corrected the text of the First Folio and gathered together much other information about the plays—possibly to indulge his interest in the theater after 1642.

If the lists are his, they may not necessarily represent the actors who performed in the original productions. The Ingenious Gentleman may, of course, have constructed the lists upon information secured from theatrical folk or, perhaps, from his friend the author. If, however, the twenty-four plays for which he furnished lists of actors represent the plays at which he "had been a Spectator . . . when they were Acted in their life-time,"

---

[15] The Second Folio does not, of course, fulfill the publishers' claim. With the plays reprinted from the First Folio are given only those prologues and epilogues which had previously appeared with them. The only important additions made in the Second Folio are certain songs, the dramatis personae for all thirty-three plays, the lists of actors, and the location of the scenes. As the scenes of action are not named in the First Folio and as the Second Folio was printed from the first, critics have not of course been justified in arguing revision from apparently confused or mistaken assignment of the action of certain plays.

he may well at times have given the names of the casts he himself had witnessed. Mr. Oliphant may, therefore, be correct—
although it contradicts his own theory—in recognizing four of
the lists[16] as suitable not for the original productions but for
later revivals, and that of *Lover's Progress* as the original cast
appended to a revision in which that cast could not have acted.

Professor T. W. Baldwin, however, apparently is willing to
accept all of the lists as those of the actors in the first performance.[17] He believes that the publishers of the folio understated
the authoritative source from which the lists were derived—
even though they obviously claimed more than was true when
they declared that the plays were printed from the authors'
original manuscripts and that several prologues and epilogues,
omitted in the earlier folio, were added here. He argues that
the Ingenious Gentleman was not what he is called in the
address "To the Reader," one who "had been a Spectator of
most of them when they were Acted in their life-time," but that
he was, indeed, an actor who had taken part in the performances
of every play to which a list was added. The plays which have
lists he dates from 1611 to 1624, all presented by the King's
Men save two which list actors belonging to the amalgamated
Rossiter-Princess company of 1613-1614. As William Ecclestone was associated with the King's Men during all of these
years save for a brief period with the Lady Elizabeth's Men
from 1611 to 1613 or 1614, Professor Baldwin thinks it was he
who sometime after 1652 entered the lists of actors in his copy
of the First Folio. Nothing is known of Ecclestone after some
time prior to June 24, 1625, when his name was omitted in the
patent granted the King's Men. Presumably, if he were still
alive, he had before that date retired from the stage. But
Baldwin sees him as the contributor some twenty-seven years
later of six rimed lines signed W. E., prefixed to the 1652
quarto of *The Wild-Goose Chase*—

a merry old gentleman of some seventy-five years, and in touch
with his old fellows, though his active connection with the company

---

[16] *Women Pleas'd, Laws of Candy, Bonduca,* and *Wild-Goose Chase.*

[17] *The Organization and Personnel of the Shakespearean Company* (Princeton.
1927), Appendix V, pp. 388-93. He does, to be sure, recognize an occasional error

had long since ceased. It seems quite probable that the actor list
of *The Wild Goose Chase* suggested a similar plan to him for the
plays of the first folio. He had thus probably amused his old age,
and instructed the younger generation by reliving the good old
days before "this late dearth of ‚wit." If so, his copy of the first
folio, which the publishers bought, almost certainly had the parts
assigned to the principal characters as in *The Wild Goose Chase*.[18]

Although it was not his intention to do so, it seems to me
that Professor Baldwin has grievously weakened the case for
these lists' having such authority as they have been assumed to
have. As I can produce no death certificate for him, I am willing to admit the possibility of the lists' having been prepared
from the notes of William Ecclestone—and to applaud the
modesty of the merry old gentleman in not assigning prominent
parts in more plays to himself. I can enjoy the irony in that
the publishers of the Second Folio, in bolstering the authority

---

[18] *Ibid.*, p. 393. The suggestion that Ecclestone was the author of these lines has
been often made. The lines, however, offer no suggestion that their author had been
an actor or had ever been in any way connected with the theater:

An Epigram upon the long lost and fortunately recovered *WILD-GOOSE
CHASE,* and as seasonably bestowed on Mr. JOHN LOWEN and Mr. JOSEPH
TAYLOR, for their best advantage.

> In this late dearth of wit, when *Jose* and *Jack*
> Were hunger-bit for want of fowl and Sack,
> His nobleness found out this happy meanes
> To mend their dyet with these *WILD-GOOSE* scenes,
> By which he hath revived in a day
> Two Poets, and two Actors with one Play.
>
> W. E.

Perhaps it is not wholly justifiable to see in the last line of this epigram an ascription
of the play to both Beaumont and Fletcher; an interest in Beaumont might be re-
awakened by the revival of a play by Fletcher alone. It may be noted, however, that
the six other signers of prefatory matter, like all modern scholars, assign the play
solely to Fletcher. The publisher, Humphrey Moseley, to be sure, declared it to be
"the noble, last, and onely remains of those incomparable dramatists," Beaumont and
Fletcher, but he is obviously referring to the quarto of *The Wild-Goose Chase* as
completing the publication of the plays of Beaumont and Fletcher, all the other of
whose previously unprinted plays he had, without distinguishing between the work of
the two men, claimed to have included in his folio of five years before. We might,
however, expect an old actor like Ecclestone to recognize a distinction, as do Lowen
and Taylor and the writers of the other commendatory verses, between a play which
Fletcher wrote alone and those in which he collaborated with Beaumont.

If Ecclestone was the author of the epigram and if he is to be identified with the
"William Eglestone" whose marriage is recorded in the register of St. Saviour's,
Southwark, on 20 February 1603, he must, as Sir Edmund Chambers remarks, have
lived to be an old man.—*The Elizabethan Stage,* 4 vols. (Oxford, 1923), II, 315.

of their volume with several false claims, overlooked or were unaware of the identity of the Ingenious Gentleman, whose earlier history could have truly given the volume the authority they wished.

Whether it was William Ecclestone or another who prepared the lists, it is almost certain that the idea of constructing such lists was conceived after the appearance of *The Wild-Goose Chase* in 1652, in which play the actors named were not the cast of the original performance but that of the revival of 1631. If it was Ecclestone who prepared the lists, would it not have been natural, even inevitable, that he should name the actors who participated in a revival while he was a member of the company even though the play had been presented earlier with a somewhat different cast? And above all, would he, twenty-eight years or more after leaving the theater and forty to fifty years after the plays were presented, stop before listing the actors of a performance he remembered, to ask himself whether the particular play had been originally presented by his company or by another? Why should an old actor "reliving the good old days" sharply differentiate between plays first presented by his company and plays which his company had presented only after earlier production by another group? I cannot believe he would.

To what extent, then, may the lists of actors be of value in revealing the dates and the stage history of the plays to which they are prefixed? If we are willing to put complete trust in the memory[19] and the accuracy of the "ingenious and worthy Gentleman," we may assume that each play with a list was acted by the company at a date at which the actors named were members of that company; we may not assume what was not claimed —that the cast was necessarily the original cast or that the company was necessarily the original producer.

[19] But we cannot put *complete* trust in his memory. He includes Nicholas Toolie among the actors in *Wife for a Month*, although that play was not licensed until 27 May 1624, almost a full year after Toolie's death. "The register of St. Giles's, Cripplegate, records the burial of 'Nicholas Tooley, gentleman, from the house of Cuthbert Burbidge, gentleman,' on 5 June 1623."—Chambers, *op. cit.*, II, 347. Toolie's will, dated 3 June 1623, made bequests to several fellow actors and named "my good friend Mr. Cuthbert Burbadge (in whose house I do now lodge)."—*Ibid.*, pp. 346-47.

II

The Knight of the Burning Pestle
and Wily Beguiled

Among the interesting features of *The Knight of the Burning Pestle* are the references and allusions made to other plays of the day. Many of these have been noted, but no one, I believe, has called attention to a striking series of parallels between *The Knight* and *A Pleasant Comedie Called Wily Begvilde*. The parallels are found in scenes xiv and xvi of *Wily*, and Act I, scene ii, and Act II, scenes iv and v, of *The Knight*.

1. In *Wily Beguiled* the heroine (Lelia) has given her love to a poor scholar (Sophos), but her father, despising the scholar's poverty, has sworn to marry her to a rich farmer's son (Peter Plodall).

In *The Knight of the Burning Pestle* the heroine (Luce) has given her love to the poor prentice (Jasper), but her father has determined that she shall marry the richer Humphry.

2. In both plays the heroine escapes to her favored lover by pretending to elope with a less fortunate suitor. (In *The Knight* the tool is Humphry; in Wily it is Churms, the lawyer, who has been wooing Lelia for himself while employed to advance the suit of Peter Plodall.)

3. In both plays the elopement is through a forest, on the other side of which the heroine claims to have a friend whose home is to be their destination.

4. In both the elopement through the forest is at night.

5. In *Wily* the Nurse tells Lelia that her brother swears

> That he will venture all,
> Both fame and bloud, and limme and life,
> But *Lelia* shall be *Sophos* wedded wife. [Ll. 1732-34.]

Before setting forth upon what he thinks an elopement, Humphry declares,

> I am resolv'd to venter life and lim
> For one so yong, so faire, so kind, so trim. [I, ii, 128-29.]

6. In both plays, after the heroine has led him to the place in the forest where she has arranged to meet the favored lover, the rejected suitor is given a severe beating.

7. When their supposed elopement is interrupted and the girls taken from them, the exclamations of Churms and Humphry are much the same:

Churms. You wrong me much to rob me of my loue.   [L. 2109.]
Humph. If it be so, my friend, you use me fine.   [II, iv, 22.]

8. In both instances the beating is spoken of as a "payment" (l. 2138 and II, iv, 29).

9. Both girls scoff at their rejected suitors:

Lelia. (*To Churms*) I must confesse I would have chosen you,
   But that I nere beheld your legs till now:
   Trust me I neuer lookt so low before.   [Ll. 2123 ff.]
Luce. Alas, poor Humphrie,
   Get thee some wholsome broth, with sage and comfrie;
   A little oile of roses and a feather
   To noint thy backe withall. . . .
   Fare-well, my pretty nump; I am verie sorrie
   I cannot beare thee companie.   [II, iv, 31-37.]

10. In *Wily Beguiled* Robin Goodfellow, Churms's accomplice, is dressed in a calfskin and, like Churms, receives a severe beating. In *The Knight* Raph, when he attempts to act as Humphry's champion, is beaten by Jasper, who, as he administers the beating, exclaims:

> With that he stood upright in his stirrops,
> And gave the Knight of the Calve-skinne such a knocke,
> That he forsooke his horse and downe he fell. [II, v, 35-37.]

11. Robin, after his beating, takes his leave with

> The diuel himself was neuer coniur'd so;   [L. 2075.]

while Humphry, under similar circumstances, cries

> The divel's dam was ne're so bang'd in hell. [II, iv, 38.]

Although *Wily Beguiled* was probably written some years before,[1] it was first printed late in 1606, having been entered upon the Stationers' Register on November 12 of that year. None of the title-pages of the six editions printed by 1638 makes any mention of its ever having been acted. If, then, the similarities I have noted represent borrowing—and their number and diversity suggest that they do—the debtor was clearly Beaumont, for *The Knight of the Burning Pestle* alludes to Day's *Travels of Three English Brothers*, which was presented in the spring of 1607.

In dating *The Knight* critical opinion has been divided between 1607 (Blackfriars) and 1610 (Whitefriars).[2] Perhaps the echoes of *Wily Beguiled* offer a slight bit of additional evidence for the earlier date.

[1] My reasons for believing that *Wily* was written in 1601 or 1602 are presented in *Studies in Philology*, XIX (1922).

[2] The evidence is briefly summarized in E. K. Chambers, *Elizabethan Stage*, III, 220-21. Sir Edmund preferred 1607, but Mr. Oliphant has argued for 1610.—*The Plays of Beaumont and Fletcher*, pp. 169 ff.

III

The Scornful Lady

When in 1904 Professor Warwick Bond edited *The Scornful Ladie,* he declared on the strength of topical allusions, that "the date of this comedy can be fixed with tolerable certainty as 1609 or 1610."[1] In so dating the play he was in agreement with most earlier writers. Ten years later, however, Professor Gayley called attention to three passages which he thought indicated a considerably later date—a date not earlier than 1613 nor later, of course, than 1616, when the play was published in quarto. In dating the play within these limits Professor Gayley has been followed by Sir Edmund Chambers and Mr. E. H. C. Oliphant,[2] although the latter suggests that there may have been an earlier version of the comedy in 1610. Fleay called attention to an allusion to the separate binding of the *Apocrypha* —"I'le hear no more of this *Apocrypha,* bind it by it self Steward" (I, i)—a question which was under discussion during the early years of James's reign in connection with both the Authorized Version and the Douay Version. As both of these versions of the Bible were completed in 1610, Fleay thought the play must have been written prior to that time.

Although this discussion may have continued for some years afterwards, an allusion to it would appear to be most apt in 1610 or earlier, and the probability of the year 1610 is increased by the certain definite echo of Jonson's *Silent Woman* (1609), first noted by Professor Gayley. In IV, i, Elder Loveless says to Lady after her woman Abigail upbraids him: "Tie your she Otter up, Good Lady folly, she stinks worse than a Bear-baiting." There can be little doubt that this speech was, as Gayley says, "suggested by the termagant Mrs. Otter and her husband of the Bear-garden, in Jonson's *Epicoene.*"[3] It may not be wholly

---

[1] *The Works of Beaumont and Fletcher,* Variorum Edition, I, 359.

[2] C. M. Gayley, *Beaumont the Dramatist* (New York, 1914), pp. 369-70; E. K. Chambers, *Elizabethan Stage,* III, 229; E. H. C. Oliphant, *The Plays of Beaumont and Fletcher,* pp. 207-14.   [3] *Op. cit.,* p. 369.

irrelevant to observe also that in both *The Silent Woman* (IV, ii) and *The Scornful Lady* (V, i) there is a reference to the "large gentlewoman" Mary Amber, whose unusual size had been celebrated in ballad during the 1580's, and that in both these comedies, as well as in *The Woman's Prize*, laughter is sought by references to the extravagant size of nightcaps worn by certain characters.[4]

Fletcher, it should be recalled, introduced into *The Woman's Prize* (which I shall show reason to ascribe to early 1611) other allusions to *The Silent Woman* and also reminiscences of *The Alchemist*. That there may possibly be reminiscences of the latter play in *The Scornful Lady* also is suggested by the appearance of the Spanish term *Verdugo* in II, i, of *The Scornful Lady* as well as in *The Alchemist* (III, ii) and *Woman's Prize* (IV, i); while Elder Loveless' charge that his Steward in his absence has made his house a place where "your Whores, like Fairies dance their night rounds" (III, ii) recalls, at least, Dol Common's impersonation of the Queen of the Fairies.

Professor Thorndike noted that *The Scornful Lady* contained, like *The Coxcomb* (1608<>1610), an allusion to Nicholas Breton's *Madcap*; like *The Woman Hater* (printed 1607), a reference to building a hospital; and like *The Knight of the Burning Pestle* (c. 1607) [and also like *Philaster* (1608<>1610)], an allusion to the *Mirrour of Knighthood*.[5] Further, in its borrowing from *The Silent Woman*, *The Scornful Lady* is, as has been noted, like *Woman's Prize* (1611). There is also a striking verbal parallel between it and *The Captain* (1609<>1612):

> . . . marry some cast *Cleve Captain,* and sell Bottle-ale.
> [*Scornful Lady,* V, iv.]

> . . . if she prove so foolish
> To marry this cast Captain, look to find her
> . . . selling cheese and prunes,
> And retail'd Bottle-Ale.   [*Captain,* II, ii.]

[4] See pp. 36 f., and with those references compare those to Roger's nightcap: "here's the walking night-cap again" (I, i); "why you wear a Night-cap" (II, i); "never again reproach your reverend nightcap" (IV, i); etc.

[5] *The Influence of Beaumont and Fletcher on Shakspere,* p. 87.

As the reference to the binding of the *Apocrypha,* the borrowings from *The Silent Woman,* and the similarity to other plays all suggest for *The Scornful Lady* a date close to the opening of 1610, it may not be amiss to re-examine the evidence which has been the basis for the later date. First there are two references to the Cleves War, the facts about which are conveniently summarized by Professor Thorndike. To his summary I have added within brackets a sentence or two from Gardiner:

John William, Duke of Cleves, died March 25, 1609. A quarrel ensued in regard to the succession, and Leopold of Austria took possession of the capitol, Juliers. [The King of France had in April 1609 "ordered his troops to march towards the frontier, in order to assure the German Protestants that he did not intend to desert their cause" and to support his declaration that he "would not allow either Austria or Spain to establish itself at his Gates."[6] Although the matter in dispute was of less immediate importance to England, yet it might fairly be expected that "James would not be content to look on when Protestant Germany was assailed by Austria and Spain."[7]] The assassination of Henry IV of France (April, 1610) interrupted his plans against Austria, but on Sept. 1, 1610, Prince Maurice of Orange took Juliers with the aid of troops supplied by France and the English forces then in the service of the States under Sir Edward Cecil.

Both of the references to the Cleves War occur in the fifth act. In scene iii, marvelling at Morecraft's transformation from usurer to gallant, Young Loveless exclaims:

> Foot, this is stranger than an *Africk* monster,
> There will be no more talk of the *Cleve* wars
> Whilst this lasts . . .

This reference is, of course, most vague. It does not imply whether or not English forces had been engaged or open hostilities commenced. It might, in fact, have been written at almost any time after John William's death.

[6] S. R. Gardiner, *History of England, 1603-1642,* 10 vols. (London and New York, 1894-96), II, 95, who cites Carew's letter to Salisbury, April 5, 1609. *S. P. France.* [7] *Ibid.*

The second allusion to the Cleves War, however, would apparently indicate, as the scene of Fletcher's comedy is the suburbs of London, that English forces, if they had not already done so, were soon expected to engage in the war. In the passage already noted as similar to one in *The Captain*, Welford wishes that, if Martha now deserts him, she may "marry some cast *Cleve Captain*, and sell Bottle-ale." Of this Sir Edmund Chambers, following Professors Thorndike and Gayley, notes that "there can hardly have been 'cast' captains until sometime after July 1610 when English troops first took part."[8]

I am not certain that Sir Edmund is justified in assuming that a captain might not be "cast" until he had been engaged in combat. On January 9, 1610, Gregorio Barbarigo, the Venetian ambassador to Savoy, wrote to the Doge and Senate that "The States have disbanded two regiments, one French, the other English. Both immediately took service with the Princes in Cleves."[9] Less than five weeks later the two Venetian ambassadors in England wrote the Doge and Senate that "The King is disposed to employ on this service the companies of English and Scotch who are in the service of the States and who, with all who have served in the late war, are still kept on foot because of the troubles about Cleves, though they are weeded of the men past service."[10] From the last lines of this quotation it is clear that in the first months of 1610 there was in England "talk of the *Cleve* wars" and that in preparation for these likely wars the troops who had served the States, some of whom had already taken "services with the Princes in Cleves," were being weeded of the unfit. In neither of the references in the play to the Cleves War, it would seem, is there anything which would not be recognized as appropriate to the early months of 1610—the date indicated by the other references which have been noted. Nor has Sir Edmund Chambers been wholly consistent with his view that "there can hardly have been 'cast'

---

[8] *Elizabethan Stage*, III, 229.

[9] *Calendar of State Papers* (hereafter cited as *C. S. P.*), *Venetian*, XI, 407.

[10] *Ibid.*, 419. The dispatch is dated February 11, 1610.

captains until sometime after July 1610." He, for instance, assigns Field's comedy *A Woman is a Weathercock* to the winter of 1609-1610;[11] yet in that play there is also an allusion to cast Cleve Captains—similar to the allusion in *The Scornful Lady* in the suggestion that such captains were most undesirable husbands. In Act I, scene ii, of Field's play, when told that Strange, his rival for the hand of one of Worldly's daughters, is "Infinitely rich," Captain Pouts exclaims: "Then, captain, thou art cast! Would I had gone to Cleveland! Worldly loves money better than I love his daughter. I'll to some company in garrison. Good-bye."

But although these references to the Cleves War may support, rather than forbid, the assignment of the play to early 1610, there is another passage in *The Scornful Lady*, which, if it has been correctly interpreted, clearly could not have been written until several years later. It may be well to quote the passage at some length. The usurer Morecraft has come to complete the purchase of Young Loveless' land:

Mor. Captain, I shall deserve some of your love too.

Capt. Thou shalt have heart and hand too, noble *Morecraft*, if thou wilt lend me mony. I am a man of Garrison, be rul'd, and open to me those infernal gates, whence none of thy evil Angels pass again, and I will stile thee noble, nay *Don Diego*,[12] I'le woo thy *Infanta* for thee, and my Knight shall feast her with high meats, and make her apt.

Mor. Pardon me Captain, y'are beside my meaning.

Young Lo. No Mr. Morecraft, 'tis the Captains meaning I should prepare her for ye.

Capt. Or provok her. Speak my modern man, I say provoke her.

Poet. Captain, I say so too, or stir her to it.   [III, ii, 11-24.]

[11] The title-page of *A Woman is a Weathercock* (1612)—the play was entered upon the Stationers' Register 23 November 1611—states that it had been "acted before the King at Whitehall, and divers times privately at the Whitefriars by the Children of Her Majesty's Revels." Chambers (*op. cit.*, p. 313), who says that the children were not at Whitefriars in 1610-11, assigned the performance of the play at court to "the winter of 1609-10."

[12] The Second Folio, from which I quote, has a period after *Diego*, but I introduce the comma found in the quarto, as it may be more favorable to the interpretation I am inclined to reject.

Calling attention to this passage, Professor Gayley wrote:

"Diego" had, of course, been for years a generic nickname for Spaniards; but Morecraft is neither a Spaniard nor in any way associated with Spaniards. . . .

The only provocation for styling Morecraft's "widow" an Infanta in this scene of *The Scornful Ladie* is that there was much interest in London at the time in a proposed marriage between Charles, Prince of Wales, and the second daughter of Philip III of Spain, the Infanta Maria. And the conjunction of the "Infanta" with a "Don Diego" has reference to the activities of the astute Don Diego Sarmiento de Acuña who had arrived as Spanish ambassador, in 1613 [May 27], "with the express object of winning James over from his alliance with France and the Protestant powers" [Gardiner, *History of England*, Vol. II]. During 1613 Queen Anne was favouring the Spanish marriage. . . . In the latter month [May, 1614], the Lord Privy Seal, Northampton, was urging the marriage upon the King; and the King soon after had signified to Sarmiento his willingness to accept the hand of the Infanta for Charles, provided Philip of Spain should withdraw his demand for the conversion of the young prince to Catholicism. In June Sarmiento was advising Philip to close with James's offer. . . . Negotiations, broken off for a time, were resumed a few weeks after the treaty of Xanten was signed; and with varying success Don Diego was still pursuing his object in December 1615. . . . Gardiner tells us, moreover, that "for some time" before Diego was created Count Gondomar in 1617 "he had been pertinaciously begging for a title that would satisfy the world that his labours had been graciously accepted by his master."[13]

Professor Gayley has presented his interpretation of the passage in a very skillful and convincing manner. But even though we accept his interpretation—and I am not convinced that we must—it hardly seems sufficient evidence for dating *The Scornful Lady* as late as 1613-1616. As all the other of the many allusions in the play would have been most apt in early 1610 and many of them stale and inappropriate by 1613, the natural assumption would be that the play was written in 1610 and that the allusion to Don Diego Sarmiento de Acuña—if such an al-

[13] *Op. cit.*, pp. 371 ff.

lusion was indeed intended—was inserted at some later time, at some time after 1613. But there are, I think, good reasons for questioning whether the dramatist intended an allusion to Sarmiento and the proposed marriage of Prince Charles and the Infanta Maria.

In the first place, the situation is not the same. In the play Morecraft ("Don Diego") is himself the suitor for the hand of the Widow ("Infanta") of a rich grocer, and she has declared that she will have him for a husband only after he has been knighted; he is not, as was Sarmiento, offering her hand to another. Again, the obvious coarseness of the passage makes it unlikely that the dramatist intended the audience to identify the "Infanta" with the daughter of the King of Spain who might soon become the Princess of Wales. Professor Gayley's interpretation rests entirely, of course, upon the identification of "Don Diego" with Don Diego Sarmiento de Acuña. Such an identification must at best remain doubtful. As Professor Gayley himself noted, "Diego" had long been a generic nickname for a Spaniard, and if it be taken in that sense, the use of "Infanta" needs no explanation, for, having used the one Spanish term, the dramatist might naturally use another to designate one whom the "Diego" was anxious to marry. With "Diego" in a generic sense, one may even see in the Captain's speech—though I think he would be quite wrong in doing so— an allusion to the discussions for some years prior to his death in 1612 of a Spanish bride for Prince Henry. But how can "Don Diego" be taken in a generic sense? Apparently Morecraft is, as Professor Gayley said, "neither a Spaniard nor in any way associated with Spaniards." The word seems, however, to have had some derived meaning which is not today immediately obvious. Morecraft, be it remembered, is a usurer who at the moment the Captain speaks is craftily engaged in buying property at a small fraction of its value. Although the Captain is eager for the deal to be consummated and would himself like to borrow money from Morecraft, he, as well as the audience, recognizes Morecraft as a villainous usurer. There would be good humor in the Captain's remark if in saying "I will stile thee noble, nay *Don Diego*," he used a term which might carry a connotation of scorn. The *New English Dictionary*, indeed, cites only such uses (under *Don* 1c):

1607 Webster, *Hist. Sir T. Wyat* . . . A Dondego is a kind of Spanish stockfish, or poor John.

c. 1626 *Dick of Devon* II. iv in Bullen's *O. Pl.* II. 39 Now Don Diego . . or Don Divell, I defye thee.

And the only definition given is:

Don Diego, a name for a Spaniard (cf. *Diego*); hence *Don Diego v.,* to cheat or 'do' (*obs.*).

The earliest illustration cited for this last use is from *The Tatler,* 1709: "Why you look as if you were Don Diego'd to the Tune of a Thousand Pounds"; but the use of the term as a verb gives evidence of its having long been used as a noun. With the term used in this sense, there would be excellent humor in the merry Captain's remark to the grasping usurer, "I will stile thee noble, nay *Don Diego*."

If, then, the term "Don Diego" should be interpreted in a generic or scornful sense, or indeed in any way other than as an allusion to the Spanish ambassador Don Diego Sarmiento de Acuña, the many allusions scattered through the play would seem to suggest a date not later than early in 1610. Although less specific than some of the allusions already cited, there is another which I think argues for the same time. In IV, i, as the curate, Roger, enters, Abigail observes: "See how negligently he passes by me: with what an Equipage Canonical, as though he had broken the heart of *Bellarmine*." On this passage Bond has the following note: "Cardinal Robert Bellarmine (1542-1621), Archbishop of Capua and a Jesuit, who engaged in controversy with James I after the Gunpowder Plot. *The Stationers' Register* contains entries of works against his writings under dates Jan. 18, 1599, Feb. 9, and Dec. 8, 1600."

The last sentence of this note is almost misleading. Such an allusion as that in the play suggests not only that Cardinal Bellarmine's was a name with which all were familiar, but also that the views he had expressed, rather than being merely theological controversy, had identified him in the public mind as one of a cruel and hard heart. Presumably the Cardinal's name would not have become such a byword to the layman before late 1607; and if the allusion was apt, if it was made at a time when the name of Bellarmine was most on people's lips, it would seem that it was introduced between 1608 and 1611. Although his name is found frequently in the *State Papers, Domestic,* and *Venetian,*[14] between late 1607 and early 1610, there is no mention of him in them prior to 1607 and extremely few references to him after 1610.

Bellarmine first achieved a wide publicity in England when on September 18, 1607, he wrote the Archpriest George Blackwell, reproaching him for having taken the oath of allegiance and urging him to retract.[15] It was against this letter of the Cardinal and two earlier breves by Pope Paul V forbidding Roman Catholics to take the oath of allegiance that King James directed his *Apology for the Oath of Allegiance* (1607/8). The Cardinal, using the name of one of his chaplains, Matthew Tortus, immediately wrote a reply containing no little personal abuse and charging that before James left Scotland "his ministers had assured the Pope that he was likely to become a Catholic, and that he had himself written to Clement, recommending the promotion of the Bishop of Vaison to the cardinalate."[16] James was deeply vexed, and the Venetian Ambassador reported to his government that "This affair is causing much talk."[17] After his former secretary had confessed that he had himself written the letter and had secured the King's signature fraudulently, James with his theologians retired to Royston to prepare his second answer. During the next few months the letters of Chamberlain and of the Venetian Ambassador make many references to the replies being prepared by James and by the Bishop of Chichester, Launcelot Andrews. In April, 1609, the King published his second answer to Bellarmine, which was appended as a preface to a reissue of his *Apology,* and a few

[14] These are the only State Papers available to me, but it would seem justifiable to interpret the times through them.

[15] *C. S. P., Domestic,* XXVIII, 370.   [16] Gardiner, *op. cit.,* II, 31.

[17] *C. S. P., Venetian,* XI, 184. 30 October 1608.

weeks later Andrews' *Tortura Torti* had appeared. Both books
were promptly answered by Bellarmine. In February, 1610, the
Venetian ambassadors report that Andrews, now Bishop of Ely,
again

has been commissioned to reply to Cardinal Bellarmin, and we understand that the King, too, while at Royston worked on the subject. At Court they say the Cardinal's book shows little learning
and less wit and that it is not worthy of the Cardinal's reputation
acquired by his other works; all the same they have taken pains
that it should not be seen, and while it was being bound Lord
Salisbury always kept a guard over it.[18]

Ely's *Responsio ad Apologiam* appeared soon afterwards.[19]
This was never answered. Instead the Cardinal turned his guns
upon another Englishman, William Barclay, who had come to
the aid of James in his *De Potestate Papae* published in London
in 1609; Bellarmine had replied in his *Tractatus de Potestate
Summi Pontificis in rebus temporalibus. Adversus Gulielmum
Barclaium*, published in Rome in 1610. It was against Bellarmine's views in this work that there appeared a flood of replies
not only in England, but also in France and Germany. Much
to the satisfaction of King James, the book was banned in both
Venice and France.

In addition to the replies by James, Bishop Andrews, and
Barclay, there were published in England during 1609 attacks
upon Bellarmine by Joseph Hall[20] and by John Raynold,[21] and
both in English and Latin, Archpriest Blackwell's justification
of Roman Catholics' taking the oath of allegiance. Early in
1610 John Donne supported Blackwell's view against Bellarmine,[22] and John Gordon published his *Antitortobellarminus*.

---

[18] *C. S. P., Venetian*, XI, 421.   11 February 1610.

[19] Chamberlain to Carleton, 6 March 1610, in Thomas Birch, *Court and Times
of James I*, 2 vols. (London, 1849), I, 108.

[20] *Peace to Rome, or her difference of opinions reckoned up out of Bellarmine and
Navarre; with a Dissuasive from Popery* (London, 1609).

[21] *Defence of the Judgment of the Reformed churches, that a man may put away
his wife for Adultery and marry another; against Bellarmine. 4to (1609).*

[22] *Pseudo-martyr. Wherein this conclusion is evicted that those of the Romane
religion ought to take the oath of allegeance* (1610). This had been entered December 2, 1609.

In 1611 appeared an English translation of Barclay, and further attacks upon Bellarmine by Richard Sheldon, Richard Thompson, and James Thomas. During these years (1609-1611) the English view was further supported by William Barlow, Morton, and Burhill against such supporters of Bellarmine as Becan and Parsons. For many years there continued attacks upon the Cardinal's views of the temporal powers of the pope, but there seems no reason to doubt that the most excited interest among the general public followed close upon Bellarmine's interference in the question of the oath of allegiance and his first insistence upon the temporal powers of the pope. Although the *State Papers, Domestic,* contain, as I have said, numerous references to Bellarmine during the period 1607-1610, there is only one reference to him from 1611 through 1625: "On August 29, 1615, Griffith Floyd upon examination stated among other things that 'Cardinal Bellarmine said that the letter written by the King to the Pope from Scotland was lost in the dispersion of Clement VIII's papers.' "

Clearly the allusion to the hard heart of Bellarmine would be much more apt between 1608 and 1610 than between 1613 and 1616. The year 1610, moreover, would agree perfectly with the date suggested by the similar references in early plays and by all, save possibly one, of the other allusions in *The Scornful Lady:* the separate binding of the *Apocrypha* (1610); the rumors of the Cleve Wars (1609), and the cast Cleve captain (1610); Jonson's *Epicoene* (1609), and *The Alchemist* (1610), to both of which Fletcher also alludes in *Woman's Prize,* early 1611. The one exception is the possible allusion to Don Diego Sarmiento. If the mention of Don Diego and his Infanta is indeed an allusion to the Spanish Ambassador's effort to arrange a marriage between Prince Charles and the Infanta, it could not have been introduced until some months after Sarmiento's arrival in England at the end of May, 1613. By 1614, however, the numerous other allusions would have lost much of their timeliness. The mere number of such allusions, it appears to me, demands that the composition of *The Scornful Lady* be assigned to 1610. It is possible that the term "Don Diego" was used in some sense similar to that given it in *Dick of Devon-shire*, where it is synonymous with "Don Devil," or in the *Tatler*, where it means "to cheat"; or it is possible that between late 1613 and March 19, 1616, when the play was entered on the Stationers' Register, there was inserted an allusion to Sarmiento and the Spanish Infanta, although the allusion was certainly not perfect, the relation of Sarmiento and the Infanta being most dissimilar to that of Morecraft and the Widow.

No critic, I believe, has ever questioned the view that the play was the joint production of Beaumont and Fletcher. If Massinger's hand could be found in the play, the probability of revision and hence of insertion, would seem much greater. Although I am far from prepared to present a claim for Massinger, there is forcibly dragged into II, i, a joke which Massinger seems to have regarded good enough to repeat twice in later plays. In spite of the fact that Lady is a woman of wealth and apparently entertains most generously, Welford's Servant reports that the "Coach-mares of the Gentlewoman's [are] the Strangest Cattel. . . . Why, they are transparent Sir, you may see through them!" In Massinger's *The Picture*, Hilario is told that he is so thin he is "transparent without dissection" (III, i), and the wasted steward, Mallfort, in Massinger's portion of *The Lover's Progress*, describes himself as so starved "You may see through, and through me" (I, i).

IV

THE WOMAN'S PRIZE, OR
THE TAMER TAMED

I

FLETCHER's *Woman's Prize, or The Tamer Tamed,* although it has generally been recognized as one of the most ingenious and rollicking comedies in the Beaumont and Fletcher canon, has for the most part been studied and discussed by critics with attention principally upon *The Taming of the Shrew.* This tendency to think of the two plays together has led not only to frequent failure to estimate fully Fletcher's comic skill but as well to several false conclusions about *The Woman's Prize.* Gayley and Oliphant wrote of it as a "continuation of" or "sequel to" *The Taming of the Shrew.* Macaulay, more guardedly, called it a "supposed continuation." Mr. D. M. McKeithan has recently declared it "not merely a sequel . . . but an adaptation." Chambers considered it an "answer" to Shakespeare's comedy. Fleay saw in it an attempt by Fletcher to ridicule his predecessor—an interpretation which greatly annoyed Ward, who viewed it rather as the younger dramatist's generous tribute to his master.

In dating *The Woman's Prize,* scholars have expressed opinions equally divergent. Fleay[1] placed it between 1613 and 1616; Thorndike[2] and Oliphant[3] assigned it to 1603 or 1604; Schelling[4] thought it written "perhaps as early as 1606, if not in 1604"; Lawrence[5] dated it 1608 and Gayley[5] "*ca.* 1615."

[1] *Biographical Chronicle of the English Drama,* I, 198.
[2] *Influence of Beaumont and Fletcher on Shakspere,* pp. 70-72; *English Comedy* (New York, 1929), pp. 192, 607-8.
[3] *The Plays of Beaumont and Fletcher,* pp. 152-54.
[4] *Elizabethan Drama,* 2 vols. (Boston and New York, 1908), I, 341.
[5] See Oliphant, p. 152, for Lawrence's views; for Gayley's see his *Representative English Comedies* (New York and London, 1914), III, lxvi-lxvii.

Recently, Professor Bond has "on stylistic grounds" advocated a date after 1617.[6]

Aside from the obvious debt to *The Taming of the Shrew*, there have been advanced only two arguments in support of the early dating, both of them allusions which, it is maintained, would have been applicable "in and only shortly after 1604." In Act I, scene iii, Sophocles reports to Petruchio that the chamber in which his bride has fortified herself is

> nothing but a mere Ostend,
> In every window pewter cannons mounted.

To Mr. Oliphant, who insists "there are few things more certain in relation to Elizabethan drama than the determination to make allusions topical," this allusion to the siege of Ostend, which ended September 8, 1604, proves that the play was written not much after if not before that date. So strongly, indeed, is he convinced of the weight of this argument that he must accept the early date even though "I find it hard to believe that Fletcher's style matured so early, and that he had his wonderful gift of vituperation in full working order at almost the commencement of his career." He is led to suggest, therefore, "that Fletcher almost entirely rewrote the play some years later, but left in the reference to Ostend."[7] Although I am willing to accept Mr. Oliphant's view that the Elizabethan dramatists sought to make their allusions topical, I am not ready to believe that a reference to such an important and memorable event as the siege of Ostend must needs be topical, an event of which Fletcher in *Love's Cure*, I, i, wrote:

> Ostend's bloody siege, that stage of war,
> Wherein the flower of many nations acted
> And the whole Christian world spectators were.

Certainly Ostend, like Waterloo and the Battle of the Marne, passed into the realm of figurative language to be used until its significance was forgotten or until its place was usurped by a siege more recent. References to it occur in several Beaumont

[6] R. Warwick Bond, "On Six Plays in Beaumont and Fletcher, 1679," *Review of English Studies*, XI (1935), 271-73.   [7] *Op. cit.*, p. 153.

and Fletcher plays. In addition to the lines quoted from *Love's Cure*, which suggest its imaginative appeal, Ostend is used in *The Coxcomb*, II, ii, to connote the strongest fortress which can be conceived:

> When they take a thief, I'll take Ostend again.

So is it used in Jonson's *Silent Woman* (1609), a play, as will be noted later, to which Fletcher seems to allude in *The Woman's Prize*. In IV, i, of Jonson's play Truewit observes:

> A man should not doubt to overcome any woman. Think he can vanquish 'em, and he shall; for though they deny, their desire is to be tempted. Penelope herself cannot hold out long. Ostend, you saw, was taken at last. You must persever, and hold to your purpose. . . .

In all these passages Ostend is clearly intended to suggest the strongest and most complete fortification which can be conceived. Noteworthy is it also, perhaps, that in both *The Silent Woman* and *The Woman's Prize* Ostend is used in connection with woman's defense against man. There is no more reason, certainly, for thinking that one more than the other must have been penned immediately after the siege.

That the second allusion which has been pointed out in support of an early date for the play is topical there can be no doubt, but it contributes little in determining a definite date for the play. In his *English Comedy* Professor Thorndike wrote:

> I think no one has called attention to the evidence for the date in I, iii, "These are the most authentic rebels next Tyrone, I ever read of." Tyrone submitted in 1603 and was in London that summer. In II, i, "It had been no right rebellion Had she held off," may also allude to Tyrone's submission. These references indicate a date of 1603-4 for the play, though they might possibly fit a date of 1607-8.[8]

It is no little surprise to find such reasoning in the writings of Professor Thorndike. Clearly he has, in the absence of all other evidence, accepted as topical the allusion to Ostend and

[8] Pp. 607-8.

is eagerly looking for supporting evidence. He completely disregards the subsequent career of Tyrone and sinks into absurdity when he suggests that the passage in II, i, "may also allude to Tyrone's submission." It is difficult to account for the "also," there being in the first passage certainly no allusion to any submission. Neither is there in the second (II, i).[9] The lines "'t had been no right rebellion Had she held off" are spoken by Petruchio when he learns that Livia, to escape marriage with the elderly Moroso, has joined his rebellious wife and her cousin in their citadel. Far from alluding to any submission, the lines merely state that the rebellion is now complete.

Although Professor Thorndike admitted that the reference to Tyrone "might possibly fit a date of 1607-8," the implication of his paragraph is that Tyrone's submission in 1603 marked the close of his career as a rebel. It did not. Having made his submission to James in 1603, Tyrone returned to Ireland and almost immediately was embroiled in fresh disputes with the government. In 1607, hearing that his arrest was imminent, he fled Ireland on September 14. Howes records that on November 16 "Proclamation was made concerning the sodayne flight of Tyrone, and the rest, wherein was declared their purpose and practice to exterpe the English Nation out of Ireland, and to conferre and yeelde the Kingdome of Ireland to the Pope, and the Earle of Tyrones soliciting forreyne princes to attempt the conquest thereof."[10] Welcomed by the Pope and by the King of Spain, Tyrone continued until his death in July, 1616, to cause uneasiness and be the subject of many reports in England. In March, 1608, William Udall wrote the Bishop of Bristol, affirming confidently that Tyrone "intends to seize Chester and head a rebellion in Ireland."[11] Late in 1609 the Venetian Ambassador in England advised his government that the King of England was "watching the movements of the Earl of Tyrone, as he holds it certain that the

[9] In Dyce's edition, II, iv. In all references to the play I follow the text of A. Dyce, *The Works of Beaumont and Fletcher*, 11 vols. (London, 1846).

[10] *Chronicles* (1615), p. 890.   [11] *C. S. P., Domestic*, March 19, 1608.

present conjunction of affairs will tempt the Pope to foment some of his old designs. I have this from a very sure source."[12] Tyrone received further publicity in England in 1610, when his lands were at last divided at the time of the plantation of Ireland. In December of that year an examination of a sailor, F. Maguir, revealed that he had met the Earl of Tyrone at the Spanish court, and that an effort had been made to persuade him to join troops to be sent by the King of Spain in the hope of inducing the Irish to rebel.[13] Rumors of the Earl's plan to invade Ireland evidently persisted as late as April, 1614, on the twenty-first of which month Carleton received a letter from Archbishop Abbott, who "asks whether the Earl of Tyrone intends to come nearer, as reported, and if a Roman nobleman has engaged his fortune to attend him in Ireland."[14] Obviously an allusion to Tyrone as the arch-rebel would have been no more topical in 1603-1604 than at any time during the following decade.

As neither the allusion to Ostend nor that to Tyrone can be recognized as offering any evidence for a definite date, there remains to support an early date merely the vague feeling that, to quote Sir Edmund Chambers, "an answer to *The Taming of the Shrew* would have more point the nearer it came to the date of the original." That, of course, would be true if Shakespeare's comedy enjoyed a brief success and then was heard no more. But is there any reason to believe that *The Shrew* was not from time to time revived? As the earliest date suggested for the composition of *The Woman's Prize* is ten years after the production of *The Shrew* and as the stage history of the latter is completely unknown, there surely can be little weight to the argument that an "answer" to it was more likely to have been written in the eleventh year after its first production than in the fifteenth or eighteenth.

Although the allusions to Ostend and to Tyrone can be of only slight value in determining a definite date for *The*

---

[12] *C. S. P., Venetian,* October 15, 1609.
[13] *C. S. P., Domestic,* December 16, 1610.
[14] *Ibid.,* April 21, 1614.

Woman's Prize, the play contains a number of other allusions which offer more particular evidence. Of these, several point to a date in or after late 1610, while one, more general, would be topical only in and immediately after the period 1607-1609. In Act II, scene ii, Bianca observes that Moroso's

> everlasting cassock . . . . has worn
> As many servants out, as the North-East passage
> Has consum'd sailors.

The existence of a northeast passage had been first suggested by Sebastian Cabot during the reign of Henry VIII, but it was not until 1553 that the search for it was begun. Of the three ships sent out in that year by the Company of Merchant Adventurers in quest of a northeast passage, two, driven far out to sea, landed on the coast of Lapland, where the crews, totaling seventy, perished of cold and hunger. The passage was again the object of English expeditions in 1556 and 1580, the latter being the last authenticated English search for the northeast passage prior to the voyages of Hudson in 1607, 1608, and 1609.[15] During the last decade of the sixteenth century, in 1594, 1595, and 1596, three Dutch expeditions sought to find the passage, and an account of the voyages was written by Gerrit de Veer. An English translation entitled *True and Perfect Description of Three Voyages* was prepared by William Philip and entered upon the Stationers' Register on June 13, 1598. The publication was, however, delayed. It was re-entered on May 15, 1609,[16] and appeared sometime during that year. There can be little doubt that its publication in 1609 was occasioned by the interest in Hudson's third voyage, on which he had sailed the month before and which, like his earlier voyages of 1607 and 1608, had as its original purpose[17] the search for a northeast passage. When, however, he was confronted by an unbroken barrier of ice near Nova Zembla, Hudson abandoned the search for an eastern passage and sailed west in hope of

---

[15] G. M. Asher, *Henry Hudson,* Hakluyt Society Publications, Ser. 1, XXVII (1860), cxxx.

[16] See the introduction to the reprint in Hakluyt Society Publications, Vol. LIV (1876).   [17] Asher, pp. iii-iv.

finding a northwest passage. On his fourth and last voyage
(1610-1611) Hudson likewise sailed to the northwest. Never
again during Fletcher's life is there recorded an English search
for a northeast passage, although in the next six years there
were no fewer than six expeditions sent in search of a northwest
passage. Possibly the two passages were at first confused in
the popular mind, and it may have been assumed that the purpose of Hudson's fourth voyage was the same as that of his
earlier attempts, but the only period during the seventeenth
century in which the English people could have been much interested in the search for a northeast passage was that of the
four Hudson voyages from 1607 to 1610-1611. That Fletcher
should refer to the northeast passage at all suggests, I think,
that he was writing in or after 1607; that he should refer to
it rather than the northwest passage as a consumer of men suggests that he was writing before September, 1611, when the
survivors of Hudson's voyage to the northwest reached England with their tragic tale of how Hudson with eight others
had by mutineers been set adrift in small boats to perish and
how on the hazardous voyage home some of the mutineers had
been killed by Eskimos and others had died of starvation. The
only comparable disaster was that of the first voyage to the
northeast in 1553. As this last voyage of Hudson was the most
disastrous of all such northern expeditions during Fletcher's
life, it is possible that Fletcher had confused the object of this
voyage with the original object of Hudson's three earlier voyages and that he is here referring to the loss of Hudson and a
large proportion of his crew. But whether that be true or not,
as the only English searches for the northeast passage between
1580 and the death of Fletcher were the voyages of Hudson
and as the account of the Dutch expeditions of the 1590's was
not printed in England until 1609, it seems hardly likely that
Fletcher would introduce a reference to the northeast passage
before 1607.

Such a view is supported by a second topical allusion which
is more definite in its suggestion of a date. In Act III, scene ii,
Petruchio, telling of the unhappiness of his first marriage, asks:

> Had I not every morning a rare breakfast,
> Mix'd with a learned lecture of ill-language,
> Louder than Tom o' Lincoln?

Although the present great bell of Lincoln Cathedral, popularly known as "Great Tom," dates only from 1855, it is the successor of two earlier great bells. The first, which had graced the cathedral during the reign of Queen Elizabeth, "was re-cast in Dean Stanton's time, Dec. 3, 1610, by Holdfield of Nottingham and Newcomb of Leicester."[18] It was hung in the northwest tower of the cathedral and "christened 'Great Tom of Lincoln,' 1610."[19]

North, in his *Church Bells of Lincolnshire*, gives an "extract from the muniments of the Dean and Chapter, headed 'Conc'neing ye greate Bell,' and bearing the date 'xxx die Januarii' of that year 1610/11. . . . On Sunday, Jan. 27, 1611, the bell having been hung up, 'range owt and all safe and well.' "[20] The allusion to the loud sound of Tom o' Lincoln would, therefore, clearly be most apt near the beginning of the year 1611.

Other allusions also point to 1610-1611. In supporting his view of a later date for *The Woman's Prize*, Professor Gayley called attention to several apparent echoes of two of Jonson's plays, *The Silent Woman* (1609) and *The Alchemist* (1610):

One of the minor characters, called Moroso, may very well be a reminiscence of Morose in Jonson's *Silent Woman* (1610), for, says Sophocles in the presence of Moroso (III, i), "I never will believe a silent woman, When they break forth they are bonfires." Fletcher's Moroso was probably attired to recall the singular appearance of Jonson's hypochondriac "with the huge turban of nightcaps on his head buckled over his ears," for, says Petronius of *The Woman's Prize* to Moroso, "Burn your Nightcap, It looks like half a winding sheet" (IV, i). In the same catalogue of advice we find "contrive your beard o' the top cut, like Verdugo's"—and in Jon-

---

[18] *Statutes of Lincoln Cathedral*, arranged by Henry Bradshaw (two parts in 3 vols. Cambridge, 1892-97), Part II, p. 604 n.

[19] W. F. Rawnsley, *Highways and Byways in Lincolnshire* (London, 1914), p. 99. Another allusion to the great sound of Tom of Lincoln is to be found in *The Nightwalker*, III, ii.

[20] Quoted in J. J. Raven, *Bells of England* (London and New York, 1906), pp. 249-50.

son's *Alchemist* we have mention of "his great Verdugo-ship" (III, ii). This name for a hangman is of rare occurrence. The coincidence of Jonsonisms in connection with a Jonsonian character of 1610 may indicate that date as the upper limit of composition for *The Woman's Prize*.[21]

Professor Gayley's suggestion that Fletcher introduced reminiscences of Jonson is rendered more likely by the references already noted, nor is it weakened by the occurrence in Act II, scene i, of *The Scornful Lady*, a play which should, I think, be assigned to 1609-1610, of both *Verdugo* and references to the nightcaps of Sir Roger. These reminiscences, however, hardly support Professor Gayley's dating of the play "c. 1615"—a date which he selects because of the general "similarity to *Wit without Money*" and because he assumes that *The Woman's Prize*, being wholly Fletcher's, was written after Beaumont's retirement in 1613. The reminiscences of *The Silent Woman*, especially if Fletcher intended the attire of Moroso "to recall the singular appearance of Jonson's hypochondriac," would indicate a date much closer to the production of that play, for *The Silent Woman* was presumably not a popular play.[22]

The date which would best suit all the allusions would appear to be early 1611. *The Silent Woman* would have been sufficiently recent to permit the audience to appreciate the similarity in the attires of Moroso and Morose. The rebel Tyrone was still feared as likely at any time to come with foreign aid to attack Ireland; in December of the preceding year the Privy Council was investigating a report that he and the King of Spain were attempting to incite an Irish rebellion. In the same

---

[21] *Representative English Comedies*, III, lxvi.

[22] This assumption is based upon Jonson's remark to Drummond that "when his play of a Silent Woman was first acted, ther was found verses after on the stage against him, concluding that the play was well named the Silent Woman, ther never was one man to say *Plaudite* to it." Against this "somewhat facetious remark," Professors Brooke and Paradise, who think that the play was popular at once, set the anonymous contemporary jingle:

> The Fox, the Alchemist, and Silent Woman,
> Done by Ben Jonson, and outdone by no man.

—*English Drama, 1580-1642* (Boston and New York, 1933), p. 528. In the present connection the question is one of little importance.

month Great Tom of Lincoln was hung in the Lincoln Cathedral. Hudson, recently convinced that the northeast passage was inaccessible or nonexistent, was exploring the northwest, the fearful tragedy of the voyage not yet enacted.

2

The relation which *The Woman's Prize* bears to *The Taming of the Shrew* has been at various times described as that of a "sequel," "continuation," "adaptation," "answer," "counterblast." None of these terms, I am convinced, accurately describes the relationship of the two plays. Although there can be no doubt that Fletcher's play was intended to recall Shakespeare's farce, *The Woman's Prize* certainly cannot properly be regarded as a continuation of the story told by Shakespeare, even though it would seem to have been so regarded by the King's Men in 1633, when it was revived by them and presented at court on the evening following a performance of *The Shrew*. These coincident revivals have, I suspect, led critics to exaggerate the similarities between the two plays and, accordingly, Fletcher's debt to Shakespeare.

Mr. D. M. McKeithan, who has published the most recent discussion of the two plays,[23] has shown that there is a rough parallelism in their dramatis personae and that several of the situations in Fletcher's play are so close to situations in Shakespeare's comedy as to suggest that Fletcher at least recalled the effectiveness of certain scenes in *The Shrew*. But the recognition of such debts as these does not forbid my questioning Mr. McKeithan's conclusion that Fletcher "deliberately set out to continue the career of Shakespeare's tamer of the Shrew,"[24] or the view previously expressed by others, that Fletcher's play was a studied sequel to Shakespeare's.

If one were preparing a continuation to *The Taming of the Shrew*, it would be natural to lay the scene in Italy. Fletcher's scene is London. As the names of most (not all) of the dramatis personae are Italian, Oliphant assumed that

[23] *The Debt to Shakespeare in the Beaumont-and-Fletcher Plays* (Austin, Texas, 1938), pp. 58-82.   [24] *Ibid.*, p. 62.

Fletcher, rewriting the play, discarded his original Italian setting in favor of an English setting. For such a revision it is
difficult to perceive the motive, or to understand how an intelligent reviser could obliterate all Italian coloring and introduce so many English allusions, and yet retain Italian names
for the principal characters. The play is crowded with local
allusions. To name but a few, there are references to Lancashire, Kingston, Lincoln, Sturbridge, and Sedgeley; to London
Bridge, Blackfriars, Smithfield, Dog's Ditch, and Thames
Street; to St. Dunstan and St. George; to Harrygroats, bear-
baiting, Puritans, and Maypoles. In IV, iii, Byancha says, "I
speak good honest English," and in V, iv, Petruchio addresses
"little England." From the last mentioned scene and from IV,
v, it is clear not only that Petruchio is, in spite of his name, an
Englishman, but also, as shown by the encouragement Maria
gives his plan to travel, that he has never been out of England.
The references to England and to things English are, indeed,
vastly more numerous in *The Woman's Prize* than are the
references to the earlier incidents in Petruchio's life as recounted
by Shakespeare.

Although there is a certain parallelism in the dramatis personae of the two plays, the similarities do not extend to characterization except in such conventional characters as the pantaloon and the servants. There are only three names in common:
Petruchio, Tranio, and Bianca (spelled Byancha in *Woman's
Prize*). Neither Katherina nor any other of the Shakespearean
characters is mentioned by name in the later play. Neither the
two Biancas nor the two Tranios have any traits in common.
The quiet sister of Petruchio's first wife merely furnishes a
name for the stouthearted cousin of his second wife; and Tranio
is promoted from the servant ranks to be a gentleman and a
friend of Petruchio. But the similarity in names has led students to seek—and find—closer bonds for the two plays than
the plays themselves can furnish. Fletcher, Mr. McKeithan has
written,

. . . retains Katherina's younger sister, Bianca (Byancha), as the
cousin of Maria and Livia. Hence, as Professor H. Ten Eyck

Perry has pointed out, Petruchio's second wife is the cousin of his first wife. The fact that Byancha is bent on seeing Maria tame Petruchio is easily explained: she desires revenge for Petruchio's brutal treatment of her elder sister Katherina, now dead.[25]

Such reconstructive criticism as this makes the plays seem very closely related indeed. But for these relationships the plays themselves offer no evidence. There is, of course, no mention of cousins Maria and Livia in *The Taming of the Shrew;* nor is there in *The Woman's Prize* any suggestion that Petruchio's first wife was named Katherina or that she was related either to Byancha or to Livia or Maria. Not only does Byancha claim no kinship with Petruchio's first wife, whom she speaks of only as "his first wife," but she reveals little sympathy with Katherina and slight knowledge of her wedded life when she testifies that Petruchio had been a quiet and reasonable man "till his first wife set him going" (I, ii; ed. Dyce, VII, 107). In placing the blame where she does, it is obvious that Byancha is not seeking "revenge for Petruchio's brutal treatment of her elder sister." Further, although Bianca of Shakespeare may well have disliked her brother-in-law, the reason should not be sought in his "brutal treatment" of her sister. The taming of Katherina, it should be remembered, required less than a fortnight, at the end of which Katherina, we are to assume, was happier than she had ever been. We should not forget that the play ends happily, with a promise that, the tumult and the fighting over, the wedded future of Petruchio and his bride is to be one of peace, love, and quiet. When in the last scene Katherina appears promptly upon her husband's command, the surprised Lucentio cries, "Here is a wonder. . . ." "And so it is," observes Hortensio. "I wonder what it bodes." To which Petruchio replies:

> Marry, peace it bodes, and love, and quiet life,
> An awful rule, and right supremacy;
> And, to be short, what not, that's sweet and happy?

This happy future promised at the close of *The Shrew* seems to have been as completely ignored by modern critics as it had

[25] *Ibid.*

been by Fletcher, who, as we shall see, has no fewer than four characters (Petruchio, Byancha, Moroso, and Tranio) suggest that Petruchio's first wife was never tamed.

Mr. McKeithan seems to suggest that Fletcher made no more changes in his "sequel" than were necessary to continue the story of *The Shrew*.

. . . Livia, like her cousin Bianca (in *The Taming of the Shrew*) is wooed by an old pantaloon and a young gentleman. Obviously, Byancha (in *The Woman's Prize*) could not be expected to persuade the man whom she had married in Shakespeare's play to marry Livia in Fletcher's play; therefore Fletcher calls Livia's young lover Rowland. He changes the name of the amorous old gentleman from Gremio to Moroso, perhaps taking the name from Ben Jonson. Tranio's name is retained, but Fletcher makes him a gentleman—as indeed he might well have been in *The Taming of the Shrew*, since he is educated, intelligent, and plays an important rôle. Fletcher possibly changed the name of Petruchio's friend, Hortensio, and the names of Petruchio's servants, Grumio and Curtis, respectively, to Sophocles, Jaques, and Pedro so as not to advertise the fact that he was getting practically all of his characters from *The Taming of the Shrew*.[26]

There is much in this passage to which I should object. There is, as has been said, no indication within the plays of the kinship of Livia and Bianca, nor is there any suggestion that Byancha was a widow—or had ever been married. The character of "Child" Rowland in no way recalls that of Lucentio. Although the name Tranio is used in both plays, I suspect that Shakespeare and Fletcher would have defined a gentleman in somewhat different terms from those used by Dr. McKeithan. And certainly I should not admit that Fletcher "was getting practically all of his characters from *The Taming of the Shrew*." If he had done so, I can see no reason why he should seek to disguise the fact. He would then definitely be writing a sequel, and in a sequel it would be both permissible and expected that he should retain the same setting and many of the characters of the original. But Fletcher has retained neither setting nor

[26] *Op. cit.*, p. 62.

characters. Not even Petruchio himself remains the same. It probably is of no significance in the present discussion that, instead of wearing the outlandish costume which contributed much to the comedy of *The Shrew* and would have proved equally effective in an answer or a sequel, Petruchio appears for his second wedding as the "trim" bridegroom (I, iii; ed. Dyce, VII, 118). Although the Petruchio of Fletcher is not without spirit, the difference in his wedding costume suggests the change his character has undergone. It is hard to understand how one even slightly familiar with the Shakespearean tamer could present him as one whose still and even temper had been lastingly distorted by the "hue and cries" of Katherina. But in Fletcher's comedy no fewer than three characters testify to Petruchio's even temper before his first marriage. Moroso recalls that his first wife

> Out of her most abundant sourness,
> Out of her daily hue and cries upon him,
> (For, sure, she was a rebel,) turn'd his temper,
> And forc'd him blow as high as she . . . .
> > [I, i; ed. Dyce, VII, 102.]

Tranio also testifies to Petruchio's earlier moderation, and makes one doubt whether his first wife had indeed ever been tamed. Up to the time of Petruchio's second marriage, Tranio tells us,

> the bare remembrance of his first wife . . . .
> Will make him start in 's sleep, and very often
> Cry out for cudgels, colestaves, any thing;
> Hiding his breeches, out of fear her ghost
> Should walk, and wear 'em yet. Since his first marriage,
> He is no more the still Petruchio
> Than I am Babylon.   [I, i; ed. Dyce, VII, 102-3.]

And Byancha warns his second wife that

> since his first wife set him going,
> Nothing can bind his rage.   [I, ii; ed. Dyce, VII, 107.]

The suggestion in the foregoing passages that the first wife had not been so successfully tamed as was Katherina is supported even by the evidence of Petruchio himself. Although Maria twits him with being "famous for a woman-tamer," Petruchio, cursing the fate that had led him to marry "this second wife, this whirlwind," asks:

> . . . . was I not well warned . . . .
> And beaten to repentance, in the days
> Of my first doting? had I not wife enough
> To turn my love too? did I want vexation,
> Or any special care to kill my heart?
> Had I not every morning a rare breakfast,
> Mix'd with a learned lecture of ill-language,
> Louder than Tom o' Lincoln? and at dinner
> A diet of the same dish? was there evening
> That e'er pass'd over us without *thou knave*,
> Or *thou whore*, for digestion?
> . . . . and did Heaven forgive me,
> And take this serpent from me, and am I
> Keeping tame devils now again?

> [III, ii; ed. Dyce, VII, 162.]

It is difficult to believe that Fletcher intended this to be a picture of the wedded life of Petruchio and Katherina. If indeed he so intended, his knowledge of the early play was slight. His "study" of *The Shrew* certainly did not extend beyond the fourth act. The passages which contradict *The Taming of the Shrew* are much more numerous than those which allude clearly and correctly to the older play.

But in spite of the numerous contradictions, it is certain that in *The Woman's Prize* as we have it an effort has been made to establish a connection with *The Taming of the Shrew*. There are 1) the appearance in both plays of characters named Petruchio, Bianca, and Tranio; 2) the subtitle *The Tamer Tamed*, and passing reference to Petruchio as "famous for a woman-tamer"; 3) allusions to Petruchio's earlier marriage. Similar situations in the course of the taming of Katherina and Petruchio or in the love affairs of Bianca and Livia, while they may reveal indebtedness on the part of Fletcher, hardly indicate an effort to identify his play as a sequel or continuation.

All of these efforts to connect the two plays may, however, easily have been introduced into *The Woman's Prize* at a time after that play had been begun. Much more numerous and convincing seem the arguments that it was not originally Fletcher's plan to write a sequel to *The Taming of the Shrew:*

1) His making no effort to establish the identity of the two Biancas or the two Tranios, and his failure to refer to any situation or to any character in *The Shrew.*

2) His changing the scene from Italy to London, and the emphasis given the fact that Petruchio is an Englishman.

3) His presentation of Petruchio, in total disregard of Shakespeare's characterization, as one whose early even temper has been destroyed by the "most abundant sourness" of his first wife.

4) His ignoring completely the end of *The Shrew* by repeated testimony that Petruchio's first wife had not been tamed, but had indeed always held the upper hand. Even after her death Petruchio would start in his sleep and hide "his breeches, out of fear her ghost should walk, and wear 'em yet" (I, i).

Inescapable seems the conclusion that *The Woman's Prize* was not originally planned as a sequel, continuation, or adaptation of *The Taming of the Shrew.* The struggle between the sexes for governance was, indeed, one of Fletcher's favorite themes. (Compare *Rule a Wife, The Spanish Curate, Women Pleas'd, The Noble Gentleman,* etc.) The suggestion for a comedy dealing with the miracle of a woman's taming her wild male need not have come from *The Taming of the Shrew.* It might have been found in numerous stories and situations. (It might even have been found in Jonson's *Silent Woman,* which abundant reference shows a favorite of Fletcher. In IV, iii, of that comedy Madame Haughty observes, "Here's Centaure has immortaliz'd herself, with taming of her wild male." "Ay," adds Mavis, "she has done the miracle of the kingdom.") But whencever came the first suggestion or inspiration, one proposing to write a comedy on such a theme—no matter at what date after 1600 he wrote—could hardly have failed to recall Shakespeare's *Taming of the Shrew.* Recall it Fletcher did, but study it he did not. He sought—perhaps soon after he began it—to associate his play with the earlier comedy by using a few remembered names and by superimposing a number of allusions to *The Shrew*. But his efforts in this direction were halfhearted. Although it would have been easy for him to have introduced allusions which would have established the relation of his characters to those of Shakespeare and would have definitely connected the two plays, the few allusions which he did introduce contradict either the events presented in *The Shrew* or the situations and characters of his own play. Far from preparing a studied continuation, Fletcher was content to rely upon either report or his own recollection—a recollection neither complete nor accurate.

V

The Date of Fletcher's
THE NIGHT-WALKER

THE COMEDY entitled *The Night-walker, or The Little Thief* was, when first printed in 1640, ascribed by its publishers solely to John Fletcher. In the form in which it is preserved, however, it has undergone additions and perhaps "corrections," presumably made in 1633. In that year appeared Prynne's *Histriomastix*, which is alluded to by name in III, iv; in May of that year, Sir Henry Herbert licensed it as "a play of Fletchers, corrected by Sherley, called *The Night Walkers*";[1] and in the following January it was "Likt as a merry Play"[2] when presented at court before the King and Queen.

Fletcher's earlier editors, because of Herbert's statement, assumed that the play "having been left imperfect by Fletcher, was corrected and finished by Shirley."[3] Modern critics have, however, preferred the view that the play had been completed by Fletcher many years before and was merely revised by Shirley in 1633. For the date of Fletcher's original comedy, no evidence has been brought forward. Macaulay observed that it "was, perhaps, as early as 1614."[4] Thorndike, after noting that "A number of allusions to books (III, 3) have not been identified," queries, "may not 'a new Book of Fools' be Armin's Nest of Ninnies, 1608?"[5] Oliphant remarks that "the verse of the Fletcher portion seems to me early in style,"[6] and that both

---

[1] J. Q. Adams, *The Dramatic Records of Sir Henry Herbert*, p. 34.

[2] *Ibid.*, p. 54.

[3] A. Dyce, *Works of Beaumont and Fletcher*, XI, 121.

[4] *Cambridge History of English Literature*, VI, 158.

[5] *The Influence of Beaumont and Fletcher on Shakspere*, p. 90.

[6] *The Plays of Beaumont and Fletcher*, p. 490. Oliphant also records the dating of the play by certain of his correspondents, whose views, I believe, are not printed elsewhere. Mr. W. J. Lawrence, because of the £2 fee collected by Herbert, thought "Shirley must have worked on an unfinished play of Fletcher's," and Mr. Wells was "inclined to date the earlier version to the same year with *The Winter's Tale*" (pp. 490 and 492). Mr. Wells's reasons for this date are not given.

in this play and in *The Woman's Prize* there is an allusion to
A Woman Killed with Kindness—an allusion, however, which I
suspect most conservative scholars will be unable to recognize.[7]
Presumably he prefers a date of 1609, for he closes his discussion of the play with the sentence: "Thorndike suggests that
'the new book of fools' referred to in the play may be Armin's
'Nest of Ninnies,' issued in 1608; and, for my own part, I am
inclined to accept that suggestion, and date Fletcher's work
accordingly."[8]

Aside from Oliphant's conviction that the Fletcherian portions of the play are in his early style, the only argument for
so early a date hitherto advanced, is the identification of "a new
book of fools" with *The Nest of Ninnies*—an identification which
at best is most hazardous in view of the continued popularity of
fool literature. It is, moreover, to be doubted whether in the
books and ballads mentioned in III, iii and iv, it was the
author's intention that in each instance an allusion be recognized.
In the former scene Lurcher and his sister Alathe, to gain
entrance into the house of Justice Algripe, appear in the street
below disguised as peddlers of books and ballads at a time when
the Justice, from a window above, is directing the defense of
his house against the siege by the mother and Nurse of his discarded bride. By hawking titles which please the Justice because
they discomfort the women, the brother and sister gain admit-
tance and, as is shown in the following scene, proceed to chastise
the Justice after having deafened the servants to the cries of
their master by giving each of them certain books or ballads to
read. In this latter scene Prynne's *Histriomastix* (1633) and
Taylor's *Hempseed* (1620) are mentioned by title, but the latter of these may well have been, like the former, added by
Shirley. A few of the titles which the pretended peddlers
hawk suggest definite allusions—such as the ballad of the
witches hanged at Ludlow, a hanging which might present very
helpful evidence for the date of the play, but of which I have
been unable to discover any record. The greater number of the

[7] The allusion is certainly to the proverb and not to Heywood's play. So again
in *The Wild-Goose Chase* (IV, iii). [8] *Op. cit.*, p. 492.

titles, however, seem most certainly not to refer to particular
books of the day but to have been coined by Lurcher and Alathe
with the view to discomforting both Algripe and the women.[9]
If, however, a particular volume is referred to in "a new book
of fools," the allusion, rather than to the *Nest of Ninnies*, 1608,
is much more likely to be to *More fooles yett*, entered upon the
Stationers' Register June 1, 1610.[10]   Not only is the title of the
latter volume more nearly that given in the play, but other
evidence indicates that Fletcher's work upon the play was completed after the beginning of 1611.

Near the opening of III, iii, as Lady impatiently awaits the
women who are to join her in railing against Justice Algripe,
Toby observes:

[9] Observe, for instance, the following dialogue in which the titles, suggested
wholly by the situation, seem coined for the moment:
   Alathe. Buy a ballad,
A ballad of the maid was got with child!
   Toby. That might ha' been my case last night: I'll ha't, Whate'er it cost me.
   [In II, ii, Toby had in the dark been mistaken by Wildbrain for Mistress New-
love.]
   Lurc. A book of walking spirits!
   Alg. That I like not.
   [In II, iv, Lurcher and Alathe had confronted Algripe, as he made his way home
through the night, with the body of his supposedly dead bride.]
   Lurc. A book of wicked women!
   Alg. That's well thought on.
   Lurc. Of rude, malicious women, of proud women,
Of scolding women!—We shall ne'er get in.
   Alathe. A ballad of wrong'd maids!
   Lady. I'll buy that.
   Lurc. A little, very little book.
Of good and godly women, a very little one,
So little you may put it in a nutshell!
   Toby. With a small print that nobody can read it.
   Nurse. Peace, sirrah! or I'll tear your books.
   Alg. Open the door and let him in; I love him.
   Lurc. A book of evil magistrates!
   [After quoting Weber's observation that this "Probably alludes to the *Mirrour for
Magistrates*, or some of its numerous imitations" (!) Dyce merely adds "Doubtful,
I think."]
   Lady. Ay, marry,
D'ye hear that, Justice?
   Lurc. And their eviller wives,
That wear their places in their petticoats!
   Alg. D'ye hear that, lady?
[10] Edward Arber (ed.), *A Transcript of the Registers of the Company of Stationers
of London; 1554-1640*, 5 vols. (London, 1875-77), III, 196.

They'll come,
Fear not, Madam, and bring clappers with 'em,
Or some have lost their old wont: I have heard
(No disparagement to your ladyship) some o' their tongues,
Like Tom-a-Lincoln, three miles off.

As I have already had occasion to note in my attempt to date *The Woman's Prize*, the great bell of Lincoln's Cathedral, founded in the minster yard in December, 1610, and christened Tom o' Lincoln,[11] was shortly after hung in the northwest tower, whence on January 27, 1610/11, it "range owt and all safe and well."[12] It may be asserted with confidence that the allusion in *The Night-walker* to the bell's great sound, which would obviously have been most apt early in 1611, was introduced by Fletcher in his original play. Not only would the allusion be much less apt in 1633, when Shirley made his additions—and there is nothing to indicate that the play was twice revised—but the fact that in *The Woman's Prize*[13] Fletcher similarly likened the voice of a scolding woman to the great sound of Tom o' Lincoln makes it reasonably certain that the simile was his. Further, that he used the allusion in *The Woman's Prize* at a time when it was both new and apt, argues perhaps that it was apt when used in *The Night-walker*.

The date about 1611, suggested by the allusion to Tom o' Lincoln, is further urged by the close similarity which *The Night-walker* bears to *The Woman's Prize* and by the indebtedness which both of these plays apparently owe to Jonson's *Epicoene* (1609). Jonson's character of Morose seems to have left a deep impression upon Fletcher, as is not surprising in view of the esteem in which Ben was held by the younger dramatist. Attention has been called to the kinship of Moroso of *The*

[11] Henry Bradshaw, *Statutes of Lincoln Cathedral*, part II, p. 604 n. Rawnsley, *Highways and Byways in Lincolnshire*, p. 99.

[12] Raven, *Bells of England*, pp. 249-50, quoting from North, *Church Bells of Lincolnshire*, an extract from the muniments of the Dean and Chapter headed "Conc'neing ye greate Bell" and dated January 30, 1610/11.

[13] In III, ii, Petruchio wonders why he should ever have taken a second wife. Had he not, he asks himself, been tortured enough during the life of his first wife:

Had I not every morning a rare breakfast,
Mix'd with a learned lecture of ill-language,
Louder than Tom o' Lincoln?

Woman's Prize, with his nightcap which "looks like half a winding sheet," to Morose "with the huge turban of nightcaps on his head buckled over his ears."[14]   Save in his name, Justice Algripe of *The Night-walker* presents an equally close borrowing.   He is a miserly pantaloon who has arranged to be married solely for mercenary gain; in one scene, at least (III, iii), the comedy is furnished by his being tormented with noise, and twice there are references to his nightcaps.   In III, i, Wildbrain, explaining why he had counselled Algripe's young wife "to make the reverend coxcomb her husband, cuckold," asks his aunt if she would be content to have Algripe's

> Anointed hams, to keep his hinges turning,
> Reek ever in your nose, and twenty night-caps
> With twenty several sweats?

And in V, ii, the Nurse reports that in their hunt for the Justice they have searched all the prisons, and

> did look among the quarters too,
> And muster'd all the bridge-house for his night-cap.

That *The Night-walker* and *The Woman's Prize* were originally written about the same time is indicated not only by their both having apparently duplicated the use of the nightcaps of Morose, by both having an allusion to Great Tom of Lincoln, and by both including a reference to the proverb of a woman killed with kindness—not, I believe, as Mr. Oliphant insists, to Heywood's play.   There are many other resemblances.   The scene of both plays is London, and both contain many references to London places.   III, iii, of *The Night-walker* presents almost exactly the reverse of the situation in *The Woman's Prize*.   In the latter play the women lock themselves in an upstairs chamber behind fortifications likened unto those of Ostend (I, iii) with the men shouting and threatening below. In *The Night-walker* it is the women who shout and threat from below, and Justice Algripe who, having locked his doors, shouts from above:

> Some new fortifications! look to my doors;
> Put double bars! . . .

[14] Gayley, *Representative English Comedies*, III, lxvi.

As in *The Woman's Prize* the besieged women are succored and seconded by a horde of City Women and Country Women, determined that woman's governance shall be maintained; so in *The Night-walker* the Lady, besieging the embattled Algripe, is joined by an unnamed number of women who make her cause theirs—an unnamed number, but enough to make the enraged Justice cry out,

> More of the kennel?—Put more bolts to the doors there,
> And arm yourselves! Hell is broke loose upon us.

The similarity of the two situations leaves little doubt that one was prepared because of the success of the other; and that little doubt is banished by the appearance in this same scene (III, iii) of the topical allusion common to the two plays—the comparison of women's voices to the great sound of Tom of Lincoln.

Of the two similar situations that of *The Woman's Prize* is infinitely the more effective, because it, as that of *The Night-walker* does not, develops directly from the plot. The scene in the latter play has no close connection with the remainder of that play and appears clearly to be an interlude introduced either because of the success of a similar situation in an earlier play or because a hasty and perhaps hurried writer, such as Fletcher many times reveals himself to have been, was quite content to use again situations previously successful.

If, to be sure, this scene in *The Night-walker* was, as I think there can be little doubt, suggested by the situation in the earlier play, the allusion to the great bell of Lincoln, as it might also have come from the earlier play, retains its value only in setting a date prior to which the scene could not have been written. As, however, the style of *The Night-walker* resembles rather Fletcher's earlier style, as all of the Beaumont and Fletcher plays with London scenes are assigned to their early years, and as the composition and the technique seem most suggestive of *The Woman's Prize*, I think it safe to assign *The Night-walker* to the year 1611—most probably to a place immediately after *The Woman's Prize*.

Although perhaps no evidence toward a date for its compo-

sition can be found in the satire which in *The Night-walker* is
directed upon a society of bell-ringers who call themselves "the
worshipful company of the knights o' the west,"[15] such satire
would have been quite timely in the year 1611. In IV, iii, after
persuading the ringers, among whom are Wildbrain and Toby,
to show their skill by ringing in the dark, Lurcher and Alathe
abscond with the clothes which the ringers have abandoned because of the strenuous exercise. The "knights of the west" are
clearly a group of amateur bell-ringers, eager for exercise and
proud of their skill. Ellacombe says that "probably the most
ancient society of which we have any certain knowledge"[16] was
that known as the Ancient Society of College Youths, whose
name, it has been claimed, was "derived from the place where
the first members were accustomed to meet and practice,—St.
Martin's, *College Hill*, Upper Thames Street."[17] The College
Youths were, however, not founded until 1637, and scholars
have agreed in viewing that society as a resuscitation of an earlier
society known as the "Schollers of Chepesyde."[18] According to
Raven,

In the library of All Souls' College, Oxford, is a MS. entitled
"Orders conceyved and agreed upon by the Company exercising
the arte of ringing, knowne and called by the name of the Schollers
of Chepesyde, in London, begun and so continued from the second
day of February, anno 1603."[19] The start seems to have been at
Candlemas. The date of the rules, however, is 1610. They are
to elect annually a Gennerall, four Wardens and a Warner, whose
function was most likely to call bobs, etc.[20]

Although the All Souls' manuscript claims 1603 for the date
of its origin, this society of amateur ringers was, it may be

---

[15] IV, iii and iv. Oliphant and Boyle agreed in viewing both these scenes as
unaltered work of Fletcher.

[16] H. T. Ellacombe, *Church Bells of Devon* (Exeter, 1872), p. 229.

[17] Canon William Thompson, *Southwark Cathedral* (London, 1906), p. 326;
Joseph Strutt, *Sports and Pastimes of the People of England*, Methuen edition
(London, n.d.), p. 236. Ellacombe (*op. cit.*, p. 231) observes, however, that "The
place called 'College Hill' did not exist before the great fire of 1666."

[18] Raven, *Bells of England*, p. 246; Ellacombe, *op. cit.*, p. 230.

[19] MS. cxix.

[20] *Op. cit.*, p. 245; Ellacombe, *op. cit.*, p. 229.

presumed from its drawing up definite rules and orders, re-establishing itself in 1610. No society responsible for so much noise could have failed to attract public notice. As Chepeside was as frequently as not referred to as "West Chepe," it is quite possible that the author intended the audience to recognize the "Schollers of Chepesyde" or West Chepe in "the worshipful company of the knights o' the west."

VI

HENRY VIII

IN A SPLENDIDLY sane article published in 1931, Mr. Peter Alexander[1] has traced the history of the conjectures which led eventually to the almost universal acceptance of the view that *Henry VIII* was written not by William Shakespeare alone but largely by John Fletcher. The belief in the play's dual authorship was first presented by Malone. Thoroughly sound had been Roderick's observation that the verse of *Henry VIII* differed from that of other Shakespearean plays; but, as Mr. Alexander points out, when Malone, with no further investigation, combined Roderick's observation with Theobald's guess that the eulogy of Elizabeth showed that the play had been first written before 1603, he presented a remarkably "casual combination of conjecture and fact" in stating that the panegyric on James was "added in 1613, after Shakespeare had quitted the stage, by that hand which tampered with the other parts of the play so much, as to have rendered the versification of it of a different colour from all the other plays of Shakespeare." Later, after Spalding and Hickson had argued for the collaboration of Shakespeare and Fletcher in *The Two Noble Kinsmen,* Spedding, acting upon a chance suggestion of Tennyson, advanced the view that Fletcher was the second author in *Henry VIII.*[2] Inevitable was the next step—taken in defiance of all the external evidence—Boyle's denial of the presence of Shakespeare and his assignment of the play to Fletcher and Massinger. Although Boyle's claim has not been without supporters—among

[1] "Conjectural History, or Shakespeare's *Henry VIII,*" *Essays and Studies by Members of the English Association,* XVI (Oxford, 1931), 85-120.

[2] Although he did not go so far as to suggest Fletcher's participation in *Henry VIII,* James Boswell (*The Plays and Poems of William Shakespeare,* 21 vols. [London, 1821], I, 560) had commented in a note on Wolsey's charge to Cromwell: ". . . I have said in a note on . . . *Cymbeline,* that this termination is perpetually to be met with in Fletcher." To illustrate, he quoted passages from *Maid in the Mill* and *Lover's Progress.*

them Robert Browning—it is Spedding's view which has for the past sixty years been generally accepted.

Mr. Alexander has done more than reveal the gradual growth in the conjectural history of *Henry VIII.* He has pointed out that characteristics which have been claimed to be peculiar to Fletcher are to be found in the later plays of Shakespeare. Although there is a change of style noticeable in *Henry VIII,* the change is less pronounced than is the change in *Antony and Cleopatra* from the style in the plays preceding it.

But I need not summarize Mr. Alexander's article. He has, however, given excellent reasons why we should not go counter to the evidence that *Henry VIII* was written by Shakespeare alone. That being true, it may seem superfluous to reprint two articles written prior to Mr. Alexander's paper, in which I question Fletcher's participation and criticize the claim for Massinger. As my method of approach is, however, so different from his, my results may serve to support his conclusion; and so widespread had become the acceptance of Fletcher's collaboration that a further questioning of it may not be altogether redundant.

I have revised and shortened my first note and, in the light of Mr. Alexander's paper, have abandoned the adjective "non-Shakespearean" in referring to the scenes which had been generally assigned to Fletcher.

I

FLETCHER AND *Henry the Eighth*

In rereading recently *The Famous History of the Life of King Henry the Eighth,* I was somewhat surprised at not finding in the parts of the play ascribed to Fletcher those peculiarities of style which I had come to consider as characteristic of him. I hastened to examine Spedding's "Who Wrote Shakespeare's *Henry the Eighth?*"[3] but I finished his discussion with more doubts than I had had before. His ascription of certain scenes

---

[3] *Gentlemen's Magazine,* August, 1850, pp. 115-23; reprinted in *New Shakspere Society Transactions,* 1874, pp. 1-18, with the title, "On the Several Shares of Shakspere and Fletcher in the Play of *Henry VIII.*"

to Fletcher seemed to me to have been made in a most summary manner. He concerned himself not at all with the plays
known to be Fletcher's, but was content simply to point out in
certain scenes of *Henry VIII* what were admitted to be characteristics of Fletcher's style. He did not show that these
characteristics were peculiar to Fletcher; nor did he suggest to
what extent they appear in Fletcher's undoubted work. In a
strict sense, Spedding cannot be said to have made any tests
whatsoever. Like Spalding and Hickson before him, he in-
dulged only in what Fleay called "higher criticism," agreeing
with Furnivall that "Counting can never be a better judge than
real criticism."[4] Though willing to admit the truth of Furnivall's observation, I am Teuton enough to demand a fairly close
agreement between counting and real criticism before assigning
parts of a play to an author for whose participation no external
evidence exists. I should demand that the characteristics upon
which the ascription is made be shown to be characteristics, and,
save in cases where the characteristics are obviously foreign to
one of two men known to have collaborated in the play, that the
characteristics be *peculiar*. Spedding, as I have said, did no
counting at all. He wrote under the influence of previous
articles by Spalding and Hickson, and apparently nominated
Fletcher as the second author in *Henry VIII* because he considered that it had previously been proved that Fletcher and Shakespeare had collaborated in *The Two Noble Kinsmen.*[5] But this
collaboration is still doubted.

Beyond the fact that Fletcher later wrote regularly for the
same company for which Shakespeare had written, there is little
evidence of their collaboration. There seems to be every reason
to question the correctness of the ascription of the lost *Cardenio*
to Fletcher and Shakespeare made by the ambitious publisher
Humphrey Moseley in 1653. Aside from the fact that *Cardenio*

---

[4] "Mr. Hickson's Division of *The Two Noble Kinsmen* Confirmed by the Stop-
Line Test," *N.S.S.T.*, 1874, p. 64.

[5] See *Gent. Mag.*, XXXIV, 381, or the reprint in *N.S.S.T.*, 1874, p. 21, where
Spedding admits the influence of Spalding and "additional light, more perhaps than
I am aware of, from Mr. Hickson himself." Fletcher had been first suggested to
him by Tennyson, who may have been influenced by Boswell's note. See footnote 2
above.

was not included in either the Shakespeare or the Beaumont and Fletcher folio, Moseley's assigning on the same day *The Merry Devil of Edmonton* to Shakespeare alone and the two plays *Henry I* and *Henry II* to Shakespeare and Davenport renders it quite possible that in the ascription of *Cardenio* Moseley was either insincere or misinformed. There remains only *The Two Noble Kinsmen,* published in 1634 as

> Written by the memorable Worthies of their time;
> Mr. John Fletcher, and ⎱ Gent.
> Mr. William Shakespeare ⎰

Scholars are perhaps about equally divided on the question of whether or not Shakespeare had a hand in the play; and if we once doubt the correctness of the title-page, there remains no trustworthy external evidence of any collaboration between Shakespeare and Fletcher.

But even should we grant that Shakespeare and Fletcher were the authors of *The Two Noble Kinsmen,* there seem to me to be many obvious differences of style between the so-called Fletcherian scenes of it and of *Henry VIII,* although the theory of collaboration demands that the two be dated at approximately the same time. In the first place, to take Furnivall's figure, the proportion of non-stop lines in *The Two Noble Kinsmen* is 1 to every 5.66 lines, whereas in *Henry VIII* it is 1 to every 3.85. The same scenes in *Henry VIII* are well larded with general truths, from which *The Two Noble Kinsmen* is remarkably free.[6] In the 1,590 lines ascribed to Fletcher in the former play, there are sixteen statements of general truths, while in 1,398 lines ascribed to him in the latter play there are only two. There is likewise in the scenes of *Henry VIII* an economy of expression far beyond the reach of the second author of the *Noble Kinsmen.* But it is not my purpose to discuss *The Two Noble Kinsmen.* I wish merely to point out that there is very little evidence for collaboration of Shakespeare and Fletcher, and that

[6] The test was applied only to the scenes of *The Two Noble Kinsmen* which Spalding, Hickson, and Littledale agreed in assigning to Fletcher: II, ii-vi; III, iii-vi; IV, i, ii; V, ii. In applying tests to *Henry VIII,* I have taken the scenes usually ascribed to Fletcher: I, iii, iv; II, i, ii; III, i, ii(*b*); IV, i, ii; V, ii-v.

in the play for which the best case can be made for such collaboration, the style of the so-called Fletcherian scenes is different
from the style of the scenes ascribed Fletcher in *Henry VIII*.

The strongest argument for Fletcher's participation in *Henry
VIII* is certainly the great number of lines ending in a stressed
extra syllable. The tendency toward the use of extra-syllabic
endings is the most pronounced characteristic of Fletcher's style,
and this tendency is most marked in certain scenes of *Henry
VIII*. I have compared the proportion here with the proportion in four of Fletcher's plays and have found that, although
the proportion in *Henry VIII* is almost twice as great as the
proportion in the Fletcherian scenes of *Philaster* and *The Maid's
Tragedy*, it is practically the same as that in *Bonduca* and *Valentinian*—a little smaller than in the former, a little greater than
in the latter. But in spite of this recognized Fletcherian characteristic in *Henry VIII*, the differences in style, as shown by
other tests which I give later, make me doubt that the scenes
denied Shakespeare were written wholly by Fletcher, that his
collaboration with Shakespeare was "direct; i.e., after making a
fairly detailed outline, each writer took certain scenes, and to all
intents, completed these scenes after his own fashion."[7] If
Fletcher had a hand in *Henry VIII*, the results of these tests
would suggest that it was not so free a hand as has come to be
believed, that either he was revising the work of another, or that
the peculiarities of his style were modified by the active collaboration of another.

A comparison of *Henry VIII* with its sources argues strongly
against Fletcher's participation. In her article, "The Authorship of Henry the Eighth," Miss Nicolson wrote:

A study of sources of the play throws little real light upon the
problem of authorship. . . . If we accept for the time being the division of scenes made by Spedding, we find that in the Shakespearean
portions there are fourteen direct borrowings from Holinshed; three

---

[7] W. A. Neilson and A. H. Thorndike, *The Facts about Shakespeare* (New
York, 1922), p. 160. The view of Miss Nicolson, I believe, differs from this only
in that she thinks that Fletcher added his scenes later; she still accepts the same
scenes as by Fletcher alone.—"The Authorship of Henry the Eighth," *PMLA*,
XXXVII (1922), 484-502.

from Foxe; one from Hall; two which may be from Cavendish or Holinshed. Fletcher has ten from Holinshed, two from Hall, four from Foxe, four which may be from Cavendish or Holinshed.[8]

When she wrote that "A study of sources throws little real light upon the problem of authorship," Miss Nicolson meant, of course, only that the source material was used in the same manner and to about the same extent in the parts ascribed to the two authors. "In no other play of Shakespeare's are the borrowings more pronounced than in this, and in no play have the historical passages been so little revised. Both authors have simply versified long passages from the chronicles. . . ."[9] But such pronounced borrowing was certainly not Fletcher's wont. It seems scarcely probable that he should here borrow so directly from his sources and never do the same again. If one compares *Bonduca*—Fletcher's only play based upon Holinshed—with the account given in either Holinshed or Tacitus, one finds practically no verbal borrowing whatsoever, although both accounts offer several excellent opportunities. Though Holinshed gives at length the prebattle prayer of Bonduca and the speech of Suetonius to his troops, Fletcher, when he wrote speeches for these leaders in the identical situations,[10] borrowed not a single word. In the whole of *Bonduca*, there are scarcely half a dozen echoes of Holinshed, and there is not an instance of even a clause from Holinshed being versified.

In view, therefore, of Fletcher's general practice and especially of his use of Holinshed in *Bonduca*, we can at least state most emphatically that the pronounced verbal borrowing in the so-called Fletcherian parts of *Henry VIII* is not characteristic of Fletcher.

Likewise several stylistic tests which I have made seem to show that certain characteristics of Fletcher's style are lacking in these scenes of *Henry VIII*. In these tests I have attempted to apply to several of Fletcher's plays and to the parts of *Henry VIII* denied Shakespeare some of the observations upon Fletch-

[8] *Op. cit.*, p. 487.   [9] *Ibid.*, p. 488.
[10] The only difference is that in Holinshed, Suetonius addresses the troops, whereas in *Bonduca* he addresses the captains.

er's style noted by Spalding in the essay which was to influence Spedding.[11]

One of the characteristics of Fletcher's style noted by Spalding was the absence of general truths. Spalding used the term "general truths" loosely to include maxims, proverbs, and concisely worded observations upon human nature. For the appearance of general truths, I examined *The Faithful Shepherdess*, the Fletcherian parts of *The Maid's Tragedy* and *Philaster*,[12] which must have been written shortly before *Henry VIII*, and *Bonduca* and *Valentinian*, which must have been written within a few years following, as Richard Burbage, who acted in both plays, died in 1618.[13] In the 590 lines of *The Maid's Tragedy* and the 619 lines of *Philaster* assigned by all critics to Fletcher, there is not a single instance of a general truth, and in *The Faithful Shepherdess* there are but three. In the 1,590 lines of *Henry VIII* ascribed to Fletcher, there are sixteen—an average of 1 to every 99.3 lines. In *Bonduca*, there are but seven—an average of 1 to every 328; in *Valentinian*, fourteen—an average of 1 to every 197.6; although it might be imagined that, inasmuch as the one is a tragedy of ancient Britain and the other a tragedy of Rome, there would be a greater opportunity for the introduction of general truths than in *Henry VIII*.

Spalding noted, too, that Fletcher was not prone to use, as were Shakespeare and Massinger, "an involved and parenthetical mode of construction."[14] This observation I have tested in the same plays, noting the introduction into the verse of parenthetical matter in the center of a clause. A few instances will perhaps best illustrate what I mean:

> Is a Wifes loss
> (For her abuse much good may do his Grace,

[11] "A Letter on Shakspere's Authorship of *The Two Noble Kinsmen*," reprinted in *N.S.S.T.*, 1876.

[12] Only the scenes which Thorndike, Fleay, Oliphant, and Boyle have agreed in assigning to Fletcher: *The Maid's Tragedy*, II, ii; IV, i; V, i(*a*), ii (Thorndike's text); and *Philaster*, I, i(*b*); V, iii, iv.

[13] Thorndike dates the two plays 1615(?) and 1615-16(?). Chambers assigns *Bonduca* to 1609◇1611 or 1613◇1614.   [14] *Op. cit.*, p. 57.

I'll make as bold with his Wife, if I can)
More than the fading of a few fresh colours,

[*Valentinian*, III, i.]

Come, chicken, let's go seek some place of strength
(The Countrey's full of Scouts) to rest a while in

[*Bonduca*, IV, ii.]

Some little memory of me will stir him—
I know his noble nature—not to let
Thy hopeful service perish too: . . . .

[*Henry VIII*, III, ii.]

In the so-called Fletcherian parts of *Henry VIII*, there are seventeen such interruptions, making an average of 1 to every 89.2 lines. Though the four such interruptions in *The Maid's Tragedy* raise the average in that play to 1 in 141, in the other plays the average is much smaller—in *Philaster* 1 to 171, in *Valentinian* 1 to 212.8, in *Bonduca* 1 to 254.3, and in *The Faithful Shepherdess* even less.

Neither does an examination of non-stop lines in the plays indicate Fletcher's hand in *Henry VIII*. Furnivall's tables in confirmation of Spedding in no way suggest the participation of Fletcher, for Furnivall gives no estimate of non-stop lines in Fletcher's plays. The interesting result of this test when applied to *The Maid's Tragedy, Philaster, Bonduca,* and *Valentinian,* is not the final figures, though these do show differences. The proportion of non-stop lines in *Henry VIII* is 1 to every 3.85 lines; in *The Maid's Tragedy* 1 to every 4.90; in *Philaster* 1 to every 4.89; in *Bonduca* 1 to every 5.40; and in *Valentinian* hardly 1 to every 6. What I think striking about the test is that of the twelve scenes ascribed to Fletcher in *Henry VIII*, in only three is the proportion of run-on lines as small as 1 in 4, and of these three scenes two have only thirty-five and forty-one lines, respectively.[15] Of the forty-seven scenes, however, in the four other plays, there are but two in which the proportion is as large

---

[15] The three scenes are III, i (184 lines); V, ii (35 lines); and V, iv (41 lines of verse).

as 1 in 4, and each of these scenes is less than one hundred lines.[16]

The most striking difference, however, between the style of *Henry VIII* and the style of Fletcher's plays lies in the repetition of words. Spalding was correct in his characterization of Fletcher as "diffuse both in his leading thought and in his illustrations. . . . He amplifies, is elaborate, not vigorous."[17] The instances of the immediate repetition of the same word are in the parts of *Henry VIII* assigned Fletcher almost negligible— there are only eleven, while there are literally masses of such repetition in the other plays examined. There is more than twice as much repetition in the 590 lines of *The Maid's Tragedy* as in the 1,590 lines of *Henry VIII,* and there is almost three times as much in the 619 lines of *Philaster.* If we take merely that type of repetition which is most frequent in *Henry VIII,* we find the instances much more frequent in Fletcher. Of the eleven bits of repetition in *Henry VIII,* six consist of the repeating of the same word with a modifying word or phrase:

O, very mad, exceeding mad, in love too   [I, iv, 27.]

This is the cardinal's doing, the king-cardinal   [II, ii, 20.]

Farewell, a long farewell, to all my greatness   [III, ii, 351.]

. . . . a frost, a killing frost   [III, ii, 355.]

O, 'tis a burden, Cromwell, 'tis a burden
Too heavy for a man that hopes for heaven   [III, ii, 384-85.]

Was it discretion, lords, to let this man,
This good man,—few of you deserve that title,—
This honest man, wait like a lousy footboy   [V, iii, 137-39.]

The following table illustrates how much more often this type appears in the plays of Fletcher.

Maid's Tragedy	590	9	1 to every 65.5 lines
Philaster	619	10	1 to every 61.9 lines
Bonduca	2,294	35	1 to every 65.5 lines
Valentinian	2,765	21	1 to every 131.6 lines
Henry VIII	1,590	6	1 to every 265.0 lines

[16] *Bonduca,* III, i (85 lines); V, ii (97 lines).
[17] *Op. cit.,* p. 11.

This table, it should be remembered, is merely for that type which represents 50 per cent of the repetition in *Henry VIII*. It is by no means true that the amount of repetition in that play is comparable to the amount in *Valentinian*, of which this type represents but a small fraction.

I have, of course, applied but a few tests to but a few plays, yet the tests have shown that between the so-called Fletcherian scenes of *Henry VIII* and certain of Fletcher's plays of about the same date, there are differences in the introduction of general truths and parenthetical constructions, and in the use of repetition and run-on lines. These stylistic differences, when considered with a use of sources unparalleled in Fletcher's plays, should, I feel, until the examination of more plays has shown other results, make us skeptical of Fletcher's participation in *Henry VIII*. They at least seem to show that the scenes assigned to Fletcher were not written by him alone "after his own fashion." They suggest that, if indeed he had a hand in the play at all, his participation was limited: either he was revising another's work, or the peculiarities of his style and method were modified by a collaborator.

2

Mr. Sykes's Case for Massinger's Part-Authorship

Most scholars have, I judge, always been skeptical, if not contemptuous, of the possibility of determining the authorship of any Elizabethan play by marshaling a host of parallel passages. But when we find such notable scholars as the late Mr. Bullen and Mr. J. Dover Wilson, in passages which I shall quote later, upholding the collecting of parallels as a method of determining authorship, we should, I think, examine carefully the method in one of the articles to which they have given their sanction. Though I cannot agree with them as to the value of such a test as it has been applied, I think that when correctly applied the collecting of parallel passages may be made a very valuable test in questions of authorship. I shall attempt to point out by illustration why the test as it has most often been applied is utterly futile, and how in some cases it may, when supported by further examination, become of real value.

The most prolific, and perhaps the most convincing, of those who have employed the parallel-passage test is Mr. H. Dugdale Sykes, who, according to Mr. Wilson, "has shown us how fruitful a method the collection of parallels can be when carried out by a fair-minded and scrupulous scholar."[18] For discussion here I select one of the articles from *Sidelights on Shakespeare*[19] which Mr. Bullen singled out for especial praise. I quote Mr. Bullen fully, for I shall have occasion to refer again to the passage he notes:

. . . after reading the articles of Robert Boyle and Mr. Sykes it is impossible to resist the conviction that though a few Shakespearean passages are to be found in *The Two Noble Kinsmen,* the play as a whole (with its merits and defects) must be given to Massinger and Fletcher. If there is little of Shakespeare in *The Two Noble Kinsmen* there is perhaps even less in *Henry VIII.* The trial-scene of Katherine (II, iv) is conducted with much dignity and impressiveness, but it follows closely—very closely—the actual wording of Holinshed; and, to show that Massinger was quite capable of writing this scene, Mr. Sykes refers the reader to *The Unnatural Combat* (IV, i), where Theocrine, pleading to her father,

> "Alas, Sir,
> Did I but know in what I give offence," &c.

recalls "in tone, phrasing and metre" the voice of Katherine.[20]

As we have a large amount of the work of each of the two authors in question, Massinger and Shakespeare, and as we have already some data on Massinger's frequent borrowing from Shakespeare, we should be able to determine more accurately the value of the parallel-passage test than we should in the case of a play for the authorship of which we have no clue, or in the case of authors whose undisputed work is limited to comparatively few plays.

I shall not pause over Mr. Sykes's introductory arguments.

[18] *Times Literary Supplement,* January 23, 1920, p. 52.
[19] Stratford-upon-Avon, 1919, pp. 18-47.
[20] *Ibid.,* Publisher's Note, pp. viii-ix.

Most of them are weak and unconvincing, and he apparently recognizes them as such when he writes: "Decisive proof of Massinger's authorship must be found, if it is to be found at all, in the language of the play."[21]

Mr. Sykes then marshals his host of parallels between *Henry VIII* and the plays of Massinger, and after presenting them, hazards: "But it will probably be agreed that the evidence already produced renders any more elaborate investigation unnecessary."[22] Though doubtless there are among his parallels some which we might question, on the whole the passages cited are surprisingly similar, and, I think, present one of the most striking arrays of parallel passages ever brought together for such a purpose. But how can he suggest that he has rendered "any more elaborate investigation unnecessary"? What has he proved other than that there exist a number of parallel passages in *Henry VIII* and various plays of Massinger? The line of investigation he began he abandoned when it was hardly a third finished. Before we are justified in drawing any conclusions whatsoever from the existence of these parallels, several other rather extensive pieces of investigation must be made.

1. One must investigate the extent of Massinger's borrowings from other Shakespearean plays. Are there, for instance, in the plays of Massinger proportionately more echoes of the ideas and phraseology of *Henry VIII* than of *Hamlet*, *Othello*, or any other of the more popular plays? Until we are able to answer this question positively, our knowledge of the recurrences in Massinger of the ideas of *Henry VIII* avails us nothing. If we must judge from the Shakespearean allusions which have been noted in Massinger—and here it seems fair to omit the parallels collected by Mr. Sykes, who searched Massinger's plays for echoes of *Henry VIII* but says nothing of echoes of other plays—we are justified in assuming, until investigation has shown the contrary to be true, that Massinger borrows as heavily from *Hamlet*, *Othello*, and *Coriolanus* as he does from *Henry VIII*. In *The Shakespeare Allusion Book* and in Appendix IV of Cruickshank's *Philip Massinger*, the number of echoes noted

---

[21] P. 22. [22] P. 43.

in Massinger are: from *Hamlet*, 11; from *Othello*, 8; from *Henry VIII*, 6;[23] from *Coriolanus*, 5.

2. Investigation must likewise show at what period in his career Massinger reveals the greatest influence of Shakespeare. Mr. Sykes admits that the style of the disputed scenes of *Henry VIII* is "more akin to Shakespeare's than is Massinger's normal style as exhibited in his later independent plays," and he suggests that "the explanation is to be found in the early date of the play, and in that alone," affirming that we should expect that "Massinger's earlier dramatic work would most strongly show the influence of his master."[24] But we have no right to entertain such an expectation until further investigation has reversed the conclusions which would be drawn from the data so far collected. The three plays in which have been noted the greatest number of parallels to Shakespeare all postdate the First Folio, and two of the three are very late plays, *The Great Duke of Florence* (1627), and *The Emperor of the East* (1631). Likewise when we examine the passages collected by Mr. Sykes, we discover not only that three of the four plays in which he saw the greatest number of parallels to *Henry VIII* were written after the appearance of the folio, but also that among the four are the two late plays mentioned above, *The Great Duke of Florence* and *The Emperor of the East*.[25] If, indeed, Massinger's earlier dramatic work most strongly showed the influence of Shakespeare, we might expect to find a large number of echoes and parallels in the scenes which Massinger contributed in his collaboration with Fletcher. However, of the

[23] This does not include what has been noted as an echo from that part of the play which Sykes ascribed to Fletcher.   [24] *Sidelights on Shakespeare*, p. 43.

[25] The five plays in which the greatest number of parallels have been recognized are:

	To Shak. Plays Other Than *Henry VIII*	To *Henry VIII* Noted by Mr. Sykes	Total
Emperor of the East (1631)..........	6	8	14
Great Duke of Florence (1627).......	6	6	12
Parliament of Love (1624)..........	8	4	12
Duke of Milan (1620)	4	7	11
Renegado (1624)...................	0	8	8

twenty-six parallels and allusions to Shakespeare which have been noted in the Beaumont and Fletcher plays, only three are found in scenes frequently ascribed to Massinger, nor is there general agreement in the ascription of these three scenes (*Knight of Malta*, IV, i; *Queen of Corinth*, I, ii; *Beggar's Bush*, V, ii). Until, then, further investigation has demonstrated that it was in his earlier plays that Massinger was most strongly influenced by Shakespeare, we must infer, with Mr. Cruickshank, "that Massinger studied the folio of 1623 carefully."[26] In Massinger's sixteen[27] independent plays more allusions to Shakespeare have been found in the last eight—those after 1626— than in the first eight—those before 1626.

3. Again, it seems hardly fair for one seeking to determine authorship by parallel passages to examine the work of one claimant without examining with equal care the work of all possible claimants. Mr. Sykes remembers to tell us only when Shakespeare does not use a similar word or phrase. I quote Mr. Sykes:

Norfolk describes to Buckingham the wonders of "The Field of the Cloth of Gold," in a speech ending with these words:

> When these suns—
> For so they phrase 'em—by their heralds challeng'd
> The noble spirits to arms, they did perform
> Beyond thought's compass; that former fabulous story,
> Being now seen possible enough, got credit,
> That Bevis was believed.

Whether contemporary spectators spoke of the two kings as "suns," we may be permitted to doubt. But that Massinger would so have "phrased 'em" we may well believe. It is one of his favourite figures of speech and it is used four times in this scene. "Fabulous story," which is nowhere to be found in Shakespeare, appears again in Massinger's *The Picture*, I, ii. . . . Nor is there in any of Shakespeare's plays a single allusion to Bevis. Massinger twice refers to that mythical hero . . . . —on both occasions to typify the extravagant and incredible.[28]

[26] A. H. Cruickshank, *Philip Massinger* (Oxford, 1920), p. 168.

[27] As a number of parallels have been noted in *The Virgin Martyr* (1621), by Massinger and Dekker, I group that here with the plays written by Massinger alone.

[28] *Sidelights on Shakespeare*, pp. 23-24.

Mr. Sykes did not think it necessary to remind us that the figure of the sun was likewise a favorite with Shakespeare, or that it appears again in *Henry VIII* in lines which Mr. Sykes ascribes to Fletcher. The figure is used in Shakespeare's other plays no fewer than eight times. To the opening lines of *Richard III*, which have probably already come into the reader's mind, I might add:

> Had princes sit, like stars, about his throne,
> And he the sun.
> > [*Pericles*, II, iii, 40.]

> Being but the shadow of your son,
> Becomes a sun and makes your son a shadow.
> > [*King John*, II, i, 500.]

> A mockery king of snow,
> Standing before the sun of Bolingbroke.
> > [*Richard II*, IV, i, 261.]

and the following which Mr. Sykes gives to Fletcher:

> Seek the king,
> That sun, I pray, may never set.
> > [*Henry VIII*, III, ii, 415.]

Finding the phrase "fabulous story" apparently but one time in the acknowledged works of Massinger, Mr. Sykes thinks its appearance in *Henry VIII* points toward Massinger's authorship. True, it appears in no other Shakespearean play. If we omit the possessive pronouns, Shakespeare uses *story* with sixteen different adjectives, and of the sixteen he repeats only one— *sad*, which appears five times. Upon examination, therefore, Mr. Sykes's observation would seem to have not more than one-seventeenth of the value he gives it. And the same is true in the case of Bevis, there being many figures to whom Shakespeare refers in but one play. Shall we question *2 Henry IV* because that happens to be the only play in which Sir Dagonet is mentioned?

Mr. Sykes's failure to inquire into Shakespeare's phrasing when noting parallels in Massinger is forcibly revealed by a strange error which he makes on page 28. There one is a bit surprised to read what is ostensibly a reproduction of *Henry VIII*, I, ii, 84 ff.:

> If we shall stand still,
> In fear our notion will be mock'd or carp'd at,
> We should take root here where we sit, or sit
> State-statues only.

"It is strange," adds Mr. Sykes, "that it has never been noticed that there is here a corruption of the text. It does not seem to have occurred to any commentator to ask himself why a person's 'notion' should be any less likely to be carped at because he was standing still. The word should be 'motion,' i.e., movement, action."

It is possible, of course, that Mr. Sykes was so unfortunate as to have access to only a carelessly printed edition of *Henry VIII*. But had he consulted the First Folio, or even another text, he would have found his judgment confirmed but his reading anticipated, for the First Folio and every one of the sixteen editions I have consulted, except two apparently edited by Sir Israel Gollancz,[29] have "motion" and not "notion." Clearly here Mr. Sykes did not, before citing what he considers parallel passages in Massinger, inquire into the possibility of parallel phrases and ideas in other plays of Shakespeare, for in no concordance could he have failed to find the passage under "motion."

The compound "state-statue" in the preceding quotation is nowhere else to be found in Shakespeare. Although Mr. Sykes was unable to find the identical combination in Massinger, he did discover in Massinger's plays eight compounds with "state" for the first element, and he concludes, therefore, that "the word 'state-statue' is, again, characteristic of Massinger."[30] But the word is thoroughly Shakespearean. It suggests Shakespeare not only in the manner of its coinage, but equally in its being

[29] One is the Temple edition, the other the Booklovers' edition, published by the University Society, New York, 1901. Possibly Sir Israel is not responsible for the text of the latter edition, though the critical notes are said to be by him and the name of no other editor or collaborator is mentioned anywhere in the volume.

[30] *Sidelights on Shakespeare*, p. 29.

used but once. In an interesting study of "The Once Used Words in Shakespeare," James Davie Butler observed that "no one class of once-used words is more conspicuous in Shakespeare than *alliterative compounds*," and he illustrates his observation by listing in what he calls a "very partial register" one hundred and thirty-five such formations.[31]

The existence of parallel passages may be due to an author's repeating himself, to imitation or influence, to chance, or to the idiom of the day. Mr. Sykes has certainly pointed out far too many parallels to permit our dismissing them as due to either of the last two; they must be due either to direct imitation or to the same author's having penned them. But surely we cannot hope to distinguish between one's imitation of another's lines and one's recollection of lines which he himself had previously penned, simply by the poetic merit of the passages and by the aptness of their use. Here, again, it seems to me, Mr. Sykes fails to take into consideration much that is essential. To illustrate, a rather extensive quotation is necessary. Mr. Sykes writes:

I will now take the famous trial-scene (II, iv) and will first quote from Katherine's speech, when she is summoned before the King:

> Alas, sir,
> In what have I offended you? What cause
> Hath my behaviour given to your displeasure
> That thus you should proceed to put me off,
> And take your good grace from me? Heaven witness,
> I have been to you a true and humble wife,
> And at all times to your will conformable,
> Ever in fear to kindle your dislike,
> Yea, subject to your countenance, glad or sorry
> As I saw it inclin'd . . . .

[31] James Davie Butler, "The Once Used Words in Shakespeare," *New York Shakespeare Society Publications*, 1886, p. 5. Might not Mr. Sykes as well claim for Massinger the Prologue to *Romeo and Juliet*, even though it was printed when Massinger was scarcely fourteen? Shakespeare nowhere else used the word "star-cross'd," which was a great favorite with Massinger and is found in *The Bashful Lover*, III, iii ("star-cross'd fortune"), *Believe as You List*, IV, ii ("star-cross'd king"), *Emperor of the East*, V, i ("star-cross'd subject"), *The Great Duke of Florence*, V, ii ("star-cross'd destiny").

> . . . . if in the course
> And process of this time you can report,
> And prove it, too, against my honour aught,
>
> . . . .
> . . . . in God's name
> Turn me away, and let the foul'st contempt
> Shut door upon me.

This, at least, say the critics, *must* be Shakespeare's—no one else *could* have written it. But after all, it is only Holinshed turned into blank verse. . . .

What reason is there to suppose that Massinger was not capable of turning Holinshed into good blank verse? And if the task was set him, how would he perform it? I will try to show that he would do it precisely in the way in which it actually has been done here.

First, with regards to the words "Alas, Sir," with which the Queen begins her appeal. No inference can be drawn from the mere occurrence of the words, because, as we have seen, they are taken from Holinshed. But is there not a very strong inference that the speech is Massinger's when we find in his plays no fewer than six speeches beginning with "Alas, Sir," and that always these words take exactly the same position in the line and accent in the metre. . . .

This is, however, a minor detail. The whole speech is typical Massinger. And it is clear, I think, not only that he wrote it, but that he regarded it with great satisfaction and recalled it some years afterwards when he came to write Theocrine's speech in IV. i. of *The Unnatural Combat*:

> Alas, Sir,
> Did I but know in what I give offence
> In my repentance I would show my sorrow . . .
> . . . . On my knees, Sir,
> As I have ever squarred my will by yours,
> And liked and loath'd with your eyes, I beseech you
> To teach me what the nature of my fault is,
> That hath incens'd you . . . .
> . . . . If that I,
> Out of the least neglect of mine hereafter,
> Make you remember it, may I sink ever
> Under your dread command, sir. . . .

Could there be anything more striking than the resemblance of these two speeches in tone, phrasing and metre? Can anyone doubt that they were written by the same man? . . .[32]

The only thing I see in the lines about which there can be little doubt is that Massinger recalled Katherine's lines when he wrote Theocrine's. When Mr. Sykes notes that Katherine's speech is taken almost word for word from Holinshed, he neglects to remind us that in several of Shakespeare's later plays many long speeches are but paraphrases of his sources. He suggests, indeed, that we know of no such paraphrases in Massinger when he asks, "What reason is there to suppose that Massinger was not capable of turning Holinshed's prose into good blank verse . . . if the task was set him?" But it is not a question of capability so much as a question of method and habit. Mr. Sykes recognizes that when he adds "if the task was set him." But who would set him such a task? We can hardly believe it would be Fletcher, the only collaborator Mr. Sykes admits, whose method was very different and who, when he turned to Holinshed in *Bonduca*, retained nothing more than the faintest verbal echo.

I have tried not to appear an advocate of Shakespeare's authorship, but simply to call attention to the incompleteness of the "parallel-passage test" as Mr. Sykes has employed it. Although Mr. Sykes's collection of parallels may be justly said to be an important contribution to the study of Massinger, it is hardly a demonstration of Massinger's part-authorship of *Henry VIII*. We are not justified surely in assigning the play to Massinger until further investigation along such lines as those I have suggested permits us to reverse conclusions forced on us by the only evidence we have.

Before we can hope to interpret properly the parallels pointed out by Mr. Sykes, we must study the plays of Massinger, first, in their relation to *Henry VIII*, and second, in their relation to the other plays of the First Folio. We must know not only to what extent Massinger repeats the ideas and phraseology of *Henry VIII*, but also to what extent he repeats

[32] *Sidelights on Shakespeare*, pp. 31-33.

the ideas and phraseology of other Shakespearean plays. We
must likewise know to what extent Massinger repeats himself
in plays admitted to be his, and we must compare with such
repetitions his echoes of *Henry VIII* and his many obvious borrowings from the works of others. Again, we must study the
relationship of *Henry VIII* not simply to the plays of Massinger, but to the plays of the First Folio as well. We must
know to what extent the characteristics of Shakespeare's style
are repeated in his various plays, and how in such repetitions
Henry VIII compares with the other plays. Finally, since it is
unanimously admitted that the style of *Henry VIII* more closely
resembles the style of Shakespeare than does the style of Massinger's later independent plays, we must demonstrate rather
than "expect" that Massinger's earlier work most strongly shows
the influence of his master. Only when these supplementary
studies have been made can the parallels noted be said to have
any value in the question of authorship.

VII

The Hungry Knave
in the Beaumont and Fletcher Plays

THOUGH THERE is prefixed to the First Folio of Shakespeare a list of "The Names of the Principall Actors in All these Playes," little success has been made in identifying the various actors with particular parts. But that Shakespeare frequently, if not regularly, had certain of his fellow actors in mind when he described his characters is suggested by the contrast which runs through so many of his plays of the tall blonde (Silvia, Helena, Rosalind) with her shorter fellow (Julia, Hermia, Celia) and perhaps by his making Hamlet "fat and scant of breath."[1] I believe there is no evidence that any of Shakespeare's predecessors were accustomed to keep in mind as they wrote the physical characteristics of their actors and the advantages or limitations which these characteristics offered or made necessary.[2] But at least this secret of Shakespeare's success the Jacobean dramatists recognized and adopted.

The plays of Fletcher and his collaborators are larded with descriptions of the physical peculiarities of the characters which are clearly suggested by the peculiarities of the actors for whom the parts were designed. It is easy to recognize certain parts written for "the tall fat fellow," John Lowen, and, with almost equal certainty, others designed for Joseph Taylor, "of middle stature, and a brown complexion."[3]

[1] See, however, Professor M. P. Tilley's suggestion, which is not without probability, that *fat* here means perspiration. "Two Shakespearean Notes," *Journal of English and Germanic Philology*, XXIV (1925), 315-24.

[2] We need not even except plays written to be acted by companies of children, for though there are constant jests on the boys' diminutive stature, they apply to boys in general rather than to individual boys.

[3] The dramatists clearly had Lowen in mind when they designed the parts of Aubrey (*The Bloody Brother*), Belleur (*The Wild-Goose Chase*), Leon (*Rule a Wife and Have a Wife*), and probably Soldier (*Nice Valour*); and they probably recognized that Taylor would take the parts of Pedro (*The Pilgrim*), Albert (*The Sea Voyage*), and Lysander (*Lover's Progress*).

In this essay I shall try to identify the actor for whom perhaps was designed one of the most frequently reappearing types
in the Beaumont and Fletcher plays—the hungry merry knave
or the comic image of famine. The frequent repetition of the
same types of characters by the Jacobean dramatists was due
certainly not wholly to the rapidity with which the dramatists
wrote and the popularity of those types, but in a large measure
to the suitability of a certain type of character to a particular
actor. This suitability of the actor is, of course, especially important where physical qualifications are demanded, as in parts
where much of the comedy depends upon the actor's extreme
thinness.

In *Bonduca* the merry hungry knave Corporal Judas is repeatedly likened unto Famine;[4] Geta in *The Prophetess* is told
by the Second Lictor,

> Your worship is a man of a spare body,
> And prone to anger.   [III, ii.]

Mallfort, the foolish steward in *The Lover's Progress*, thus
describes his wasted body:

> Last Lent, my Lady call'd me her Poor John,
> But now I am grown a walking Skeleton,
> You may see through, and through me;   [I, i.]

and similarly Lazarillo in *Love's Cure* complains that

they tell me in *Sevil* here, I look like an Eel, with a mans head: and
your neighbor the Smith here hard by, would have borrowed me th'
other day, to have fish'd with me, because he had lost his Angle-rod.
     [II, i.]

In this last play, to be sure, there are two thin men; though
Lazarillo's thinness is made much the more ridiculous, Bobadilla refers to his own "slender hanches" (I, ii), and Clara
rails upon him as

> *Signior Spindle* . . .
> You Dog-skin-fac'd rogue, pilcher, you poor *John* . . .
> Now, thou lean, dry'd, and ominous visag'd knave.   [II, ii.]

---

[4] Several times in II, iii, and IV, ii. Cf. V, i, where Hengest calls him "the
lean rogue."

In *The Spanish Curate,* also, both Lopez and his sexton Diego seem to be thin, although little comedy is developed from their hunger as Leandro soon supplies them with means.

In *The Queen of Corinth* there are said to be three pictures of lean famine—Onus, his Uncle, and his Tutor, though Onus obviously represents the most exaggerated picture. In II, iv, Euphanes speaks of them as "these thin Cubs," and Sosicles in III, i, describes them as "a treatise of famine divided into three branches." That the thinness of Onus was, however, the more exaggerated and more comic is shown by Uncle's statement that "I have try'd to famish him" (IV, i) and by the following dialogue:

Era[*ton*].   He's exceeding meagre.
Tut[*or*].   His contemplation—
Unc[*le*].   Besides 'tis fit
Learners should be kept hungry.
Nea[*nthes*].   You all contemplate;
For three such wretched pictures of lean famine
I never saw together.   [I, iii.]

And the Page rails upon them in language which suggests that one of them (the Uncle?) was tall as well as thin:

Ye Crow-pick'd heads, which your thin shoulders bear
As does the Poles on Corinth Bridge the Traitors: . . .
His Page is able to swindge three such whelpes:
Uncle, why stand ye off: long-man, advance.   [IV, i.]

These three parts have nothing to do with the plot and are so small as to suggest that they were inserted for no other reason than the fun to be got out of the ridiculous thinness of Onus.[5]

---

[5] Possibly *The Sea Voyage* also presents three thin comics. In IV, iii, when Clarinda observes "Me thinks ye look but thin," Morillat, Franville and Lamure cry:

Mor. Oh, we are starved, . . .
Lam. We are all poor starv'd knaves.
Fran. Neither liberty nor meat, lady.
Mor. We were handsome men . . .
But now we look like rogues, like poor starv'd rogues.

The three rogues, abandoned on a desert island, have, of course, been without food for some time. No further comedy, however, is derived from their thinness, and no suggestion is offered as to whose is the most extreme.

Finally in *Women Pleased* Penurio, who is addressed as "Leangut" (III, ii), replies to the question "what wind blew you?"

> Faith 'tis true,
> Any strong wind will blow me like a Feather,
> I am all Air, nothing of earth within me,
> Nor have not had this month, but that good Dinner
> Your Worship gave me yesterday, that staies by me,
> And gives me ballast, else the Sun would draw me.   [II, iv.]

The only effort which has been made to study the casting of these rôles is, I believe, that of Professor T. W. Baldwin in his volume *The Organization and Personnel of the Shakespearean Company*. Although he does not attempt to identify the actor for every part I have discussed, he assigns the principal "lean-gut" rôles to no fewer than three actors. The part of Geta *(The Prophetess)* to John Shanke; those of Onus *(The Queen of Corinth)* and Mallfort *(Lover's Progress)* to Thomas Pollard; those of Judas *(Bonduca)*, Penurio *(Women Pleased)*, and Lopez *(The Spanish Curate)* to Nicholas Toolie.[6] Against some of these assignments there seem to me to be several good arguments. First of all, there exists no evidence that either Pollard or Toolie was exceptionally thin. Indeed, Professor Baldwin, although he recognizes that the authors "cut the play to fit the actors" and that "specific allusions to personal characteristics probably are to be attributed to the actor who took the part, rather than to the author's idealized picture,"[7] assigned to Pollard the part of the Lieutenant in *The Humorous Lieutenant*, who is described as "a goodly man" and of whom it is said, "I do believe a horse begot this fellow; He never knew his strength yet." As *The Humorous Lieutenant* was most certainly written between *The Queen of Corinth* and *Lover's Progress*, Pollard, if the three parts were written for him, must have found an amazing tonic which he soon thereafter discontinued.

The only parts which Nicholas Toolie is definitely known to have taken are those of Barnavelt's wife in *Sir John van*

---

[6] See Appendix IV, pp. 373-87.   [7] *Ibid.*, p. 373.

Olden Barnavelt (1619) and of a madman in Webster's *The Duchess of Malfi* (1619-1623). Although there exists no evidence that he was, he may, of course, have been thin, and may well have taken some of the "lean-gut" rôles, for in certain of the plays, as has been noted, there seem to have been two or even three actors whose thinness was sufficiently exaggerated to provoke comment or laughter. That the more extreme pictures of famine, "the walking skeletons," were, however, not designed for Toolie is indicated by the fact that the plays in which they appear do not all fall within the period of Toolie's service with the company. He was presumably a member of the King's Men from 1605, or earlier, to his death in 1623.[8] He had, therefore, been with the company for a decade or more before the part of the thin rogue appears and, which is more important, the part continues in plays written after his death.[9]

Although some of the "thin" rôles may have been taken by Toolie or by Pollard, or by other members of the company, I am inclined to believe that all of the parts for the extremely thin comedian were designed for one particular actor, that Fletcher and his collaborators were capitalizing the physical peculiarities of an actor just as today we see the moving pictures capitalizing fatness, thinness, crossed eyes, and the like. First, it is to be noted that in their first presentation of the hungry knave, Lazarillo in *The Woman Hater*, c. 1606, he is not referred to as thin; indeed his being always attended by a small page suggests that Lazarillo, in size at least, follows in the Falstaff tradition. The first of the Beaumont and Fletcher plays in which we have sport furnished by the leanness of the comedian is *Bonduca*, which, if the list of principal actors preceding the play in the folio is to be trusted, must have come between 1609 and 1611 or between 1613 and 1614.[10] There seems to be every reason to accept the later date.[11]

---

[8] See Edwin Nungezer, *A Dictionary of Actors and of Other Persons Associated with the Public Representation of Plays in England before 1642* (New Haven, 1929), p. 375.

[9] Especially in Massinger's *The Picture* (1629), discussed later.

[10] Chambers, *Elizabethan Stage*, III, 228.

[11] Earlier critics had agreed in dating the play between 1615 and 1618. The other plays I have noted are dated as follows: *The Queen of Corinth c.* 1617,

Moreover, there is evidence which points to the King's Men having at just about this time acquired the services of an actor who later was to establish a reputation as a comedian and who was, as is shown by a part clearly written for him, remarkably thin.[12] I refer to John Shanke. Of Shanke's thinness and of my other reasons for identifying him with the parts noted, I shall speak later. First I wish to show that, though historians have dated his connection with the King's Men several years later, it is quite possible that Shanke was a member of that company before we find in the Beaumont and Fletcher plays any sport made of a comedian's thinness—that is, by 1614.

Although Shanke had been on the stage for many years, he is first mentioned as a member of the King's Men when his name appears last in the patent of March 27, 1619. Collier, followed by his other biographers,[13] assumed, therefore, that he had only shortly before transferred from the Palsgrave's Company. His name appears for the last time among the Pals-grave's players in the patent of January 4, 1613, where it stands thirteenth in a list of fourteen.[14] He is not mentioned as a member of this company when on October 31, 1618, the company leased the Fortune from Edward Alleyn.[15] It would seem, therefore, that he left the Palsgrave's Company, presumably to join the King's Men, sometime between these two dates. However, that Shanke had not just recently joined the King's Men when his name appears in the patent of March 27, 1619, is certainly the natural conclusion to be drawn from his testimony in 1635 that he had "of his owne purse supplied the companye for the service of his Majesty with boyes, as Thomas

---

Women Pleased 1619-1620, *Love's Cure* c. 1621 (Chambers, III, 232), *The Prophetess* 1622, *The Lover's Progress* 1623.

[12] The "lean fool of the Bull" referred to in a ballad in *Turner's Dish of Stuff or a Gallimaufry* and identified by Fleay (*A Chronicle History of the London Stage, 1559-1642* [London, 1890], p. 375) as "Thomas Greene, the Queen Anne's player at the Bull," has, of course, no connection whatsoever with the Beaumont and Fletcher plays.

[13] Fleay in his *Chronicle History* is characteristically contradictory, giving two dates for his joining the King's company. On p. 269 he gives 1619, while on p. 375 he has "c. 1616." Knight in *D. N. B.* says "presumably 1619."

[14] J. T. Murray, *English Dramatic Companies*, 2 vols. (London, 1910), I, 211.

[15] *Ibid.*, I, 212.

Pollard, John Thompson deceased (for whom he paid 40 li),"
etc.[16] Thompson first appears in the list of principal actors preceding *The Laws of Candy*, variously dated 1619-1621, but
Pollard appears in the list for *The Queen of Corinth*, which
scholars have pretty well agreed in placing in 1617.[17] Unless
this play has been dated several years too early or unless Shanke
bore false testimony, it would seem that he was already an
important business member of the company in 1617. His occupying a position of such responsibility at this time, moreover,
would indicate that he had not even then only recently joined
the company. Indeed it seems likely that Shanke had become
affiliated with the King's Men within a comparatively short
time after he is last recorded as a member of the Palsgrave's
Company, 1613. It is, therefore, not impossible that he did
take the part of Judas in *Bonduca*, that shortly after his company acquired the services of the "lean fool" Fletcher began
to introduce parts for him.

It is true that his name does not appear among the eight
listed as the principal actors in *Bonduca*. This absence, however,
does not, I think, present any great difficulty. The part of
Judas is hardly a principal part. Apparently Shanke was never
regarded as a great actor,[18] and though he became one of the

[16] *Ibid.*, II, 152. It is hardly possible that Shanke's statement means only that
he had maintained or boarded these boys. The natural interpretation is, I think,
that he had paid the purchase price.

[17] Boyle, thinking he recognized the hand of Beaumont, dated it earlier. Fleay
dated it once 1618 and again *c.* 1617. Oliphant and Macaulay agree on "probably
1617." Thorndike gives *c.* 1617.

[18] That Shanke was, however, popular both as an actor in and as an author
of jigs is shown by the following jingles:

> Rounce, Robble, Hobble, he that writ so high big,
> Basse for a ballad, John Shank for a jig.
> [*Choyce Drollery, Shak. Society Papers*, III, 173.]

> That's the fat foole of the Curtin,
>   and the leane foole of the Bull:
> Since *Shanke* did leaue to sing his rimes,
>   he is counted but a gull.

These lines appear in a stanza of William Turner's "Dish of Lentten stuffe" (reprinted by Hyder E. Rollins [ed.], *Pepysian Garland* [Cambridge, 1922], p. 35),
which Professor Baskervill dated "about 1613."—*The Elizabethan Jig* (Chicago,
1929), p. 118. Clearly the allusion is to the order which, as a result of disturbances
at the Fortune, was issued by the General Session of the Peace at Westminster,
October 1, 1612, to "abolishe all Jigges Rymes and Daunces after their playes

two principal shareholders in both the Globe and Blackfriars, he seems never to have taken other than small parts. He is listed, as we have seen, in the patent of 1619, but his name does not appear among the actors in any play before 1622. Of the twenty-five plays for which the principal actors are named, nineteen of which come after 1619, in only two lists does he appear, and one of these, *The Wild-Goose Chase*, is exceptional in listing twelve principal actors whereas all the others name eight or less. In *Bonduca* there are three comic parts, the love-sick Junius, the merry captain Petilius, and the hungry knave Judas. No two of these could have been taken by the same man. Of the eight actors named only two are known to have taken broad comic parts, Toolie, who acted one of the madmen in *The Duchess of Malfi*, and Robinson, who, as he is praised by Jonson in 1616 as a portrayer of women's parts, almost certainly took one of the female rôles. Apparently Toolie was also still acting women's parts, for he took the part of Barnavelt's wife in 1619. In the three women's parts and the three comic parts there is again no opportunity for an actor's doubling. It seems indeed quite probable that the part of the hungry knave was not considered important enough to warrant its portrayer's appearing among the principal actors. And the same is true of the other parts I have noted. In only *The Prophetess* does Shanke's name appear in the list of principal actors, but the part of Geta in that play is the only one of these comic rôles which approaches importance.

In addition to the coincidence that Fletcher, having first presented the hungry comedian as a fat gourmand, substituted the starved image of famine at the very time at which Shanke may have joined the company, the little we know of Shanke emphasizes his physical fitness for such parts. In his *Historia His-*

And not to tollerate permitt or suffer anye of them to be used vpon payne of ymprisonment and puttinge downe and suppressinge of theire playes."—Quoted by Baskervill, *ibid.*, p. 116. Professor Baskervill (p. 119) suggested that if Shanke joined the King's Men soon after 1613, when his name last appears among the Fortune plays, "the prohibition of jigs may have had something to do with the change. It is perhaps possible, too, that 'leaue to sing his rimes' reflects the change from a company that featured him prominently in jigs to one in which the jig was at least relatively neglected."

trionica (1699), Wright wrote that "Pollard and Robinson were comedians; so was Shanke, who used to act Sir Roger in *The Scornful Lady*."[19] *The Scornful Lady*, however, having been written some years before 1613, the authors obviously could not have had Shanke in mind when they designed the part of Sir Roger, who, indeed, is not referred to as lean and of whose appearance the only hint is found in Abigal's speaking of him as "My little Levite"—perhaps an indication that the play was prepared for the Children of the Chapel, by whom it was performed.

The only other parts known to have been taken by Shanke are that of an undescribed servant in *The Wild-Goose Chase* and that of Hilario in Massinger's *The Picture*, before both of which plays twelve actors are listed rather than eight as customary in the Beaumont and Fletcher folio. Much of the comedy furnished by Hilario depends upon his extreme thinness. When Ubaldo and Ricardo first see him, the former exclaims, "What skeleton's this?" and Ricardo answers, "A ghost! or the image of famine!" And just before they enter, Hilario describes for us his wasting body:

> I look'd this morning in my glass, the river,
> And there appear'd a fish call'd a *poor John*,
> Cut with a *lenten* face, in my own likeness . . . .
> A surgeon passing by ask'd at what rate
> I would sell myself; I answer'd, For what use?
> To make, said he, *a living anatomy*,
> And set thee up in our hall, for thou art *transparent*
> *Without dissection;* and indeed he had reason
> For I am scour'd with this poor purget to *nothing*.   [III, i.]

Compare with these the lines in *The Lover's Progress* in which the foolish steward Mallfort describes his body:

> Last *Lent*, my Lady call'd me her *Poor John*,
> But now I am grown a *walking Skeleton*,
> You may *see through, and through me*.
> Leon. Indeed you are much faln away.
> Mal. I am a kind of *nothing*.   [I, i.]

[19] Quoted by Chambers, *op. cit.*, IV, 371.

I have italicized certain phrases to emphasize the similarity of the passages. It is perhaps worth noting that, with the exception of the first two, which are combined, the characteristics are repeated in exactly the same order. Both passages were, no doubt, written by Massinger, and I think there can be little doubt that they were written with the same actor in mind, that the later part was designed especially for Shanke because of his success in the earlier.

From these self-descriptions it is but a short step to those of Lazarillo *(Love's Cure)* and Penurio *(Women Pleased)* which I quoted earlier. All four are so similar as to suggest that they were intended to be spoken by the same comedian. The other lean characters which I have noted, though they do not indulge in such pathetic descriptions of their wasted bodies, furnish the same sort of broad comedy. As the lean comedian first appears in the Beaumont and Fletcher plays at a date which seems to agree with that at which Shanke must have joined the King's Men, I think it highly probable that all of these comic pictures of famine were designed especially to capitalize his ridiculous thinness.

VIII

The Attitude toward the Duello in the Beaumont and Fletcher Plays

NUMEROUS writers have called attention to the Jacobean dramatists' continued presentation of duelling as "an important feature in their portraits of contemporary society."[1] The many passages in the plays in which duelling is presented have, however, been most variously emphasized and interpreted. In a note on *A King and No King*, IV, iii, Dyce credits the playwrights with a large share in the public awakening to the absurdities of the duel: "Duelling with all its absurd punctilios was the passion of the age; and there seems every reason to believe that what mainly contributed to the suppression of such follies was the ridicule with which they were treated by most of our early dramatists."[2] Creizenach, noting that "This ridicule is, however, mainly directed against pretended fire-eaters who make use of a vaunted expertship in the rules in order to trump up pretexts for avoiding an encounter," observes that no hero was more popular than the haughty young cavalier, whose conduct in matters of honor was regulated by the duelling code: "in *Bussy d'Ambois,* when the hero comes to court and is pardoned by the King for having killed three men in a duel, Chapman expends all his eloquence in seeking to justify the 'law of reputation, which to men exceeds all positive law.' "[3]

In the plays of the Beaumont and Fletcher canon there are several instances in which ridicule is directed against "swordsmen," who are regularly shown as cowardly pretenders to honor and valor, and against quarrelsome gulls, who are made to fur-

[1] Sir Sidney Lee, *The Autobiography of Edward, Lord Herbert of Cherbury,* Appendix IV, p. 182.

[2] *The Works of Beaumont and Fletcher,* II, 310.

[3] Wilhelm Creizenach, *The English Drama in the Age of Shakespeare* (Philadelphia and London, 1916), p. 141.

nish sport by penning challenges to their betters. But such ridicule is not an attack upon the duel itself. As Lord Bacon testifies, those who most frequently sought to settle their differences
by the duel were young men of the gentry and the nobility.
The dramatists of the early seventeenth century would not
have honestly and correctly interpreted their world had they
satirized the custom of duelling or had they portrayed a society
without an exaggerated esteem for honor—honor in the sense
in which it had been borrowed from France. In not one of the
Beaumont and Fletcher plays can there be said to be any ridicule or satire of duelling as an institution. There are, however,
two entirely different attitudes toward duelling to be found in
the plays. A study of these different attitudes, both in the man-
agement of the plots and in the speeches of the characters, has
convinced me that they are to be explained not by different
authorship, not perhaps by Fletcher's changing convictions, but
principally by the dates at which the plays were written. In
other words, I believe that in those plays in which we have
challenges and duels and in which the playwright obviously applauds or condemns the challenger or duellist, we have a valuable clue to the dates of composition.

Duelling had been introduced into England from France.
"To impetuous Frenchmen . . . the duello was indispensable,
and when Englishmen imitated French social customs, they
adopted unconsciously the most characteristic feature of French
social life—that sensitive regard for what the Frenchmen called
their honour."[4] It has been estimated that during the first
eighteen years of the reign of Henry IV, 1589-1607, four thousand Frenchmen met their deaths in duels.[5] Although Henry
IV, recognizing the loss which his kingdom suffered from these
bloody practices, published a severe edict against duelling in
1602, the duel became no less common, for the King, either
because of the severity of his edict or because he shared his
countrymen's sensitive regard for honor, distributed his pardons
freely. Quoting M. de Chevalier, Abraham Bosquett informs
us that

[4] Lee, *op. cit.*, p. 179.   [5] Lee, *op. cit.*, p. 180.

in the province of Linnoisin there were killed six-score gentlemen in the space of only six or seven months; and that in ten years' time there had been granted above six thousand pardons, and one hundred and twenty of them in one expedition to Piedmont.

It was justly observed of Henry the Fourth of France, that his private countenance did more to promote duels than his public edict could do to restrain them, and that they would never cease till the King ceased to intermeddle in them.[6]

According to the same authority, "The passion, or rather rage, for duelling, was carried to its highest pitch in the reign of Louis XIII [1610-43]. When acquaintances met, the usual inquiry was not then as now,—'What is the news of the day?' but, 'Who fought yesterday?' "

It was during the same period that duelling assumed importance in England. King James, before coming to England, had in 1600 established a law in Scotland making it murder to kill one in a duel held without royal sanction.[7] There had been no special legislation in England against duelling[8] when about 1613 James and his ministers first took steps to curb this rapidly spreading abuse. Although the records show that before that time duelling had not been rare, the number of duels recorded for 1613 is vastly greater than in the preceding years. On September 6 of that year Sir Edward Sackville and Lord Bruce of Kinlos fought the famous duel, described long afterwards by Steele in the *Guardian* from Sackville's own manuscript narrative, in which Lord Bruce was killed and Sackville severely wounded. After telling of this conflict in a letter to Sir Robert Cotton dated September 10, 1613, the Lancaster Herald, Nicholas Charles adds: "There is also a quarrel between my Lord of Essex and Mr. Harry Howard, and one of them is gotten over, but there were letters sent to the Archduke and the French King to prevent their desperate proceedings. There is also talk of a quarrel between my Lord of

---

[6] *A Treatise on Duelling* (London, 1818), pp. 107-8.

[7] A. W. Renton and M. A. Robertson, *Encyclopaedia of the Laws of England,* vide Duel, 2d ed. (London, 1907), V, 27-28.

[8] J. F. Stephens, *History of the Criminal Law in England,* 3 vols. (London, 1883), III, 100.

Rutland and my Lord Danvers, as also of other nobles and gentlemen of good quality."[9] On the preceding day Chamberlain had written Carleton: "Though there yet be in shew a settled peace in these parts of the world, yet the many private quarrels are very great, and prognosticate troubled humours, which may breed dangerous diseases, if they be not purged and prevented." And after referring to the Bruce-Sackville combat, Chamberlain reports:

Here is speech likewise that the Lord Norris and Sir Peregrine Willoughby are gone forth for the same purpose, and that the Lord Chandos and Lord Hay are upon the same terms; there was a quarrel kindling betwixt the Earls of Rutland and Montgomery, but it was quickly quenched by the King, being begun and ended in his presence. But there is more danger betwixt the Earl of Rutland and the Lord Danvers, though I heard yesterday it was already or upon the point of compounding. But that which most men listen after is what will fall out betwixt the Earl of Essex and Mr. Henry Howard, who is challenged and called to account by the Earl for certain disgraceful speeches of him. They are both gotten over, . . . with each of them two seconds.[10]

It was at this time apparently that James and his advisers determined to take decisive action against this rage for duelling. On the fifteenth of October, James issued a proclamation prohibiting reports of duels. Five weeks after the Bruce-Sackville conflict, Sir Francis Cottington addressed to Lord Northampton, at his lordship's command, an account of the punishment accorded duellists in Spain.[11] King James issued a second proclamation February 4, 1613/14—this time "Against Private Challenges." "To this time and occasion" belongs, thought Spedding, an undated paper printed by Dalrymple from an original in Lord Bacon's handwriting and entitled "A Proprosition for the repressing of singular Combats and Duels."[12] Following

[9] Ellis, *Original Letters,* 2d ser., III, 234; quoted by Lee, *op. cit.,* pp. 180-81.
[10] Quoted by Lee, *op. cit.,* p. 181. Printed in Birch, *Court and Times of James I,* I, 272.
[11] Letter CCLXVII in Ellis, *Original Letters,* 1825, III, 107-10.
[12] James Spedding, *The Letters and Life of Francis Bacon,* 7 vols. (London, 1861-72), IV, 396.

closely Bacon's advice set forth in this Proposition, *His Majesty's Edict against Private Combats* was published late in this year. "The composition" of this edict, says Spedding, "having been left to the care and taste of the Earl of Northampton, it is difficult to get at the matter for the art." It had little effect upon popular opinion, and certainly did little to curb the abuse. Bacon, as the King's Attorney General, determined to achieve results, and accordingly brought before the Star Chamber the following January the case of Priest and Wright "to see if this court can do any good to tame and reclaim that evil which seems unbridled. And I could have wished," continued Bacon, "that I had met with some greater persons, as a subject for your censure, . . . but finding this cause on foot in my predecessor's time, . . . I thought to lose no time in a mischief that groweth every day." The present case, he adds, "may serve for a warning until example may be made in some greater person; which I doubt the times will but too soon afford."[13]

Priest and Wright were not charged with actual combat, but Priest with writing and sending a letter of challenge and Wright with carrying it. As a result of Bacon's arguments the court sentenced both to fine and imprisonment; and "to nip this practice and offence of duels in the head, which now did overspread and grow universal, even among mean persons,"[14] the court further ordered that the decree, together with Bacon's speech, be published, and the Justices of Assize be

required by this honourable Court to cause this decree to be solemnly read and published in all the places and sittings of their several circuits, and in the greatest assembly; to the end that all his Majesty's subjects may take knowledge and understand the opinion of this honourable Court in this case, and in what measure his Majesty and this honourable Court purposeth to punish such as shall fall into like contempt and offences hereafter.[15]

Even this well-publicized threat of punishment seems to have had small effect in curbing the number of duels. A few

[13] *The Works of Francis Bacon*, ed. Basil Montagu, 16 vols. (London, 1826), VI, 108-9.

[14] *Decree of the Star Chamber against Duels*, Spedding, *Letters and Life*, IV, 415.

[15] *Ibid.*, p. 416.

years before, in the eyes of many an Englishman the Earl of Montgomery had forfeited his reputation as a gentleman by failing to draw his weapon or challenge one Ramsey, a Scotsman, who had switched him in the face. That most of the courtiers were more careful of their reputation and continued to seek satisfaction in duels is shown by a letter from Bacon to Lord Villiers in 1616 wherein he writes:

> Yesterday was a day of great good for his majesty's service, and the peace of this kingdom concerning duels, by occasion of Darcye's case. I spake big . . . I was bold also to declare how excellently his Majesty had expressed to me a contemplation of his touching duels; that is, that when he came forth and saw himself princely attended with goodly noblesse and gentlemen, he entered into the thought, that none of their lives were in certainty[,] not for twenty-four hours[,] from the duel; for it was but a heat or a mistaking, and then a lie, and then a challenge, and then a life. . . . his majesty were touched with compassion to think that not one of his attendants but might be dead within twenty-four hours by the duel.[16]

On the thirteenth of February following, King James visited the Star Chamber, where upon "a case of challenge 'twixt two youths of the Inns of Court—Christmas and Bellingham—he took occasion to make a speech about duelling, wherein he was observed to bestow many good words on the Spanish nation and to gall the French more, which he since interprets to be only touching that point."[17]   Late in the same year Lord Carew, writing Sir Thomas Roe of the capture of one who had slain Art Wingfield in a duel, observes that it is thought he "will hardlye escape the rigor of the law, the Kinge beinge a professed enemie to duells, and therefore little hope of favour is lefft for dvellistes."[18]

The dramatist who then essayed to write plays portraying the life and manners of his time could hardly have disregarded so prominent a feature as the duel. It may be assumed that his

[16] *The Works of Francis Bacon*, XII, 240.

[17] Chamberlain to Carleton, 22 February 1617, Birch, *op. cit.*, I, 456. See also Camden, *Annals*, 12 February 1617, and the letter of the Venetian Secretary in England to the Doge and Senate, 24 February 1617, *C. S. P., Venetian*.

[18] *Letters of George Lord Carew*, Camden Society, LXXVI (1859), 133.

attitude toward the duel—if expressed at all—might be qualified by the attitude presented in the source which he used, by the attitude of the society of the time, and perhaps, if the play was written after James's active participation in the campaign against the duel and if the play was designed with the hope of its being presented before the King, by the desire to present a view pleasing to the monarch.

In the plays of the Beaumont and Fletcher canon there is, as has been said, no satire upon the duel or upon the duellist. There is, to be sure, satire upon gulls who foolishly pretend to valor or who have an exaggerated esteem for their nonexistent honor. In *The Queen of Corinth* the middle-aged ward, Onus, is persuaded to pen a challenge to the deserving favorite, Euphanes:

> If he refuse you, yours is then the honour;
> If he accept, he being so great, you may
> Crave both to choose the weapon, time, and place,
> Which may be ten years hence in Calicut
> Or underneath the Line, to avoid advantage;   [IV, i.]

but when Onus delivers the challenge into the hands of Euphanes' page, he is by him soundly swinged. Onus with his uncle and tutor is put to flight, but without loss of honor, for, as the Tutor explains, "He is a boy, And we may run away with honour" (IV, i). A similar ridicule of the codified systems of honor and of the escapes which such systems offered the coward is seen in *A King and No King* (IV, iii), where two "gentlemen of the sword" debate and decide in the negative the question whether Bessus has lost honor by having been kicked by Bacurius. They argue that as "the valiant man is known / By suffering and contemning" and as Bessus had laughed aloud upon being kicked, he is truly valiant. In *Love's Pilgrimage* (especially in V, v) ridicule is directed at the formal regulations governing the quarrel and the duel in the reverence in which the lame but pugnacious old Sanchio holds the rules of Caranza. And in *The Little French Lawyer*, after a duel has been arranged between the gull Sampson and the little advocate who had miraculously become valiant and quarrelsome, their clothes are conveyed away and they, undressed and near dead with cold, are quickly cured of their valiant humor.

These are the only passages in the plays which ridicule any phase of the duel. The first three clearly satirize not duelling but only the systematized regulations governing it, while in all save old Sanchio ridicule is aimed at foolish or cowardly pretenders to valor who seek to ape their betters. There is, however, frequent recognition not only of the prevalence and costliness of duels but also of the trivial causes for which they were fought. In *Nice Valour* the cowardly Lapet states that his forthcoming book entitled *The Kick* will, by lessening the number of duels, save a "hundred gentlemen a week" (IV, i); Dorilaus in *Lover's Progress* exclaims when told that two of his friends have killed each other in a duel:

> . . . the plague, war, famine,
> Nay, put in dice and drunkenness (and those
> You'll grant are pretty helps), kill not so many
> (I mean, so many noble)

as do duels fought over women (II, iv).

The trivialities which provoked many duels are suggested in his sister's explaining to Monsieur Thomas that his sweetheart, Mary, is disgusted by "all your quarrels, and the no-causes of 'em" (I, ii). In *Wife for a Month* Evanthe, hurt by the thought that her husband's continence is due to fear of the tyrant Frederick, exclaims:

> Dare men fight bravely
> For poor slight things, for drink, or ostentation,
> And there endanger both their lives and fortunes,
> And for their lawful loves fly off with fear?   [IV, iii.]

The Second Brother in *Nice Valour* observes that

> the difference of long tags
> Has cost many a man's life;   [III, i.]

and Cleremont in *The Little French Lawyer*, distinguishing between his former and his present mood, admits that while he will not bear calmly a blow or an insult to friend or mistress, yet

> I'll not quarrel with this gentleman
> For wearing stammel breeches; or this gamester
> For playing a thousand pounds, that owes me nothing;
>   . . . nor five hundred
> Of such-like toys, that at no part concern me.   [I, i.]

The observation that many duels were fought for trivial causes constitutes, of course, no more of an attack upon the fashion of duelling than did the presentation of the pretenses to valor of quarreling gulls and feigned gallants. Indeed, the manner in which these latter are represented in the earlier plays may well be interpreted as a defense of the practice of the day. The heroes of the early plays are quick to challenge and quick to fight; one who refuses to fight or seeks escape through technicalities was hooted or laughed at as a coward. So Protaldy is revealed a coward when, upon the brave and honest Martel's challenging him:

> Now draw your sword and right you,
> Or render it to me,

he gives over his sword with

> If wearing it may do you any honour,
> I shall be glad to grace you; there it is.
>   [*Thierry and Theodoret*, II, iii.]

For an ancient wrong, the wise and honest Bacurius insists upon a duel with Bessus when rumor reports that that coward has become valiant (*King and No King*, II, i, and III, ii). Melantius is, Amintor says, "as slow to fight with words as he is quick of hand" (*Maid's Tragedy*, I, ii). Amintor under normal conditions was certainly as quick to right his reputation, even though he draws his sword against his friend only when Melantius charges him with cowardice and threatens to "fix a scandal upon thy name for ever" (III, ii). He will not at first accept the challenge of the disguised Aspatia, but the explanation is his old love for her:

> Thy sister is a thing to me so much
> Above mine honour, that I can endure
> All this—Good gods! a blow I can endure:

> But stay not, lest thou draw a timeless death
> Upon thyself.   [V, iv.]

Although, he says, he "would endure yet, if I could," when she kicks him, he must right his honor by killing her.

The hero of *Monsieur Thomas* is "truly valiant" and constantly fighting duels (I, ii, and IV, iv). Accepting the challenge of Hemskirk "To the repairing of mine honour," the noble Goswin exclaims,

> If I do not,
> Let no man think to call me unworthy first:
> I'll do't myself, and justly wish to want her [Bertha].
> > *[Beggars' Bush*, III, iv.]

All the principal characters in *The Chances* "wear a sword to satisfy the world" and esteem the duel the proper method of sustaining their honor and reputation.

In none of the plays so far mentioned is there any speech either condemning the practice of duelling or suggesting any avenue other than single combat by which a gentleman who fancied himself wronged might satisfy himself to the world. In a much more extended manner this same view is set forth in *Love's Cure*, *Nice Valour*, and *The Elder Brother*.

The theme of this first play is, of course, the power of Love to bring out hitherto retarded masculine and feminine virtues. When Lucio, who has been reared as a girl, is dressed in proper male attire and turned over to Bobadilla to be trained in the use of arms, the steward is assigned a difficult task. Trying to arouse some manhood in him, Bobadilla cries:

> Suppose me now your father's foe, Vitelli,
> . . . answer me as you would Don Vitelli;

and Lucio answers:

> ". . . forget, sir, and forgive,
> 'Tis Christianity: I pray, put up your sword;
> I'll give you any satisfaction
> That may become a gentleman. However,
> I hope you are bred to more humanity
> Than to revenge my father's wrong on me

That crave your love and peace." La you now, Zancho,
Would not this quiet him, were he ten Vitelli's?   [II, ii.]

The audience is expected to agree that Lucio is still a "craven chicken." So, too, the audience should agree that the decision of Genevra is just when, Lamoral having snatched from Lucio the glove with which she had just favored him, Lucio kneels and asks its return:

> *Genevra.* Kneel to thy rival and thy enemy!
> Away, unworthy creature! I begin
> To hate myself, for giving entrance to
> A good opinion of thee. For thy torment,
> If my poor beauty be of any power,
> Mayst thou dote on it desperately! but never
> Presume to hope for grace, till thou recover
> And wear the favour that was ravish'd from thee.   [IV, i.]

Love, however, makes a man of Lucio. He soliloquizes:

> My womanish soul
> . . . I feel departing from me;
> And in me, by her beauty, is inspir'd
> A new and masculine one, instructing me
> What's fit to do or suffer. Powerful Love,
> That hast . . .
> Rous'd sleeping manhood in me.   [IV, iv.]

In *Nice Valour* are presented the stories of the cowardly Lapet and of Shamont, who is described as one that

> has that strength of manly merit in him,
> That it exceeds his sovereign's power of gracing;

as one who is

> so jealous
> Of honour's loss or reputation's glory,

that he hates

> The man, from Caesar's time, or farther off,
> That ever took disgrace unreveng'd.   [I, i.]

When, to attract his attention, the Duke touches Shamont with his riding whip, the favorite turns angrily to discover who had so insulted him. He cannot avenge himself upon the Duke:

> Never sat shame cooling so long upon me
> Without a satisfaction in revenge;
> And Heaven has made it here a sin to wish it . . .
> I have lost my peace and reputation.   [II, i.]

Shamont, therefore, takes an abrupt leave of the court. Although the title of the play might indicate the contrary, the absurdity of such nice valor is never suggested in the play. Upon Shamont's departure the Duke gives the order,

> Upon your love to goodness, gentlemen,
> Let me not lose him long,   [II, i.]

and later makes many such remarks as,

> What a great worth's gone with him!   [IV, i.]

> . . . h'as no vice
> But is more manly than some other's virtue.   [IV, i.]

Lapet, on the other hand, is one

> Will make you sick at heart, if baseness do't.   [I, i.]

Not only will he receive mildly blows from any one, but he is publishing a volume called *The Uprising of the Kick, and the Downfall of the Duello*. Although La-Nove observes to Lapet,

> Bring that to pass, you'll prove a happy member,
> And do your country service: your young bloods
> Will thank you then, when they see four-score,   [IV, i.]

it is La-Nove who remarks that the book is awaited by "all the cowards in the town," and that once it is out, cowards can easily be found at church-corners where books are sold. Possibly it was intended that *Nice Valour* should ridicule secondarily a too nice worship of reputation, but certainly the chief object of ridicule is the coward unmindful of honor.

The third of these plays, *The Elder Brother*, contains the clearest defense of that code of honor which demanded a scru-

pulous care of reputation and a readiness to defend it with the
sword.   The theme of the play, similar to that of *Love's Cure*,
is the power of Love to provoke manly virtue.   The elder
brother, Charles, is a scholar who, until he sees and falls
in love with Angellina, has been interested only in his books.
Transformed by his love for her, he wins and carries her away.
His younger brother, Eustace, accompanied by two other courtiers, seeks them out, but Charles snatches Eustace's sword and
the two courtiers are afraid to draw theirs.   Later Eustace begins to see these courtiers in a truer light, as they urge him not
to take the affront with such dejection; at court, they say, one
would not.   Eustace asks:

Piety, then
And valour, not to do nor suffer wrong,
Are there no virtues?
    Egremont.   Rather vices, Eustace.
Fighting! what's fighting? it may be in fashion
Among provant swords, and buff-jerkin men:
But wi' us that swim in choice of silks and tissues,
Though in defence of that word *reputation*,
Which is indeed a kind of glorious nothing,
To lose a dram of blood must needs appear
As coarse as to be honest . . . .
    Eust.   My sword forced from me too, and still detain'd,
You think, 's no blemish . . . .
And yet you wear a sword.
    Cowsy.   Yes, and a good one,
A Milan hilt, and a Damasco blade,
For ornament; no use the court allows it . . . .
    Eust.   I'll borrow this . . . .
And now I have it, leave me! y' are infectious,
The plague and leprosy of your baseness spreading
On all that do come near you: such as you
Render the throne of majesty, the court,
Suspected and contemptible.   [V, i.]

Eustace, his eyes opened to the baseness of his former advisers,
although he recognizes that he has little hope of regaining
Angellina, determines that

My honour, unto which compared she's nothing,
Shall, like the sun, disperse those lowering clouds,
That yet obscure and dim it. Not the name
Of brother shall divert me; but from him,
That in the world's opinion ruin'd me,
I will seek reparation, and call him
Unto a strict account.   [V, i.]

And later in the same scene he says to Charles and his uncle,
Miramont,

Though I am lost to all deserving men,
To all that men call good, for suffering tamely
Insufferable wrongs, and justly slighted,
By yielding to a minute of delay
In my revenge . . .

This change in Eustace, this determination to avenge by the
sword any loss of reputation, the audience was obviously expected to applaud as do both Charles and Miramont.

In all of the plays so far mentioned there are, save in the
mouths of patent and ridiculous cowards, only two speeches
which may be interpreted as directed against the duel and the
prevailing sense of reputation. In *Nice Valour*, as has been
seen, La-Nove remarks to the cowardly Lapet that, should his
forthcoming book abolish duels, "you'll prove a happy member,
and do your country service." And in *Love's Cure*, when the
King has allowed the families of Vitelli and Alvarez to settle
their old enmities by duel, Saavedra, who had previously not
practiced what he now preaches, urges that they will

let not daring
(Wherein men now-a-days exceed even beasts,
And think themselves not men else) so transport you
Beyond the bounds of Christianity . . . .
Oh, will you then, for a superfluous fame,
A sound of honour, which, in these times, all
Like heretics profess (with obstinacy,
But most erroneously), venture your souls?
'Tis a hard task, thorough a sea of blood
To sail, and land at Heaven.   [V, iii.]

This argument, which Saavedra's actions argue that he himself scarcely believes, is rejected by the principals. It is at best half-hearted dissuasion and is necessary to the plot.

Although it might at first be thought that the attitude presented in these plays toward the duel was determined largely, if not wholly, by the story which the dramatists had chosen, that view seems unlikely when one considers how in many of the later plays, where, too, the plots demand that the heroes fight duels, there are introduced strong and eloquent arguments against the practice of duelling. It is rendered more improbable by the general agreement that, with the exception of *The Elder Brother*, none of the plays so far discussed should be dated after 1615. Although its most recent editor, Mr. Greg, prefers to believe that Fletcher "left the play unfinished at his death, and that it was completed by Massinger,"[19] some support for the view of Mr. Oliphant and Mr. Lawrence, that Fletcher's portion of *The Elder Brother* dates from 1614,[20] is given by the fact that in all the plays definitely dated after 1615 which contain discussions of duelling there are arguments cited against it. Moreover, such arguments are to be found only in plays which are generally held to have been written or revised in or after 1616.[21]

The most eloquent speeches against duelling are to be found in *Custom of the Country*, in *The Pilgrim*, and especially in *Lover's Progress*, three plays which with general assent have been dated, *c.* 1619, 1621, and *c.* 1623. Less important in the plot and less extensive but hardly less eloquent appeals against duelling are found in *The Queen of Corinth*, usually placed about 1616, in *Wit without Money*, which I shall try to show was either written or revised in 1620, and in *The Little French Lawyer*, generally dated *c.* 1620. In addition, there is in *The*

---

[19] *The Works of Beaumont and Fletcher*, Variorum Ed., II, iii. This suggestion was, I believe, first made by Fleay.

[20] *The Plays of Beaumont and Fletcher*, p. 231.

[21] The one qualification of "generally held" which may be necessary is in the case of *Wit without Money*, which I shall try to show should be dated about 1620, rather than about 1614, as most scholars once held. That there is in this play an attack upon the duel argues, I believe, in favor of the date I have suggested; or at least that it was written or revised after 1616.

Night-walker, probably written before 1614 but certainly revised later, an argument against duels which is twice repeated. As Heartlove and Wildbrain prepare to fight, Maria, whom they think dead, appears and stops them:

> Was I not late, in my unhappy marriage,
> Sufficient miserable, full of all misfortunes,
> But you must add, with your most impious angers,
> Unto my sleeping dust this insolence?
> Would you teach time to speak eternally
> Of my disgraces? fight, then, and kill my honour!
> Fight deadly, both: and let your bloody swords,
> Through my reviv'd and reeking infamy,
> (That never shall be purg'd) find your own ruins!
> Heartlove, I lov'd thee once; and hop'd again
> In a more blessed love to meet thy spirit:
> If thou kill'st him, thou art a murderer;
> And murder never shall inherit Heaven.   [III, ii.]

The last line perhaps recalls the appeal of Saavedra in *Love's Cure*, but more important, I believe, is Maria's earlier argument that fighting for a woman's honor is less apt to defend it than to bring it into discredit—an argument advanced by Olinda in *Lover's Progress*:

> To what may love, and the devil jealousy, spur you,
> Is too apparent; my name's call'd in question;
> Your swords fly out, your angers range at large:
> Then what a murder of my modesty follows;   [I, ii.]

in *The Wild-Goose Chase* (*c.* 1621) this idea is accepted by De-Gard, who in reply to Lugier's advice, "Keep your sword close," replies:

> I will, sir,
> And will be still directed; for the truth is,
> My sword will make my sister seem more monstrous; [III, i.]

and it is much more eloquently presented by the reformed Roderigo in *The Pilgrim*, who, when Pedro asks "Is not [our mistresses'] honour ours?" replies:

> If they be virtuous;
> And then the sword adds nothing to their lustre,
> But rather calls in question what's not doubted:
> If they be not, the best swords and best valours
> Can never fight 'em up to fame again.   [IV, iii.]

The same idea is again expressed by Lysander in *Lover's Progress* as he reconciles Lydian and Clarange:

> That part of noble love which is most sweet,
> And gives eternal being to fair beauty,
> Honour, ye hack to pieces with your swords;
> And that ye fight to crown ye kill,—fair credit.   [II, iii.]

This "fair credit" is often lost, not alone by the woman whose honor is the subject of duels, but, as we are told by the wise Governor of Lisbon, Manuel du Sosa, by one who seeks honor by engaging in duels. In *The Custom of the Country* Don Duarte has won fame (or infamy) for himself as a successful duellist. From the dramatist, however, he receives no such sympathy as had been accorded that gallant brawler and sender of challenges for "no-causes," Monsieur Thomas. Duarte is portrayed as a quarrelsome bully, whose duelling successes lead his uncle the Governor to warn:

> Prosperity does search a gentleman's temper
> More than his adverse fortune. I have known
> Many, and of rare parts, from their success
> In private duels, rais'd up to such a pride,
> And so transform'd from what they were, that all
> That lov'd them truly wish'd they had fallen in them.
> . . . ere Don Duarte
> Made trial of his valour, he indeed was
> Admir'd for civil courtesy; but now
> He's swol'n so high, out of his own assurance
> Of what he dares do, that he seeks occasions,
> Unjust occasions, grounded on blind passion,
> Ever to be in quarrels; and this makes him
> Shunn'd of all fair societies.   [II, i.]

And to Duarte, he says:

> . . . are you valiant?
> Waste not that courage, then, in brawls, but spend it
> In the wars, in service of your King and country.   [II, i.]

The idea that by fighting with his countrymen the duellist is un-patriotically weakening the fighting strength of his country is suggested in *The Island Princess* (IV, iii) and repeated twice in both *Lover's Progress* (II, iv; IV, iv) and *The Little French Lawyer* (I, i; II, i). One of these passages from the former play I shall quote later; in *The Little French Lawyer* the idea is found in an harangue in which Cleremont attacks duelling as

> That daring vice from which the whole age suffers.
> The blood of our bold youth, that heretofore
> Was spent in honourable action,
> Or to defend or to enlarge the kingdom,
> For the honour of our country and our prince,
> Pours itself out with prodigal expense
> Upon our mother's lap, the earth that bred us,
> For every trifle; and these private duels,
> Which had their first original from the French,
> And for which to this day, we are justly censur'd,
> Are banish'd from all civil governments;
> Scarce three in Venice in as many years;
> In Florence they are rarer; and in all
> The fair dominions of the Spanish king
> They are never heard of; . . .
> And I have heard that some of our late kings
> For the lie, wearing of a mistress' favour,
> A cheat at cards or dice, and such like causes,
> Have lost as many gallant gentlemen
> As might have met the Great Turk in the field
> With confidence of a glorious victory . . .   [I, i.]

Although it is true that Cleremont later disavows these senti-ments, explaining that

> I then came from confession,
> And 'twas enjoin'd me three hours for a penance
> To be a peaceful man, and to talk like one,

and that he later overlooks no opportunity of participating in duels, it is equally true that no such passages are to be found in the plays prior to 1616. His later combats are integral to the plot; his words here are not. Nor can one as he reads these lines fail to recall that at the trial of Billingham and Christmas in February, 1616/17, King James "took occasion to make a speech about duelling, wherein he was observed to bestow many good words on the Spanish nation and to gall the French."

In *Wit without Money*, upbraiding the suitors of Lady Heartwell, Valentine calls them "people Betray'd into the hands of fencers', challengers', Toothdrawers' bills"; and arguing against marriage, he asks what comfort is to be got from children:

> . . . come to years once,
> There drops a son by the sword in 's mistress' quarrel,—
> A great joy to his parents! [II, ii.]

Whereas in the early plays the valiant had been quick to draw their swords in defense of their reputation and none but cowardly pretenders sought escape, in these later plays the truly valiant often both condemn duelling and seek to dissuade their challengers. In *The Queen of Corinth*, which, if correctly dated *c.* 1616-1617, would appear to be the earliest play in which the changing attitude of the dramatists is to be detected, Conon in challenging Crates is careful to make clear that he does so not because of the many wrongs Crates has done him, but rather in the hope of reconciling the brothers Crates and Euphanes. Although he recognizes that one may fight upon just grounds, he insists,

> . . . I did ne'er affect these bloody men,
> But hold 'em fitter be made public hangmen
> Or butchers call'd, than valiant gentlemen. [IV, iv.]

In *The Island Princess* (IV, iii) the hero, Armusia, when challenged by Ruy Dias, professes that he would prefer to be his friend, that the Portugals should not fight among themselves. When, in *The Pilgrim*, Pedro, having told us in an aside that his challenge is to test the reformation of the brave but formerly cruel Roderigo, demands that Roderigo "do him right," Roderigo refuses to fight. Nor can Pedro persuade him by urging his mistress' honor. Remarking in a passage already quoted that "the sword adds nothing to their lustre," Roderigo proves his awakening to virtue by continuing:

> To fight because I dare, were worse and weaker
> Than if I had a woman in my cause, sir,
> And more proclaim'd me fool; yet I must confess
> I have been covetous of all occasions,
> And this I have taken upon trust for noble,
> The more shame mine.   [IV, iii.]

It is, however, in the *Lover's Progress* that the attacks upon duelling are most numerous and eloquent. Speeches by Olinda and Dorilaus condemning duels have already been quoted. But it is by the hero of the play, Lysander, that the institution of duelling is most logically and most thoroughly condemned. It should be noted, moreover, that he who so earnestly preaches against duels is one whose skill with the sword and whose courage and sense of honor are repeatedly demonstrated, one who is able to say toward the close,

> I will not, like a careless poet, spoil
> The last act of my play, till now applauded,
> By giving the world just cause to say I fear'd
> Death more than loss of honour.   [V, i.]

Alcidon makes it clear that Lysander did all that could be expected to avoid his duel with Chrysanthes and Cloridon:

> In brief, a challenge was brought to Lysander
> By one Chrysanthes; and as far as valour
> Would give him leave, declin'd by bold Lysander:
> But, peace refus'd, and braves on braves heap'd on him,
> Alone he met the opposites, ending the quarrel
> With both their lives.   [IV, i.]

Lysander himself, however, finds no comfort in the realization that the duel was forced upon him and sees in it no excuse for what he terms murder:

> . . . this hand,
> Of late as white as innocence, and unspotted,

> Now wears a purple colour, dy'd in gore;
> My soul of the same tincture. Purblind passion,
> With flattering hopes, would keep me from despair,
> Pleading I was provok'd to it; but my reason,
> Breaking such thin and weak defences, tells me,
> I have done a double murder; and for what?
> Was it in service of the king? his edicts
> Command the contrary: or for my country?
> Her Genius,[22] like a mourning mother, answers,
> In Cloridan and Chrysanthes she hath lost
> Two hopeful sons, that might have done their parts
> To guard her from invasion. For what cause, then?
> To keep the opinion of my valour upright
> I' the popular breath; a sandy ground to build on!
> Bought with the king's displeasure, as the breach
> Of Heaven's decrees . . .   [IV, iv.]

Twice later does he exclaim against the foolish worship of false honor or reputation which leads to acts against civil allegiance and religion's law. Still lamenting his actions in that duel which had been forced upon him, he promises:

> . . . to the king,
> To whom I stand accountable for the loss
> Of two of his lov'd subjects' lives, I'll offer
> Mine own in satisfaction; to Heaven
> I'll pay my true repentance; to the times
> Present and future I'll be register'd
> A memorable precedent to admonish
> Others, however valiant, not to trust
> To their abilities to dare and do;
> And much less, for the airy words of honour,
> And false-stamp'd reputation, to shake off

[22] This passage recalls the speech of Clara in *Love's Cure* (I, iii):

> Or think you
> Your countryman, a true-born Spaniard, will be
> An offering fit to please the Genius of it [your house].

She is, however, not condemning duels or even duels between fellow countrymen. As she later tells Vitelli, in a plea for whose life these lines appear,

> I see thee worthy,
> And therefore now preserve you for the honour
> Of my sword only.

> The chains of their religion and allegiance,
> The principal means appointed to prefer
> Societies and kingdoms.   [V, ii.]

And shortly before, when he had met Lydian in a hermit's
dress, he had asked himself:

> But wherefore do I envy, and not tread in
> This blessed track? Here's in the heart no falsehood
> To a vow'd friend, no quarrel seconded
> With challenges, which, answer'd in defence
> Of the word *reputation*, murder follows:
> A man may here repent his sins, and, though
> His hand, like mine, be stain'd in blood, it may be
> With penitence and true contrition wash'd off.   [IV, iv.]

In spite of their verbal similarity, there is, of course, a world
of difference between these condemnations of "the word *reputation*" spoken by one who is brave and honorable and that condemnation given by the cowardly courtiers of *The Elder
Brother*:

> Though in defence of that word *reputation*,
> Which is, indeed, a kind of glorious nothing,
> To lose a dram of blood must needs appear
> As coarse as to be honest.   [V, i.]

These two passages well illustrate, I believe, the changing
attitudes toward duelling to be found in the plays. In the early
plays the dramatists, even though they may not have personally
approved duelling, were content to portray favorably a society
in which it was approved and to laugh with that society at those
insensible to honor. To accept the suggestion that this very
definite change took place about 1616 one need not greatly alter
the present tentative chronology. He must accept, (1) what
few have ever doubted, that the original form of *Nice Valour*
was written before 1616; (2) that Fletcher's share in *The Elder
Brother* was, as Mr. Oliphant and Mr. Lawrence have held,
written before 1616; (3) that perhaps some lines were inserted
in *The Night-walker* (known at least to have been revised by

Shirley); and (4) that *Wit without Money*, as I shall later give reasons to believe, was composed or revised after 1616.

If one refuses to accept the suggestion that there was a definite change either in the dramatists' opinions or in their policy, the alternatives remaining to him are to ascribe the different attitudes wholly to the sources used—in other words, to chance— or to account for them by assigning certain views to certain of the collaborators. Unless the assignment of scenes hitherto attempted is quite wrong, the second of the alternatives seems quite untenable, for to Fletcher alone are given both *Monsieur Thomas* and *The Pilgrim*, to Fletcher and Massinger the whole of both *The Elder Brother* and *Lover's Progress*. Unless, therefore, one is able to believe that, by a remarkable sequence of chance, the sources which the dramatists chose before 1616 demanded that their characters take one attitude toward duelling, and the sources which they happened to choose after that date demanded that their characters take an opposite attitude, one must assume that the change in attitude is to be explained by a change in either the opinions or the policy of the dramatists themselves. Such an assumption seems quite logical when we recall the part which King James was taking in the campaign against duelling and the fact that all but one *(The Nightwalker)* of the plays containing passages against duelling are known to have been acted by the King's company.

IX

The Date of Love's Pilgrimage and Its Relation to The New Inn

I

Love's Pilgrimage was "renewed" and, it has been generally assumed, revised in 1635. As a result of Dyce's misreading of Malone, it was supposed that the play had been left incomplete at the time of Fletcher's death in 1625 and that it was "revised and finished" by Shirley ten years later. Although the fallacy of that view has long been noted, no evidence has, I believe, been advanced in an effort to determine the date of composition.[1] There are in the play, however, what seem to me to be two, or perhaps three, allusions to contemporary events which suggest very definitely the date at which the play must have been started.

As a general rule there is, I admit, great danger in attempting to date an Elizabethan play by topical allusions, which may well have been inserted at almost any time by a dramatist or a reviser, perhaps even by an actor. Allusions may be of little value unless there is complementary evidence of another sort. Where, however, there are references to events which follow immediately the earliest possible date at which the play could have been written, such references would seem surely to indicate the time at which the play was composed. So it is, I believe, with the references in *Love's Pilgrimage*.

As Cervantes' *Las dos Doncellas*, the ultimate source of *Love's Pilgrimage*, was not allowed for publication in Spain until August, 1613, the play certainly cannot have been composed before 1614. I am not so certain as some critics have been of Fletcher's small knowledge of Spanish, but there is good reason to believe that for the plays based upon the *Novelas*

[1] Mr. W. J. Lawrence, according to Oliphant, *The Plays of Beaumont and Fletcher*, p. 435, assigns it to 1614; Professor Thorndike, in his edition of *The Maid's Tragedy and Philaster* (Belles-Lettres Series, Boston, n.d.), dates it "1614?"

Ejemplares Fletcher used the French translation of 1615.[2]
If the French rather than the Spanish was used, *Love's Pil-grimage* could not have been started before 1615. The ref-erences to which I shall call attention, alluding as they do to events between late 1615 and the end of 1616, suggest 1616 as the date at which the play was written.

All of these allusions were to events on the continent, but that these events were closely followed and well known in Eng-land is shown by reports and letters. The accounts of these events, therefore, I quote from English sources, for the actual dates of the events are here less important than the dates at which they were discussed in England.

The scene of *Love's Pilgrimage* is, of course, Spain. In Act I, scene i, Incubo says to Phillipo:

> Sir, the French,
> They say, are divided 'bout their match with us.

There can be no doubt that the reference here is to the civil war in France occasioned by the opposition of the Prince of Condé and other nobles to the double alliance with Spain ar-ranged by the Queen Mother, whereby the young Louis XIII was betrothed to Anne of Austria, daughter of Philip III of Spain, and the Spanish prince, afterwards Philip IV, to Princess Elizabeth of France. Anne and Louis were married on Novem-ber 24, 1615, Philip and Elizabeth one year later to the month. Although there had been French opposition to the alliance with Spain for some time before the first marriage, the allusion to the French being divided would best fit the period between the rebellion headed by the Prince of Condé in the summer of 1615 and the pardon accorded the rebels—all save Condé—late in 1616. That England had watched with interest the French al-liances with Spain, we have the testimony of the Venetian Am-

---

[2] *Les Nouvelles de Miguel de Cervantes Saavedra où sont contenues plusieurs rares Adventures, & memorables Exemples d'Amour, de Fidélité, de Force de Sang, de Ialousie, de mauuaises habitudes, de charmes, & d'autres accidents non moins estranges que veritables.* Traduictes d'Espagnol en François: Les six premières par F. De Rosset. Et les autres six, par le Sr. D'Audiguier. Avec l'Histoire de Ruis Dias, & de Quixaire Princesse de moluques, composée, par le Sr. Dr. Bellan. *A Paris Chez Iean Richer . . .* M.DC.XV.

bassador, who on 23 October 1615, wrote to the Doge and Senate: "Here they were eagerly awaiting the issue of . . . the marriages between France and Spain, from which will arise, in great measure, the negotiations about the prince."[3] And how closely the sequence of events, especially the civil strife, was watched in England is revealed by the full accounts sent Sir Thomas Roe, the English ambassador to the far distant Great Mogul, by Lord George Carew. In February, 1615, Carew wrote:

> Monsieur de Silerie is gone into Spayne to consummatt the mariage of the King his master, but the event is very doubtfull, the Frenche princes beinge so opposite vnto it. The assemblye of the three Estates is dissolved . . . and France is divided into so great factions as troubles is expected.[4]

In January, 1616, Lord Carew wrote that the preceding summer the marriage of the King and the Infanta had been "as muche consummated as by proxie canne by required," and that at the moment

> The Prince of Condie, with sundrye of the peers and noblesse of France, are in armes, and the whole boddie of the Religion are ioyned with them, so as they are very stronge in horse and foote; . . . The iniquitie of the murder of Kinge Henry 4, the displacinge of corrupt councillors about the kinge, *the inconveniences which may ensue by the matche with Spayne,* and the confirmation of the former Edicts in the behalfe of the Religion, are the chiefest poyntes and motiffs of this disturbance in France: . . .[5]

In February, Carew recorded that the Duke of Vendome, Henry IV's natural son, had joined the princes to avenge the death of his father, "which, *with the mariadge with Spayne,* was one of the principallest causes thatt moved the princes to take armes."[6] In April[7] Carew writes that a general peace has been concluded, but under August he notes that on the twenty-second the Prince of Condé had been arrested, that other noblemen had fled Paris,

---

[3] *C. S. P., Venetian,* p. 50.

[4] *Letters from George Lord Carew to Sir Thomas Roe,* Camden Society, LXXVI (1859), 3.   [5] *Ibid.,* pp. 24-25.

[6] *Ibid.,* p. 30.   [7] *Ibid.,* p. 33.

and that "The common people of Paris, hearinge of the arrest, in furye they sacked the Marshall de Ancres [one of the principals of the Spanish party] house, and made pilladge of his goodes. . . ."[8] Under September[9] Carew records the commitment of Condé to the Bastille and the King's forgiveness of the other nobles who had been in arms against him. No other mention is made of civil discord until the account under May, 1617, of the assassination of d'Ancre, which seems to have been plotted because of the Marshall's arrogance and not because he had once been active in the Spanish alliances.

Information concerning the troubles in France was perhaps not current among the masses of London until some weeks after it had reached one so keen upon the scent of news as Lord Carew, but with the reconciliation between the King and nobles in September, 1616, and the second Spanish-French marriage in November of that year, the reference to the French being "divided 'bout their match" with Spain would seem to lose its aptness.

Two other allusions in the play seem, with less certainty, to point to the autumn of 1616. Six lines after the mention of the Franco-Spanish marriage, Incubo asks:

> What do you hear
> Of our Indian fleet? they say, they are well return'd.

To be sure, richly laden ships from India were not uncommonly arriving in either England or Spain, but it is unlikely that Fletcher, who in the preceding speeches, and, indeed, throughout the play, so carefully keeps his Spanish locale, should here refer to an English fleet. Such fleets were, of course, so common that Incubo's question might ordinarily be thought of no value at all in dating the play. It is, however, a matter of record that in the autumn of 1616 the whole of western Europe was awaiting with interest the return of a Spanish Indian fleet to confirm rumors of the fabulous wealth it bore.

Under November, 1616, Lord Carew wrote Sir Thomas Roe: "The 19. I received letters out of Spayne. The West Indies fleet is daylye expected";[10] and in the same month the Venetian Secretary wrote from London to the Doge and Senate:

[8] *Ibid.*, p. 41.   [9] *Ibid.*, p. 45.   [10] *Ibid.*, p. 58.

It is understood that at the island of St. Vincent there are some twenty ships of Algiers, which are awaiting the Spanish fleet to attack it. If they succeed it will be a matter of great moment in the present state of affairs, since there is a great scarcity of money both in Spain and in Flanders, and for some while they have been supporting themselves by the hope of this fleet. The Spaniards say that His Catholic Majesty's share in it will amount to 6 millions, but it is not believed that it will even come to half that.[11]

In January of the next year Carew wrote Roe of the fleet's safe arrival at Lisbon:

We have newes of the Lord Rosse's safe arryval att Lisbone, and thatt a fewe dayes before his cominge thether the West Indie Fleete (enforced by fowle wether) came into thatt porte richlye laden, to the valew of 20 millions of ducatts, whereof 9 millions in silver and gold was presentlye (sent) overland vnto Madrid.[12]

Such a cargo could hardly fail to excite the curiosity and kindle the imagination. One may be sure that Lord Carew and the Venetian Secretary were not the only ones in London interested in its return. During the month of November, 1616, when it was said to be "daylye expected," there must have been many rumors concerning it.

There is in the play, finally, what may be an allusion to a third incident about which the streets of London must have buzzed during late October of 1616. In the same scene in which I recognize the other allusions, I, i, one of the hostlers complains of the strange way in which the horse of one of the guests has cast his shoes.

> He had four shoes,
> And good ones, when he came; 'tis a strange wonder,
> With standing still he should cast three.

Less strange but equally wondrous, perhaps, was the casting of its shoes by Lord Hay's horse in Paris shortly before the date suggested by the allusions already mentioned.

On July 12[13] Lord Hay left London for Paris, sent by King James ostensibly to felicitate the French King on his recent

[11] *C. S. P., Venetian*, p. 358.   November 24, 1616.
[12] *Op. cit.*, p. 76.   [13] *Ibid.*, p. 38.

marriage. The journey had been delayed to permit the Ambassador and his train to equip themselves in the utmost splendor. After describing the gorgeous dress of the embassage, Wilson recounts the following incident, which was apparently prearranged rather than accidental:

And some said (how truly I cannot assert) the Ambassador's Horse was shod with Silver-shoes, lightly tack'd on; and when he came to a Place where Persons, or Beauties of Eminency were, his very Horse prancing and curveting, in humble Reverence flung his Shoes away, which the greedy Understanders scrambled for; and he was content to be gazed on and admir'd, till a Farrier, or rather an Argentier in one of his rich Liveries, among his Train of Footmen, out of a Tawny Velvet Bag took others, and tack'd them on; which lasted till he came to the next Troop of Grandees: And thus with much ado he reach'd the *Louvre*.[14]

In October "the Lord Hay retourned frome his employment in France, where he was feasted beyond belief."[15] During the remaining months of 1616 there must have been many stories current in London concerning the extravagance of his reception, the richness of his retinue, and, no doubt, the casting of his horse's shoes. If the play was being written in the autumn of 1616, as I think the allusion to the Franco-Spanish match conclusively proves, it seems not unlikely that the misfortune befalling the horse at the inn in Ossuna may have been suggested by the casting of its shoes by Lord Hay's horse in Paris.

2

I do not insist upon the allusion to the behavior of Lord Hay's horse; it is not necessary to dating *Love's Pilgrimage* in 1616. It serves, however, as a transition to another problem—the relation of *Love's Pilgrimage* to Jonson's *New Inn*—as these lines are among those common to both plays. The similarity of the two plays is succinctly summarized by Mr. Oliphant:

[14] *The Life and Reign of James, The First King of Great Britain*, by Arthur Wilson. Reprinted in Vol. II of [Bishop Kennett's] *A Complete History of England* (London, 1706), p. 704. For this reference I am indebted to one of my students, Miss Kathryn Robb.   [15] Carew, *op. cit.*, p. 47.

. . . about a dozen lines in I, 1a are identical or almost identical with lines in II, 2 of Jonson's *New Inn* . . . ; while I, 1b is almost a duplicate of much of III, 1 of the same play, twenty-four out of seventy-four lines (omitting the first one and the last five) being absolutely identical with lines in Jonson's play, while only six are altogether peculiar to *Love's Pilgrimage*.[16]

Langbaine called attention to the similarity and accused Fletcher of the theft, although Fletcher had been dead for four years when *The New Inn* was first presented. It has been suggested that Jonson was the renewer of *Love's Pilgrimage* in 1635 and that he at that time may have borrowed these lines from his own *New Inn*, which had been hissed from the stage six years before, and then, as an appeal from the verdict of the theater, printed in 1631. But Mr. Tennant, and he is followed by the most recent editors[17] of Jonson, believes that Jonson had no connection with *Love's Pilgrimage*, and rejects Mr. Oliphant's claim that some of the lines common to both plays show the unmistakable metrical characteristics of Fletcher. Mr. Oliphant's suggestion is "that Jonson commenced a revision of *Love's Pilgrimage*, . . . gave it up, and, when he commenced *The New Inn*, took a few of his own lines from the earlier play, and also lifted, with some alterations, the only piece of Fletcher's work he had left in the only scene he had meddled with."[18]

Mr. Oliphant uses only the argument that certain lines common to both plays show the peculiarities of Fletcher's meter. I agree; but apparently to some, such as Professor Tennant and the recent editors of Jonson, the argument has not been convincing. But there are other reasons for believing that some of the similar passages appeared first in *Love's Pilgrimage*, whence they were inserted into *The New Inn*. Both plays introduce a number of Spanish words and phrases, which, although

[16] *Op. cit.*, p. 439. The lines in *The New Inn*, according to the numbering in Vol. IV of C. H. Herford and Percy Simpson (eds.), *Ben Jonson* (10 vols., Oxford, 1925), are Act II, scene v, 48-69, and Act III, scene i, 57-168.

[17] George Bremner Tennant, *The New Inn*, Yale Studies in English, XXXIV (New York, 1908); Herford and Simpson, *Ben Jonson*, II, 198-200.

[18] *Op. cit.*, p. 439.

they seem thoroughly Jonsonian, are much better suited to the earlier play where the scene is laid in Spain than to *The New Inn,* where the scene is English. Many of the Spanish terms of the latter play do not appear in the first, but one phrase is used for comic effect throughout both plays and particularly in the lines which are almost identical. In *Love's Pilgrimage* (I, i) and in *The New Inn* (II, v) the respective hosts are criticized at length for appearing *in cuerpo.* The phrase goes much more naturally with *Love's Pilgrimage.* It appears frequently in Cervantes' *Novelas,* Fletcher's source, and, apparently some years before Jonson wrote *The New Inn* Fletcher (or his collaborator), who never hesitated to repeat, had used the same phrase with humorous intent in *Love's Cure,*[19] where the scene is likewise laid in Spain. There, in II, i, Pachieco Alasto says to Lazarillo: "Boy: my Cloake and Rapier; it fits not a Gentleman of my ranck to walk the streets in Querpo." Compare *Love's Pilgrimage* (I, i):

> *Inc.* Call for thy cloak and rapier
> *Diego.* How!
> *Inc.* Do, call,
> And put 'em on in haste; alter thy fortune,
> By appearing worthy of her. Dost thou think
> Her good face e'er will know a man *in cuerpo?*
> . . . call, I say—
> His cloak and rapier here!

Such a Spanish phrase may well have found its way into the English slang of the day,[20] but the other similarities in the two plays show that it was not by mere chance that it appears in *Love's Pilgrimage* and *The New Inn.* As Fletcher or one of his collaborators used it in another play, and as it appears in the *Novelas Ejemplares,*[21] the indication would seem to be that Jonson was the borrower. If there was in the horse's casting

---

[19] Many have placed the date of *Love's Cure* from sixteen to nineteen years before 1625, and almost every dramatist of the time has been advanced as a collaborating author.

[20] *A New English Dictionary* cites the passages in *Love's Cure* as the earliest noted appearance in English.

[21] I have not been able to examine the 1615 French translation.

his shoes a reference (and certainly the date of *Love's Pilgrim-age* suggests there was) to the behavior of Lord Hay's horse in Paris in 1616, Jonson is again the borrower, for little fun could be got from the allusion when *The New Inn* was written ten years later.

I do not argue that the passages similar or identical in the two plays were all borrowed by Jonson. It may well have been, as Mr. Oliphant suggested, that Jonson began a revision of *Love's Pilgrimage* and, having abandoned his plan, later put parts of his revision to use in *The New Inn*.[22]

[22] *The Bloody Brother* may present a somewhat similar case if, as some have believed, Jonson either contributed to or later revised that play. For echoes of *The Bloody Brother* in Jonson's plays and masques, see Charles Crawford, "Ben Jonson and *The Bloody Brother*," *Shakespeare-Jahrbuch*, XLI (1905), 163-76.

In the passage common to both *Love's Pilgrimage* and *The New Inn* there is a satirical thrust at the "grazier." I do not know how often he is the object of attack by Jonson, but Fletcher shoots at him often. (Compare *Wit without Money*, I, i [Dyce, IV, 110]; *The Pilgrim*, I, ii [Dyce, VIII, 14]; *Woman's Prize*, IV, ii [Dyce, VII, 179]; *Wit at Several Weapons*, I, ii [Dyce, IV, 23].)

X

Nice Valour, or the Passionate Madman

Erudition has its dangers for an editor. He must keep ever on his guard lest he be misled into recognizing allusions which his author could never have intended. The Rev. Alexander Dyce was more erudite but also more guarded than were most of the early editors of our drama; yet in his preface to *Nice Valour, or the Passionate Madman* a fancied recognition of an allusion led him not only to create an imaginary history for the play but to ignore completely the obvious meaning of the passage he cited. In this brief preface Dyce declared that

In act v. sc. 3. mention is made of a piece called *Fisher's Folly*, which was first printed in 1624, the year preceding that of our author's death; and I am inclined to believe, either that *The Nice Valour*, though it may have been brought out by Fletcher himself, was afterwards altered to its present shape by some other dramatist, or that it was left unfinished by the author, and was completed for the stage by a second playwright.[1]

Since Dyce's time those who have written on Beaumont and Fletcher have, I believe without exception, accepted the allusion and with increasing confidence pronounced 1624 the earliest possible date for the extant form of the play.[2] But this allusion is an impossible creation of Dyce's fancy, and any suppositions made upon it must be discarded.

In V, iii, the foolish Lapet is boasting of the financial success to be enjoyed by his forthcoming volume. "'Twill much enrich the Company of Stationers," he says; "'Tis thought 'twill prove a lasting benefit." "Is 't possible," asks Moulbazon,

---

[1] *Works of Beaumont and Fletcher*, X, 295.

[2] For instance, Oliphant, *The Plays of Beaumont and Fletcher*, p. 444, observes: "There is another reason why the play is not to be looked upon as of a single date: in V. 3 there is an allusion to "Fisher's Folly," published in 1624; yet the play was not licensed by Herbert, and must therefore date not later than May, 1622."

"such virtue should lye hid, And in so little Paper?" "How!"
exclaims Lapet:

> . . . why there was the Carpenter,
> An unknown thing; an odoriferous Pamphlet,
> Yet no more Paper, by all computation,
> Than *Ajax Telamon* would use at once.
> Your Herring prov'd the like, able to buy
> Another *Fishers* Folly, and your *Pasquil*
> Went not below the mad-caps of that time,
> And shall my elaborate *Kick* come behind, think you?

Although in this as well as in a previous passage in the
scene there are allusions to several pamphlets of the day, it is
most unlikely that Dyce and his followers are correct in seeing
in the statement, "Your Herring prov'd . . . able to buy Another
Fishers Folly" an allusion to the reply which the Puritan divine
George Walker addressed in 1624 to Fisher the Jesuit and entitled *Fisher's Folly unfolded, or the Vaunting Jesuites Vanity
discovered in a challenge of his (by him proudly made, but on
his part poorely performed).*[3] As Walker's pamphlet could
have sold for only a few pence, there would have been little
point to the words "able to buy Another *Fishers* Folly." Further, the pamphlet presumably passed through only one edition;
there is no reason to believe that it was widely known, or even
that it was likely to be recognized by an audience under such
an abbreviated title. It is safe to say that the great majority
of any audience, even in 1624/25, would have thought first not
of any controversial pamphlet but of what George Walker must
himself have had in mind when he gave his pamphlet the title
Fisher's Folly unfolded—the extravagantly magnificent mansion which Jasper Fisher, a man of modest means, had erected
near Bishopsgate during Elizabeth's reign, and which very soon
became popularly known as Fisher's Folly. Stow makes the
following comment upon it:

Next to that ["a faire house, of late built by John Powlet"] a
far more large and beautiful house, with gardens of pleasure, bowling
alleys, and such like, built by Jasper Fisher, free of the goldsmiths,

---

[3] See Dyce's note, *op. cit.*, X, 363.

late one of the six clerks of the chauncerie and a justice of the peace.
It hath since for a time been the Earl of Oxford's place. The
queen's majesty Elizabeth hath lodged there. It now belongeth to
Sir Roger Manars ["to Master Cornewallos"[4]—1st. ed., p. 128].
This house, being so large and sumptuously built by a man of no
greater calling, possessions, or wealth (for he was indebted to many)
was mockingly called Fisher's folly, and a rhythm was made of it,
and other the like, in this manner:

> "Kirkebyes Castell, and Fishers Follie,
> Spinilas pleasure, and Megses glorie."[5]

During the reign of James I the house became the residence of
first the Campbells and then the Hamiltons. Records show,
however, that it continued to be popularly known under the
name "Fisher's Folly." In January, 1615, "the Lord of
Argyll's house, called Fisher's Folly," was offered to the East
India Company, but held unfit for their service;[6] and when on
March 12, 1624/25, Chamberlain wrote Carleton of the Marquis of Hamilton's death, he reported that "his body was carried, with much company and torchlight, to Fisher's Folly, his
house without Bishopsgate."[7] Later in the seventeenth century
the house was occupied by the Earls of Devonshire and called
Devonshire House, but that its earlier name and history were
still remembered in 1660 is shown by a broadside ballad of that
year, entitled "The Entertainment of Lady Monk at Fisher's
Folly," in which appear the lines:

> Y' are a welcome guest
> Unto our board, whose presence makes us jolly,
> Since you vouchsafe to come to Fisher's Folly;
> So called from the Founder, a lackwit
> Who built the house, but could not finish it. . . .[8]

---

[4] Sir William Cornwallis purchased Fisher's Folly from the Earl of Oxford
in 1588.—Margaret Sefton-Jones, *Old Devonshire House by Bishopsgate* (London,
1923), p. 99.

[5] Stow, *Survey of London*, Everyman Library Ed. (London, 1912), pp. 149-50.

[6] 10 January 1615, *Cal. East Indies*, p. 368.

[7] Birch, *Court and Times of James I*, II, 504.

[8] Quoted by H. B. Wheatley, *London, Past and Present*, 3 vols. (London, 1891),
II, 48.

Obviously the allusion in Lapet's speech is to Jasper Fisher's house and not to George Walker's Puritan pamphlet. No argument in support of this view is needed in that an allusion to the former makes sense whereas an allusion to the latter renders the passage completely meaningless. Basing his hopes for the financial success of his forthcoming volume, *The Kick,* upon the large returns brought in by other small pamphlets, Lapet observes that the "Herring"—obviously a pamphlet—"prov'd . . . able to buy [i.e., enabled the author or, more likely, the publisher to buy] Another *Fishers* Folly"—a large and beautiful house like that built by Jasper Fisher.

As there is no reason for assuming that there is also an allusion to Walker's *Fisher's Folly unfolded,* we must discard the general view that *Nice Valour* in its present form must date after the publication of that pamphlet in 1624. If, however, in the words "buy Another *Fishers* Folly" there is implied a recent sale of that magnificent house, the allusion may yet contribute toward the dating of one version of the play. Certainly there would have been more point to the reference if the house had a short time before changed hands upon the payment of a great sum, or if it had recently been offered for sale. There was only one sale of this property during the reign of King James.

Sir William Cornwallis, who had purchased Fisher's Folly from the Earl of Oxford in 1588, although he leased it to Sir Roger Manners for an indefinite period commencing in 1602,[9] owned it until 1609, when, after the death of his wife, Dame Lucy, he "desyred that a particion" "of all the . . . mannors lordshipps messuages landes ten[emen]ts and hereditam[en]ts" "should be made in his life tyme to prevent future disagreament amongest" his four daughters.[10] He accordingly in an indenture dated March 15, 7 James I [1608/9], "in consideracon of a competent some of lawfull money of England" "graunted bargained and sould" to his youngest daughter Anne and her husband, Archibald Earl of Argyle, "that Capitall Messuage or Mansion howse with thappurtenñces wherein one Jasper ffisher

[9] Margaret Sefton-Jones, *op. cit.,* pp. 105-6.
[10] Close Roll 54/1983.

sometyme inhabited and wherein the said Sir Willm̃ Corn-
wayleys now inhabiteth . . . lyinge and being in the parishe
of Saint Bottolph without Bishopsgate."[11]   It was, as has been
noted, the home of the Earl in 1615 when he offered it unsuccessfully to the East India Company. This offer was probably
occasioned by the Earl's increasing debts which three years later
led him to flee to the continent to escape his creditors.

Before his flight, however, Argyle had disposed of Fisher's
Folly. In an indenture dated 3 June, 14 James I [1616], two
of the Earl's kinsmen by marriage, Sir Charles Cornwallis and
Sir Edmund Wythypoll, acting "with the assent and consent
and appoyntment of the right honorable Archebald Erle of
Argill" sold the mansion house "wherein one Jasper ffisher
sometyme inhabited" to Anne Lady Harrington "in consideration of the sum of foure thousand pounds."[12]   Fisher's Folly
for a while later was the residence of Lady Harrington's daughter, Ben Jonson's friend, Lucy Countess of Bedford, who was
named her mother's executrix in a will proved June 1, 1620.
About two years later, however, the cost of its upkeep caused
the Countess to lease the property to the Marquis of Hamilton,[13] who lived there until his death in March, 1624/25.

Such seems to have been the history of the ownership and
occupancy of Fisher's Folly during the reign of James I—during the period in which *The Nice Valour* must have been written. Although the Earl of Argyle may have paid or promised
to pay a sum in addition, the great house really passed into his
possession as dowry of his wife. The only actual sale of the
property between 1588 and 1625 was in 1616, when Lady Harrington purchased it for £4000. As has been said, the Earl was
apparently eager to dispose of the property for more than a year
previous to the sale to Lady Harrington. If, therefore, there is
a timely allusion in the words "able to buy Another *Fishers
Folly*," the years 1615 and 1616 would appear to be the time
when such an allusion would have been most apt. But before

[11] *Ibid.*
[12] 14 James I. 30th Part. Roll 2313 (33).
[13] Margaret Sefton-Jones, *op. cit.*, p. 123.

accepting an allusion, let us examine the other evidences for
dating the play.

As we must discard the allusion to *Fisher's Folly unfolded*,
it is no longer possible to state that the play was revised "after
1624"; and I am not sure that we are justified in saying the
play has been revised, unless by "revised" we mean that it has
been telescoped and sadly tampered with. Evidences of telescoping are numerous. *Nice Valour* is much the shortest play
in the Beaumont and Fletcher canon. Three of the five acts
(I, II, IV) have only one scene each. The one scene of Act I
is especially episodic; into this scene all the characters of any
importance are introduced, the appearance of many being forced,
brief, and quite unrelated to what precedes or follows. The
care of the Passionate Madman is entrusted to "his kind brother"
and to La-Nove, but his brother is never seen nor again heard of.
Shamont, the Duke's dearest friend, has been absent but two
days, yet upon his return he knows few of those who have lived
in the court for years. At the opening of the scene La-Nove,
who has been courtier and steward for at least five years (IV, i;
Dyce, X, 348), has to inquire who Shamont is, yet he greets him
familiarly and is by Shamont at the end of the scene character-
ized as

> . . . this dear Gentleman, my absolute friend,
> That loves a Soldier far above a Mistress,
> Thou excellently faithful to 'em both.

There is no need to list the many contradictions. Mr. Oliphant has listed more than enough to show how unsatisfactory
is the text.[14] His suggestion, however, that the text we have
may be a first draft "which for some reason or other never
reached the intended final form,"[15] is, I think, contradicted by
the evidence of telescoping. The text has clearly suffered much
after leaving its author, whether we call it revision, recension,
curtailment, or mere vandalism. The crudity of the technique
in Act I would certainly suggest that the reworker was not an
experienced or even a capable dramatist. As, however, *Nice*

---

[14] Oliphant, *op. cit.*, pp. 443-44.   [15] *Ibid.*, p. 441.

Valour has clearly been altered, internal evidence, unless it favored a very early date, could hardly be used in arguing the date of original composition.

In the passage in which Lapet alluded to Fisher's Folly, it will be recalled that there were allusions—unfortunately most of them vague—to certain pamphlets which had apparently proved remunerative. The identification of these allusions is, however, uncertain. That to *"The Carpenter,* an unknown thing,*"* Dyce identifies as a reference to *A little Tractate, entituled The Carpenter,* which was appended to Henoch Clapham's *Theological Axioms or Conclusions,* etc., 1597.[16] I can offer no more acceptable suggestion.[17] The piece called "your *Herring,"* which "prov'd . . . able to buy Another *Fishers* Folly," may possibly have been *A most strange and wonderfull herring, taken on 26 no. 1597 neere vnto Drenton, Norway;*[18] but more probably the reference was, as has been suggested, either to *Nashes Lenten Stuffe . . . With a new Play, never played before, of the praise of the Red Herring, &c,* 1599, or to *A herrings tayle,* 1598.[19] All of these pieces, however, are so early as to be of no assistance in dating the play.

It is no easier to identify the intended allusions in the lines,

> . . . your *Pasquil*
> Went not below the mad-caps of that time . . .

Although Nicholas Breton was not alone in writing of *Pasquil* and of mad-caps, it seems reasonable that one if not both of the pamphlets alluded to were by him. He used such titles much more frequently than did any other author; in *The Scornful Lady* there is an allusion to Breton's prolificacy and to, perhaps, the large editions in which his pamphlets were printed. Roger says that he

---

[16] X, 362, note.

[17] Less acceptable is, I feel, *Trigonum Architectomium or the Carpenter's Squire, that is a table serving for the measuring of board, glasse, stone and such like playne and sollids,* by William Bedwell, entered on the Stationers' Register March 1, 1613/14.

[18] A. W. Pollard and G. R. Redgrave (eds.), *A Short Title Catalogue,* Bibliographical Society (London, 1926), No. 13239.

[19] *Ibid.,* No. 4614. See Dyce's note, X, 362.

undertook, with labour and expense,
The recollection of those thousand pieces,
Consum'd in cellars and tobacco shops,
Of that our honour'd Englishman, Ni[ch] Br[eton].[20]

[II, i.]

It is almost certainly to one or more of Breton's pamphlets that Mother alludes in *The Coxcomb* when she asks Alexander: "Do you read *Madcap* still?"[21] Most of these pamphlets by Breton appeared close to 1600. *Pasquils mad-cap and map-cappes message*[22] (1600) was followed in the same year by *The second part of Pasquils Mad-cap, intituled the Fooles-cap.*[23] In 1600, too, appeared *Pasquils mistresse,*[24] *Pasquils passe and passeth not,*[25] and *Pasquilles swullen humoures;*[26] and in 1602 *Old map-cappes new galli-mawfry;*[27] and in 1612 *Cornu-copiae, Pasquils nightcap.*[28] In addition to these pamphlets by Breton there was the anonymous pamphlet, *Pasquils jest, mixed with Mother Bunches merriments*[29] (1604). In such a confusion of titles it seems hardly possible to designate a particular pamphlet as that alluded to in *The Nice Valour*. Further, the passage in the play is ambiguous in another respect.

> Your Herring prov'd the like, able to buy
> Another *Fishers* Folly, and your *Pasquil*
> Went not below the mad-caps of that time.

It is not clear whether "of that time" refers to the time of *Pasquil* or to the time of *Herring*. Under the first interpretation, the allusion would seem to be to the pamphlets crowded into 1600; but if the meaning be that some later *Pasquil* proved as popular as the earlier *Mad-caps*, the allusion may be to the pamphlets of 1604 or 1612. Only if the latter interpretation

---

[20] Dyce was the first to expand the abbreviation; *Works*, III, 28, note. Dyce (X, 363, note), without giving reasons, thinks the lines in *Nice Valour* refer to works by two authors.

[21] Weber identified the allusion as to *Pasquils Mad-cap, and Mad-cappes Message* (1600); Dyce preferred *Olde Mad-cappes new gally-mawfry* (1602). Both were by Breton.

[22] *Short Title Catalogue*, no. 3675.   [23] *Ibid.*, no. 3677.
[24] *Ibid.*, no. 3678.   [25] *Ibid.*, no. 3679.
[26] See *ibid.*, no. 3666.   [27] *Ibid.*, no. 3673.
[28] *Ibid.*, no. 3639.   [29] *Ibid.*, no. 19451.

were meant can the reference be of any assistance in dating the play; and it is perhaps prejudicial to that interpretation that the other references in the passage seem to be to pamphlets printed prior to 1600.

Other volumes Lapet alludes to in his speech immediately preceding the one quoted, and here again those which can be identified had appeared first prior to 1600. His *Kick*, he says,

> will much enrich the Company of Stationers.
> 'Tis thought 'twill prove a lasting benefit,
> Like the *Wise Masters,* and the *Almanacks,*
> The hundred *Novels,* and the Book of *Cookery,*
> For they begin already to engross it
> And make it a Stock-book, thinking indeed
> 'Twill prove too great a benefit, and help,
> For one that's new set up . . .

The *Seven Wise Masters of Rome, A C. Merry Tales,* and the *Book of Cookery*[30] had all been popular and frequently printed during the sixteenth century. Probably the dramatists had in mind no particular almanacs, but rather the stipulation of the patent granted the Stationers' Company on October 26, 1603, that in the future all annual almanacs and prognostications were to be published not as private enterprises but for the benefit of the company as a whole.[31] Although there may well have been effort made by some stationers to have the "lasting benefit" of the other three volumes transferred to the Company, I have found no evidence that they were successful. None of the three appears among the stock-books listed in the Stationers' Register—which are almost certainly incomplete lists. Al-

[30] Dyce, who worked without such aids as *The Short Title Catalogue,* observed: "What particular cookery-book is meant here, it would be useless to inquire." There can be little doubt, I think, that the reference is to *A Booke of Cookrye, gathered by A. W. and now newlye enlarged,* which was printed by J. Allde in 1584 and republished by E. Allde in 1587, 1591, and 1594. See *Short Title Catalogue,* nos. 24895-24898.

[31] On December 3, 1588, Richard Watkins and James Roberts had been granted the exclusive license to print almanacs and prognostications for twenty-one years from May 12, 1588. Wilkins had died *c.* 1599, and in 1603, Roberts presumably being willing, a new patent was granted to the Company of Stationers. See Eustace F. Bosanquet, *English Printed Almanacks and Prognostications: A Bibliographical History to the Year 1600,* Bibliographical Society (London, 1917), pp. 8-9.

though there are no extant copies of any edition of the *Seven Wise Masters* or of *A C. Merry Tales* published between 1600 and 1647, the rights to both volumes were transferred within nine days in the autumn of 1615—October 29 and November 6. As there were a large number of books concerned in each transfer, there is no reason to believe that a new edition of either was then contemplated; but as the transfer in each case was occasioned by the death of the former owner,[32] there may well have been a widespread feeling that it was time for the "lasting benefit" of these popular volumes to be "engrossed" by the Company.

In this same scene (V, iii) some have recognized still another literary allusion—an allusion which, if it can be affirmed, would materially limit the dates of the play's composition. Reed made the suggestion, apparently accepted by Dyce,[33] that a few lines later there is an allusion to Selden's *The Duello, or Single Combat*, entered on the Stationers' Register late in 1609 and published in 1610. To one looking through his new book Lapet observes:

> What have you there now? oh Page 21 . . .
> Mark how I snap up the *Duello* there.

Earlier Lapet had given the full title of his volume as "the Uprising of the *kick;* and the downfall of the *Duello*" (IV, i). Although the immediate presence of allusions to so many other pamphlets may urge that a literary allusion is intended here, it is certainly questionable whether there is an allusion to Selden's *Duello* or to any other volume. From the general tone of the play as well as from particular passages, the allusion seems to be rather to the widespread practice of duelling and perhaps to the gathering efforts to discourage such a costly code of honor.

Indeed, the treatment which the fashion of duelling receives

[32] *A C. Merry Tales,* was, on October 29, 1615, entered to William Jaggard among books "which were heretofore entered to James Roberts." The *Seven Wise Masters* was among the books entered to Purfoote, Jr., "which were Copies of Master Thomas Purfoote his father deceased," November 6, 1615.

[33] X, 363, note.

in *Nice Valour* offers, I believe, some definite suggestion for the date of the play's composition. As has been noted in Essay VIII, in all the Beaumont and Fletcher plays definitely dated after 1615 which contain discussions of duelling, there are arguments cited against the practice; while in the plays which can be dated prior to 1616, the dramatists accept without questioning the current view that a gentleman must defend his reputation with the sword. As has been noted too, *Nice Valour* reveals, as the earliest plays do not, an appreciation both of the dreadful cost of the fashion of duelling and of the trivial causes for which many duels were fought. La-Nove assures Lapet that if his book accomplishes the "downfall of the *Duello*,"

> you'll prove a happy member,
> And do your Countrey service: your young blouds
> Will thank you then, when they see fourscore.   [IV, i.]

There may, too, in the story of Shamont be ridicule of a too nice worship of reputation. On the whole, however, the authors seem not antagonistic to the prevailing fashion. No eloquence is, as in the later plays, employed to urge the folly and the wrong of duelling. Scorned and laughed at are those characters who reveal themselves as insensible to wounded reputation, ready to excuse or justify the peaceful acceptance of an insult. Lapet's condemnation of the duello is, La-Nove says, awaited "by all the cowards in the Town."

If the theory which I advanced in Essay VIII is correct, the treatment accorded duelling in *Nice Valour* argues strongly that the play was composed not later than the close of 1615 or at latest the opening of 1616. Unless the few lines which seem to condemn the duello were introduced at the time of revision, we perhaps may see in *Nice Valour* the transition from the dramatists' first attitude to their later hostility, and accordingly hazard for the play a date close to 1615.

On entirely different grounds Mr. W. J. Lawrence has suggested that the play was written in 1615. His suggestion was made in a note to Mr. Oliphant, from whom I quote:

Lawrence supplies me with the following interesting note: "IV. i:

'*Lapet.*   I hope

To save my hundred gentlemen a month by it,

Which will be very good for the private house.'

Weber thinks this a reference to some playhouse; but he fails to see the significance of the use of the word 'house' in the singular. To begin with, this was doubtless a local allusion, as the play in all likelihood was a Blackfriars play. The question is, at what time after 1610 was the Blackfriars the sole private theatre? The Whitefriars closed December, 1614, and never reopened; Rosseter's Blackfriars patent is dated June 3, 1615, and the theatre was used late in 1615 or early in 1616; the Cockpit was opened *circa* March, 1617. The safe date would be the spring of 1615." Is Mr. Lawrence quite correct in his facts? There was perhaps a gap in 1616-7 between the closing of Porter's Hall (Rosseter's Blackfriars) and the opening of the Cockpit, which might have been a time when there was only one private theater; Porter's Hall was probably not a private house (it is not so treated by Chambers); and, so far from Whitefriars never reopening after December, 1614, when the occupying company's lease expired, it was certainly in use as a theater as late as 1621; nor do I see why, even on his own assumptions, Mr. Lawrence should prefer the spring of 1615 to a later part of the year.[34]

Other objections which he raises later, Mr. Oliphant is able to reconcile to Mr. Lawrence's date, but he rejects it finally because "The play was obviously written for a boys' company— the singing characters show that. If the revised version had not also been for a boys' company, it seems natural to suppose that the singing would have been cut out."[35] *Nice Valour*, with six songs, Mr. Oliphant rejects as an adult company's play, yet he has no hesitation in accepting as plays written for the King's Men, *The Mad Lover*, with seven songs, *The Loyal Subject* and *Valentinian* with five each, *Bonduca* and *The Pilgrim* with four each. He is quite willing to accept 1616 as the date for *The Mad Lover*[36] and assigns *The Loyal Subject* to 1618. In the former of these plays there are the same number of singing

[34] Oliphant, *op. cit.*, pp. 444-45.   [35] *Ibid.*, p. 447.

[36] Oliphant wrote that he could have come no closer than 1615-1618 except for word from Mr. W. J. Lawrence that the play was acted in 1616. He sees no objection to Mr. Lawrence's dating.

parts as in *Nice Valour,* most of the songs being by Stremon, "a soldier that can sing," as most of those in *Nice Valour* are by the Passionate Lord. In *The Loyal Subject* there are even more singing parts. His chief reason for rejecting Lawrence's dating, therefore, seems weak.

If we accept Mr. Lawrence's argument, any date in 1615 would presumably be satisfactory; and if we prefer to believe that Porter's Hall was not considered a private theater, the period in which there might be a reference to *"the* private house" may be extended to include both 1615 and 1616. To be sure, we cannot be certain that Lawrence's interpretation is correct. As Mr. Oliphant observed, the words "the private house" may mean not "the only private house" but merely "this private house." If, however, we hypothesize 1615 as the date of the play's composition, there is perhaps some other evidence to support it. It must be confessed that most of this evidence is slight and much of it subject to more than one interpretation; but as there have been no other suggestions for a date, one is justified in urging a tentative date on the basis of inconclusive evidence.

1) Of least certainty is the assistance afforded by a doubtful interpretation of the lines

> Your Herring prov'd the like, . . .
> . . . and your *Pasquil*
> Went not below the mad-caps of that time.

These lines must have been written in or after 1612 if the correct interpretation is: *Pasquils nightcap* (1612) sold as well as did the Mad-cap pamphlets (1600) of the time of the *Herring* (1598-1599).

2) Fisher's Folly, which he had acquired in 1609, was in January, 1615, offered by the Earl of Argyle to the East India Company, and in June, 1616, sold to Lady Harrington. If this magnificent house had recently been sold, or if it were known that it could be purchased for a good big sum, there would have been more point to the remark that the returns from some trifling pamphlet had been sufficient to enable the author (or publisher) to "buy another Fisher's Folly."

3) There would likewise in the late autumn of 1615 be more point in a reference to the "lasting benefit" of the *Seven Wise Masters of Rome* and *A C. Merry Tales,* as both of those old favorites, after a century of popularity, were re-entered upon the Stationers' Register at that time. To what extent, however, such a re-entry might be publicly known is uncertain, but it is unnecessary to assume that it would have been known to all in the theater, or to any save the dramatist himself.

4) The treatment accorded the duello is for the most part like that found only in plays prior to 1616, yet the recognition of the dreadful cost of such a fashion and, possibly, the ridicule of a too nice observance of the current code of honor seem to lead directly to the attacks upon duelling found in the plays from 1616 on.

5) And, finally, there is Mr. Lawrence's interpretation of "the private house," which, if correct, would indicate a date within 1615 or 1616.

Each of these arguments, as I have already admitted, is slight and most of them are drawn from passages which lend themselves to more than one interpretation. Furthermore, even if they be allowed greater weight because of their variety and their number, they obviously cannot be said to furnish evidence for the date of the play's original composition. It is conceivable that all of these passages were inserted at the time of revision. We can never determine the earliest possible date of any of these plays when no external evidence exists and when no source is known.

No source for *Nice Valour* has ever been suggested. Although I should not urge it as the source of the play, an incident at the court of King James which was later recorded by Wilson, is in some respects so similar to the main plot of *Nice Valour* that it would, I think, be recognized as having offered suggestions to the dramatist if it could be shown that it occurred shortly before the play was composed. In the play the Duke, to attract the attention of a favorite, Shamont, touches him with his riding whip. Shamont, who is described as a "gentleman of the Chamber" and of whom the First Gentleman says

> There is not such a curious piece of courage
> Amongst man's fellowship, or one so jealous
> Of honour's loss, or reputation's glory,   [I, i.]

turns angrily to avenge so base an insult. When, however, he discovers that it was the Duke who had touched him, he cries:

> Never sate shame cooling so long upon me,
> Without a satisfaction in revenge,
> And heaven has made it here a sin to wish it.
> . . . . Oh, y' ave undone me! . . . .
> Cruelly undone me;
> I have lost my peace and reputation by you:
> Sir, pardon me; I can never love you more.   [II, i.]

He, thereupon, immediately departs from the court and, until the end of the play, cannot be induced to return.

The incident which Wilson relates was intended to illustrate the vacillating character of King James:

Another time, at *Theobalds*, the King wanted some Papers that had Relation to the *Spanish* Treaty, so hot in Motion, which raised him highly into the Passion of Anger that he should not know what he had done with them, being things so Material, and of such Concernment: And calling his Memory to a strict Account, at last he discharged it upon *John Gib*, a *Scotchman*, who was of his Bedchamber, and had been an old Servant to him. *Gib* is called for in haste, and the King asks him for the papers he gave him; *Gib* collecting himself, answer'd the King, he received no Papers from him. The King broke into extream Rage, (as he would often when the Humour of Choler began to boil in him) protesting he had them, and reviling him exceedingly for denying them; *Gib* threw himself at the King's Feet, protesting his Innocency, that he never received any, and desired his Life might make Satisfaction for his Fault, if he were guilty. This could not calm the King's Spirit, tossed in his Tempest of Passion; and overcharging with it, as he passed by *Gib* (kneeling) threw some of it upon him, giving him a Kick with his Foot. Which Kick infected *Gib*, and turned his Humility into Anger; for, rising instantly, he said, Sir, *I have served you from my Youth, and you never found me unfaithful; I have not deserved this from you, nor can I live longer with you with this Disgrace; Fare ye well, Sir, I will never see your Face more:* And away he goes from the King's Presence, took Horse, and rode towards *London*. Those about the King put on a sad Countenance to see him displeased, and every Man was inquisitive to know the Cause: Some said, the King and *Gib* were fallen out; but about what? some Papers of the *Spanish* Treaty, the King had given him, cannot be found. *Endimion Porter* hearing it, said, The King gave me those Papers, went presently and brought them to the King, who being becalmed, and finding his Error, called instantly for *Gib*; Answer was made, he was gone to *London:* The King hearing it, commanded with all Expedition to send Post after him to bring him back, protesting never to Eat, Drink, or Sleep till he saw Gib's Face. The Messenger overtook him before he got to *London;* and *Gib* hearing the Papers were found, and that the King sent for him with so much Earnestness, returned to the Court. And as he came into the King's Chamber, the King kneeled down upon his knees before *Gib*, intreating his Pardon, with a sober and grave Aspect, protesting he would never rise till *Gib* had forgiven him; and though *Gib's* modesty declined it with some humble Excuses, yet it would not satisfie the King, till he heard the Words of Absolution pronounced. So Ingenuous was he in this Piece of Passion! which had its sudden Variation from a stern and furious Anger, to a soft and melting Affection, which made *Gib* no Loser by the Bargain.[37]

There are, obviously, many differences between the play and the incident related by Wilson. In the play there is no charge or misunderstanding: the Duke's act which makes Shamont feel disgraced is not a kick given in anger to one who kneels with humility, but is a switch with a riding-whip merely for the purpose of attracting his attention. It may be noted, however, that the Duke, confessing that he, like all humans, is "subject to impetuous passions," recognizes that he may strike an attendant in anger. After Shamont's departure, therefore, he dismisses all the gentlemen attending him and orders that their places be filled by

> grooms,
> Men more insensible of reputation,
> Less curious and precise in terms of honor,
> That if my anger chance let fall a stroke,

---

[37] Arthur Wilson, *The Life and Reign of James, the First King of Great Britain,* in *A Complete History of England* (1706), II, 760-61.

> As we are all subject to impetuous passions,
> Yet it may pass unmurmur'd, undisputed;
> And not with braver fury prosecuted.   [IV, i.]

As King James willingly admitted that he had been wrong, swearing to remain on his knees until he had received Gibb's forgiveness, so the Duke of *The Nice Valour* promises Shamont that

> where any wrong
> Bears my impression, on the hasty figure
> Of my repented anger, I'm a Law
> Ev'n to my self, and doom my self most strictly
> To Justice, and a noble satisfaction.   [IV, i.]

Although there are obvious differences, there are also striking similarities between the play and the incident narrated by Wilson. If the incident preceded the play, it does not appear impossible that the dramatists may have embroidered and changed to suit their ends a story which had been told them of a subject's angry departure from his sovereign because of actions which according to his code of honor brought disgrace upon him. The dramatists would, certainly, hardly have dared to present upon the stage a literal re-enactment of King James's behavior, and the differences between play and anecdote seem no greater than the changes which would have been necessary to permit the play to be performed. In both stories the sovereign, according to the contemporary code of honor, casts disgrace upon an old and honored friend—a gentleman of his chamber. (A blow with a riding-whip, something to be used on animals, was only slightly less insulting than a kick;[38] and it may be noted that in the subplot of *Nice Valour* there is Lapet, who submits to being kicked—indeed expects to be, and is writing a book to show that a kick brings with it no loss of honor.) In both stories the insult is wrought by the sovereign, upon whom the disgrace may not be avenged. Both subjects show the

---

[38] One may recall Osborne's story of the insult offered Philip Herbert, Earl of Montgomery, by John Ramsay, who switched him in the face at the Croydon races in 1607, and "Herbert not offering to strike again, there was nothing spilt but the reputation of a gentleman."

same noble anger, courageously declare that they cannot over-look such disgrace, and depart pronouncing the bold resolve never to serve again the master who has brought such shame upon them. In the play, of course, Shamont, though but "a gentleman of the Chamber," is in the end married to the sister of his lord, a good fortune which Gibb did not enjoy. But, as I have said, I do not wish to suggest that this incident at court can be regarded as the source of the play. At most the drama-tists could have borrowed only a situation upon which to build their plot. The characters in the play can owe nothing to King James and Gibb.

Furthermore, it is difficult to date the incident related by Wilson. It appears, indeed, that Wilson has confused the par-ticipants, for John Gibb seems not to have been of the King's Bedchamber for some years prior to Endymion Porter's connec-tion with the court. Porter, having been reared in Spain, upon his return to England entered the service first of Edward Vil-liers and then of George Villiers, Duke of Buckingham, by whose influence he entered the service of Prince Charles about 1620. John Gibb's career is difficult to trace. It is the more vague because his son, Henry Gibb, was also of the King's Bedcham-ber during part of the time that his father was, and there are many references no more specific than "Gib of the Bedchamber." Henry is first referred to as a "Groom of the Bedchamber" when he was granted an annuity of £200 on 31 July 1613,[39] and for some years he continued to be the recipient of rich gifts, as his father had been during the first part of the reign. If Wilson confused the father and son and really meant Henry Gibb, he may have been correct in making Endymion Porter the third actor in the farce of errors. However, not only his naming him John rather than merely Gibb, but his designating him as a Scotchman who had spent his life in James's service, argues that it was John whom he meant, as perhaps does also the fact that Endymion Porter's share in the Spanish match later was so well known that his name would tend to creep into any stories dealing with the Spanish business. The claim

[39] *C. S. P., Domestic*, LXXIV, 195.

"I have served you since my youth" might possibly fit either of the Gibbs, though it would seem inexact in the mouth of Henry until the very end of James's reign. The elder Gibb came with James from Scotland. Shortly thereafter "Mr. *Gibb*, a Scottish Gentleman of the King's Bedchamber," was sent by his master with a reprieve for Markham, Grey, and Cobham.[40] In 1605/6, in addition to a New Year's gift of ten ounces in guilt plate,[41] he received £3000 "out of Recusants' lands and goods."[42] John Gibb was still of the Bedchamber on July 5, 1614, when a yearly pension of £200 was granted to James Gibb "on surrender of a like pension by John Gibb, his father, Groom of the Bedchamber."[43] An entry two years later to the week, July, 1616, suggests that John had before then surrendered his office, for the grant is made "to Henry Gibb of the Bedchamber, for the benefit of his father, John Gibb, of lands called Brading, Isle of Wight, which have been much overflowed by the sea, and are to be inclosed at his expence."[44] From the grant's being made to Henry and from his office only being mentioned, the conclusion would be that the father was no longer of the King's Bedchamber. But for a while earlier, at least, father and son both seem to have served in that capacity. How the two were distinguished is suggested by a letter from Chamberlain to Carleton (9 September 1613) in which he says that "young Gib of the Bedchamber" had been sent to try to stop the duel between the Earl of Essex and Mr. Henry Howard.[45] But Chamberlain uses no such distinguishing adjective when on April 30, 1616, he informed Carleton that Sir Robert Carr and "Gibb of the Bedchamber" had been "confined for burning letters and papers."[46] Nor is Camden more definite in recording in his *Annals*, 23 April 1616, "Robert Carre of Ancram, and Gibbs, being examined by the Chancellor,

---

[40] Sir Ralph Winwood, *Memorials of Affairs of State*, 3 vols. (London, 1725), II, ii.

[41] John Nichols, *Progresses of King James I*, 4 vols. (London, 1828), I, 599.

[42] *Ibid.*, II, 43.   [43] *C. S. P., Domestic*, LXXVII, 241.

[44] *C. S. P., Domestic*, LXXXVIII, 381. 11 July 1616.

[45] Birch, *op. cit.*, I, 272.

[46] *Ibid.*, p. 401. Reporting the same event to Carleton two days earlier, Sir George Goring refers to him merely as "Mr. Gibb."—*C. S. P., Domestic.*

are acquitted the next Day." It would seem, therefore, that
John Gibb had surrendered his post some years before Endymion Porter was connected with the court.

The fact that Endymion Porter and the Gibbs belonged
to rival factions makes it further unlikely that they would have
been employed at the same time in the Spanish business. Porter, a protégé of the Villiers family, owed his court career
entirely to Buckingham. The Gibbs, however, perhaps as
Scotchmen, were close to the earlier favorite, Somerset. Somerset and the elder Gibb both had accompanied James when he
first came to England. When Chamberlain wrote Carleton on
July 20, 1615, that "Young Gibb, of the bedchamber, is willed
to absent himself," he added that this reproof "is taken for
an ill sign and cross below to somebody else,"[47] referring certainly to the signs already apparent of Somerset's crumbling
fortunes. In April, 1616, charged with burning letters and
papers, Gibb was arrested with Sir Robert Carr of Ancram,[48]
whose appointment to the Bedchamber had been brought about
by Somerset.[49] And when in January, 1621/22, Somerset and
his countess were released from the Tower, they went, Chamberlain reported, "to Mr. Gibbs's, by Otelands."[50] It seems
probable, therefore, that such a situation as that described by
Wilson, if John Gibb and not Endymion Porter was concerned,
would have occurred during the ascendancy of Somerset, at a
time most likely when James, after the death of Salisbury, was
serving as his own secretary. Salisbury had died May 24, 1612,
and for some years thereafter James refused to appoint a successor, conducting all business himself with the assistance of
Somerset. In the Spanish business, indeed, he in 1613 gave
Somerset a free hand.[51]

As the Gibbs were affiliated with Somerset, it seems hardly
likely that either of the Gibbs would have been in any way con-

[47] Birch, *op. cit.*, I, 367.
[48] Camden, *Annals*, 23 April 1616; Chamberlain in Birch, *op. cit.*, I, 401;
Sir George Goring to Carleton (*C. S. P., Domestic*), 28 April 1616.
[49] Rev. Thomas Lorkin to Sir Thomas Puckering, July 15, 1613. Birch, *op.
cit.*, I, 256.
[50] Letter to Carleton, 19 January 1621/22; Birch, *op. cit.*, II, 286.
[51] See Gardiner, *History of England, 1603-1642*, II, 148, 231, 327.

cerned with the Spanish business after Somerset's fall or after the rise of Buckingham. It would appear that there was no time at which a paper might have been entrusted to either John Gibb or Endymion Porter. If we are justified in assuming that Wilson has erred in naming the two, it is easy to understand how the error was made. Aside from the King, the only important figure in the incident was John Gibb, the Scotchman. Him Wilson correctly named. The name of the unimportant third figure he did not recall, but he did recall that Endymion Porter had played an important part in the proposed Spanish match for Prince Charles, that he had indeed been sent to Madrid to prepare for Charles's visit to the Infanta. What could have been more natural, therefore, since the third figure was so unimportant in his story, than for him to introduce the name of Endymion Porter?

If this suggestion be correct, the incident in all probability took place at some time when, after the death of Salisbury, the Spanish business was entrusted largely to Somerset. The outside date would be 1615, when Camden records,

The Seals are taken from *Somerset:* He is commanded by the Lord *Wotton* to lay down the Staff, the Badge of the King's Chamberlain, and to appear before the Delegates, by whom he is sent to the Tower.

As we have seen, slight though it be, what evidence there is suggests that *Nice Valour* was prepared for the stage in late 1615 or during the first months of 1616. If such was the case, the play presumably followed after no great interval the misunderstanding between James and his faithful follower. Possibly the dramatists were seeking to please by suggesting a less humiliating explanation. More likely if there was a relation between incident and play, the dramatists simply recognized that the incident afforded an excellent dramatic situation and proceeded to remodel it to the extent necessary to allow stage presentation.[52]

[52] To Professor Evelyn May Albright of the University of Chicago I am under obligation for a careful reading of my manuscript and for several helpful suggestions. She ingeniously suggests that if *Nice Valour* was based upon the incident

In this discussion there have been, I recognize, a great many "if's," "possibly's," and "presumably's." Such uncertainty there must be where the evidence is so meager. But I believe that until some more specific evidence is at hand, we may accept for the play the tentative history here outlined.

---

at court between King James and Gibb, resulting censorship may explain both the mangled form in which the play has come down to us and the subservience in Fletcher's later plays to James's views on duelling.—Cf. Essay VIII.

XI

THE OLD LAW

The Excellent Comedy, called the Old Law; or A new way to please you, was first printed in 1656 and upon its title-page was ascribed to "Phil. Massenger. Tho. Middleton. William Rowley." In the modern efforts to trace its stage history there has been little agreement. Since the days of Steevens it has been generally, but not unanimously, supposed that the play in its original form dates from 1599,[1] since in III, i, it is said that Gnotho's wife was "born in *an.* 1540, and now 'tis 99." As in that year Massinger was only sixteen and Rowley probably even younger, it has been necessary to assume that their shares in the play were contributed in later revisions. Fleay accordingly suggested that Massinger's share (of which he seemed to have had doubts) was added about 1615, and Rowley's "before (not long before) the death of Dr. Butler in 1618 [29 January 1617/18]. See ii. 1, end."[2] E. E. Morris, after an elaborate study of the versification of the three parts, was more confident of the appearance of Massinger, whose revision he thought followed rather than preceded that of Rowley. No two of the authors, he was convinced, worked on the play together. He accepted 1599 as the date of the original play by Middleton, assigned Rowley's recension to a date "after 1616," and suggested that Massinger's version may have been prepared for presentation before the King and Queen as part of the coronation ceremonies in 1625.[3]

---

[1] That is, practically all printed notices of the play date its original composition in 1599. No doubt much of the unprinted opinion has been influenced by the article of Mr. Mark Eccles (referred to later) to discard so early a date. The early date had also been questioned by Dr. Furnivall (see *Shakspere Allusion Book* [London, 1932], I, 143) as well as by others mentioned later.

[2] *Biographical Chronicle,* II, 100.

[3] "On the Date and Composition of *The Old Law,*" *Publications of the Modern Language Association,* XVII (1902), 1-70. Morris offers this suggestion as a guess which has the merit of explaining the statement upon the title-page that the play was "Acted before the King and Queene at Salisbury House" and the nature of the Massinger additions, which he believes reveal an intent to glorify royalty.

Mr. C. W. Stork, however, preferred to believe that the play was written by Middleton and Rowley "in conjunction with Massinger"[4]—apparently denying the earlier view that there had been two independent revisions. Indeed, he rejected the evidence for an early version in 1599 by declaring the scene containing it to have been written by Rowley—a lad about fourteen in 1599. He offered no further suggestion, however, than that "Mr. Fleay's date for the revival, 1615, may well be the date of composition." So, too, was the 1599 date questioned by Professor Gayley,[5] who suggested a date 1614-16, and by Mr. Arthur Symonds, who, though doubting Massinger's participation in the play at all, saw the hand of Rowley "not so much in the actual writing of the comic parts as in the whole conception of the main scenes and characters,"[6] and accordingly regarded the play as the product of collaboration.

There is one—and only one—argument for the 1599 date. That the fortunes of youth may not be kept from them until they are too old to relish them, the Duke of Epire has proclaimed a law that men at eighty and women at sixty must be put to death. In III, i, the happy but impatient Gnotho has come to the parish clerk to find out the exact age of his old wife, Agatha. The clerk reads to him the entry in the parish register: "Born in *an.* 1540, and now 'tis 99. By this infallible record, sir, (let me see,) she is now just fifty-nine, and wants but one." But even one year is too long for Gnotho to postpone his purposed second marriage. He therefore suggests that the clerk alter the entry so that Agatha's time may be up.

Gnotho. . . . Come, I know you, being a great clerk, cannot choose but have the art to cast a figure.

Clerk. Never, indeed, neighbor: I never had the judgment to cast a figure.

Gnotho. I'll show you on the back side of your book,—what figure's this?

Clerk. Four with a cipher, that's forty.

---

[4] *William Rowley*, Publications of the University of Pennsylvania, Series in Philology and Literature, XIII (1910), pp. 48-49.

[5] *Representative English Comedies*, III, lv.

[6] *Cambridge History of English Literature*, VI, 69-70.

Gnotho. So! forty; what's this now?

Clerk. The cipher is turned into a 9 by adding the tail, which makes forty-nine.

Gnotho. Very well understood; what is't now?

Clerk. The 4 is turned into 3; 'tis now thirty-nine.

Since the audience could not see the marks Gnotho was making, it was, of course, necessary that the alteration be such as could be briefly explained by the dialogue and easily followed by the spectators. It was further necessary that the alteration increase Agatha's years by one. Much too involved would be an exposition of how a five might be turned into a four, or a six into a five. True Gnotho does not explain how he makes the change from "49" to "39," but the audience, able to appreciate the ease with which the first change has been made from "0" to "9," understands fully what Gnotho is doing and demands no further explanation. As no numeral may be so easily changed to the one immediately preceding it as a zero may be changed into a nine, it seems likely that an author, regardless of the year in which he was writing, would have selected as a date to be altered one ending in a zero. He would likewise have selected 1540 rather than 1550 or 1560 because, as Mr. Eccles has pointed out, "the practical playwright preferred a round number to which his hearers could at once add sixty, the age of compulsory death." Mr. Eccles' discovery that Middleton was christened April 18, 1580, and hence probably several years younger than had usually been thought, makes it most unlikely that he, the oldest of the three, could have written so excellent a play in 1599. "There is no real evidence," Mr. Eccles states, "that Middleton turned professional playwright before 1602."[7] Obviously we must discard either the date 1599 or all three of the authors mentioned on the title-page.

A further reason for questioning the theory of a 1599 version of *The Old Law*, even though one advance new authors for the play, may be an indebtedness to later plays of Shakespeare. The echo of a line such as "Alas, poor ghost,"[8] if due

[7] Mark Eccles, "Middleton's Birth and Education," *Review of English Studies,* VII (1931), 431-41.   [8] See *Shakspere Allusion Book,* I, 143.

to other than chance, may, of course, have been inserted at a
later date; but there is, I believe, a similarity between *The Old
Law* and *King Lear* in both theme and action, which would at
least have made the former play more timely and more logically motivated if it followed Shakespeare's tragedy. *The Old
Law* is indeed merely a comic treatment of the theme so trag-
ically presented in *Lear*—the struggle between Youth and Age,
the desire of youth to obtain its inheritance while able to enjoy
it most. This struggle between Youth and Age is, of course, a
perennial theme, and, although it is less frequent, I believe, in
late Elizabethan drama than its prevalence at other times and
in other types of literature might suggest, it may well sound
ridiculous to urge a relationship between two plays dealing with
that age-old theme. If, however, there was a likelihood that
The Old Law was composed during a time when *Lear* was on
the stage, the similarity of the two plays could obviously be
more readily admitted. I believe that it can be shown that *The
Old Law* was at least being worked upon at a time when *Lear*
was probably still upon the boards. But, first, let me illustrate
the similarity in theme.

Goneril defends her unnatural actions toward her father by
claiming that

> Old fools are babes again; and must be used
> With checks as flatteries,—when they are seen abused;
>
> [I, iii, 19-20.]

and Edmund, after his father has read the forged letter, falsely
asserts that he has heard his brother "oft maintain it to be fit,
that, sons at perfect age, and fathers declining, the father should
be as a ward to the son, and the son manage his revenue" (I, ii,
77-79). The forged letter is indeed the theme of much of *Lear*
and of the whole of *The Old Law:*

> This policy and reverence of age makes the world bitter to the
> best of our times; keeps our fortunes from us till our oldness can-
> not relish them. I begin to find an idle and fond bondage in the
> oppression of aged tyranny; who sways, not as it hath power, but
> as it is suffered. [I, ii, 49-55.]

The reason for the dissatisfaction of youth given in this letter is exactly the reason given in *The Old Law* for the decree that old men at eighty and women at sixty are to be put to death—that their lives are "tedious to their successive heirs, whose times are spent in the good of their country, yet wanting the means to maintain it, and are like to grow old before their inheritance (born to them) come to their necessary use" (I, i, 144-48). In both plays we find the contrast between the kind and grateful child, who seeks to shelter his father from unjust power, and the cruel and ungrateful child, who seeks his father's death that he may the sooner inherit. The themes of the two plays are identical, even though the treatments they receive are far apart.

The likeness of the two plays hardly extends to verbal similarity. Pure chance may account for the few parallel expressions. The old Lysander's describing himself as

> a poor old man, that now can reckon
> E'en all the hours he has to live,   [II, ii, 77-78.]

is only faintly reminiscent of Lear's description of himself as "a poor old man, As full of grief as age" (II, iv, 275-76). Hardly more striking is the resemblance between Lear's ironical cry "Age is unnecessary" (II, iv, 157) and the aged Antigona's insistence that the "laws extend not to desert, sir, But to unnecessary years" (II, i, 105). Of much more significance, however, seems to be the use of the same simile in describing mixed emotions, even though the verbal similarity be slight. The pathetic and beautiful lines in which the Gentleman describes, to Kent, Cordelia's emotion upon receiving his letter:

> . . . patience and sorrow strove
> Who should express her goodliest. You have seen
> Sunshine and rain at once: her smiles and tears
> Were like, a better way: . . .   [IV, iii, 18-21.]

—however odious they may render a parody, may well have suggested the First Courtier's description of a widow lamenting the death of her husband:

> I ha' known a widow laugh closely, my lord,
> Under her handkercher, when t' other part
> Of her old face has wept, like rain in sunshine. [II, i, 161-63.]

Obviously this verbal similarity is not of much significance when viewed alone, but when it is recalled that the themes of the two plays are so alike as to suggest that *The Old Law* is a comic rendering of the struggle depicted in *Lear*, one may question the use of the simile's being mere coincidence—especially if *Lear* was being acted at a time when *The Old Law* was being written or revised.

It will be recalled that *King Lear* was one of the ten plays which in 1619 were printed in quarto by Jaggard—some of them with fraudulent dates upon their title-pages, the *Lear* quarto bearing the date 1608. The only logical explanation which has been offered for Jaggard's substitution of fraudulent dates is that the Lord Chamberlain had, at the request of the King's Men, intervened to prevent the publication of their plays without their consent, and that Jaggard had accordingly resorted to the fraudulent substitution of the dates and of the publishers' names borne by earlier quartos of the plays.[9] If the King's Men objected so strenuously to the plays being reprinted, it may be assumed that some of them were still part of the company's repertory. Of the ten plays which Jaggard then printed, only five of them carry fraudulent dates. It may be that the three dated 1619—the quartos of *2* and *3 Henry VI* are undated—had been republished before the Lord Chamberlain intervened; or it may have been that the company's objection extended only to those upon which the fraudulent dates appear and that their objection was motivated by these plays still being acted from time to time. Against this view it may be said that one of these, *1 Sir John Oldcastle*, did not belong to the King's company, and was of such a nature as to have lost most of its box-office value. Of the plays fraudulently dated, however, *Lear* is the only one written after 1600, and if the King's Men objected to the republication because they were still acting some of the plays, then certainly *Lear* was the one most likely to have been recently or still upon the stage.

Within the year preceding the effort of the Lord Chamberlain to prevent the republication of these plays, *The Old Law*

---

[9] See E. K. Chambers, *William Shakespeare*, 2 vols. (Oxford, 1930), I, 133 ff.

was, it would seem, either being written or undergoing revision. In II, i, Simonides, preparing to enjoy his inheritance, discharges all of his old father's retainers except the coachman and the footman. To the latter he gives the reason for his retention: "You can win me wagers, Footman, in running races" (ll. 254-55). There can be little doubt, I feel, that there is here an allusion to an event which Chamberlain, for want of other news, recounted to Sir Dudley Carleton in a letter dated April 10, 1618:

We were never at so low an ebb for matter of news, especially public; so that we are fain to set ourselves a work with the poorest entertainment, that you have lightly seen, or heard of; as on Wednesday, with a race of two footmen from St. Albans to Clerkenwell; the one an Englishman, belonging lately to the Countess of Bedford, but now to the king; the other an Irish youth, that lost the day, and I know not how much money laid on his head. The sums no doubt were very great, when my Lord of Buckingham, for his part, went away with £3000; and, it is said for certain, there was more than twice as much won and lost that day. The Irish youth serves Sir ———— Howard, a younger son of the lord treasurer, and the general opinion is, that if the race had been shorter, and the weather and ways not so extreme foul, our man had been put to the worse, though he had made good proof of himself heretofore; and 'tis a very lusty, able fellow, but carried it now by main strength, so that the other gives over 'twixt this and Highgate, when he was not twice his length behind him. This story were not worth the telling, but that you may see we have little to do, when we are so far affected with these trifles, that all the court, in a manner, lords and ladies, some farther off, some nearer, went to see this race, and the king himself, almost as far as Barnet: and, though the weather was so sour and foul, yet he was scant *fils de bonne mère*, that went not out to see; insomuch, that it is verily thought there was as many people as at the king's first coming to London. And, for the courtiers on horseback, they were so pitifully bewrayed and bedaubed all over, that they could scant be known, one from another. Besides divers of them came to have falls and other mishaps, by reason of the multitude of horses.[10]

[10] Reprinted in Birch, *The Court and Times of James I*, II, 71-72.

Although there may have been many instances during the period when footmen were raced for wagers, the humor of the reference would seem certainly to demand from the audience a recollection of such heavy bets and such disorder and mischance as accompanied the race described by Chamberlain.

There is, however, another definite allusion within *The Old Law* which was cited by Fleay[11] as introduced prior to Dr. William Butler's death, January 29, 1617/18. At the end of the same scene (II, i), after the Butler has suggested that the discharged retainers recoup their fortunes by seeking out widows of nine-and-fifty, the Cook exclaims: "Oracle butler! oracle butler! he puts down all the doctors a' the name." I can, however, see no reason why this allusion to the famous physician could not have been made shortly after his death as well as during his life. Indeed the news of the death at the age of eighty-two of such a famous and eccentric character would certainly have stimulated the relating of anecdotes about him—not a few of which have been preserved—and have caused the doctor's fame to be much greater during the months immediately following his death than ever it had been during his lifetime. It would appear to me, therefore, that rather than urge a date before Dr. Butler's death, the allusion to his oracular powers strengthens the identification of the allusion to the racing footmen, and argues that the scene was being written (or rewritten) in the spring of 1618.[12]

I confess I can see no reason for saying rewritten. Massinger has never been assigned a substantial share in the play; the

[11] *Biographical Chronicle*, II, 101.

[12] I am not certain that there may not be a third topical allusion in the opening of III, i. Gnotho tells the Parish Clerk to be covered:

> . . . remember yourself, you are clerk.
>
> *Clerk.* A small clerk, sir.
>
> *Gnotho.* Likely to be the wiser man, sir; for your greatest clerks are not always so, as 'tis reported."

Unless Gnotho's last speech was accompanied by some suggestive pantomime, the audience could hardly have recognized a reference to the corpulent Marco Antonio de Dominis, Archbishop of Spalato, who had settled in England late in 1616 and had, no doubt, already begun to display the avarice and irascibility which made him so unpopular among the people. The only reason for suspecting a possible allusion here to the bulky ecclesiastic is that Middleton was later to bring him on the stage as the Fat Bishop in *A Game at Chess*.

conception has been always attributed to Middleton or Rowley; and the allusions noted are in scenes which clearly belong to one or both of them. As there can no longer be any reason to cling to the theory that the play was originally composed in 1599, there is no reason to believe that the parts of at least Middleton and Rowley were not produced in collaboration or at least prepared at the same time. They are known, of course, to have collaborated both before and after 1618, their earliest joint play, *A Fair Quarrel*, having been acted and printed in 1617, while their *World Tost at Tennis* was, shortly after its presentation, published in 1620. Whether or not Massinger had any share in the play,[13] or, if he did contribute, whether his contribution was made at the original writing or at the time of a later revision, *The Old Law* should be dated 1618.

[13] Many critics have expressed their inability to see in *The Old Law* anything suggestive of Massinger. The doubts of Fleay and Arthur Symond's have already been noted. A. H. Bullen wrote: "Probably Massinger did no more than revise the play on the occasion of its revival at the Salisbury Court Theatre; I doubt whether he added a single scene."—*The Works of Middleton*, I, xv. Emil Koeppel thought it "just possible" that Massinger revised it, "but, if he did so, he carefully abstained from any material alterations. No trace of his individual style is to be discovered in the existing text."—*C. H. E. L.*, VI, 165. Canon A. H. Cruickshank observes that the play "does not owe much to Massinger . . . it may have owed its association with his name to revision on his part . . . the humor is not his, but better; his phraseology is markedly absent; the prose scenes show another conception of art. . . ." —*Philip Massinger*, pp. 141-42.

If *The Old Law* is the joint effort of Rowley and Middleton, the logical dating of it would be very close to 1618, even though it contained no topical allusions to support that date.

XII

THE NOBLE GENTLEMAN

THE RECORDED stage history of *The Noble Gentleman* begins on February 3, 1625/26, on which date it was licensed as by John Fletcher. Twenty-one years later it appeared in the first folio of the Beaumont and Fletcher plays, preceded by a prologue which implies that the play is the work of both Beaumont and Fletcher and states that it was popular "twenty years agoe." The evidence of this prologue may, however, be of doubtful value. Not only is the date of its composition unknown, but its belonging to *The Noble Gentleman* may be questioned by its appearing again prefixed to the 1649 quarto of *Thierry and Theodoret*.

There have been only three efforts to date the play. Weber, judging doubtless by the date of the license that the play was never acted until after Fletcher's death, conjectured that "being left imperfect by that poet, some of his friends finished it, perhaps Shirley."[1] Dyce and Fleay, though they would substitute others instead of Shirley as the redactor, accepted Weber's suggestion that the play was left unfinished by Fletcher.[2] To Mr. Oliphant, however, it seems that the Fletcherian portions of the play are in Fletcher's early style rather than his late style, and that the hand of Beaumont should be recognized in much of what the revisers have left of the original play. He sees indeed two revisions. He thinks that the play was first written about 1606 by Beaumont (and Fletcher?), that it was revised by Fletcher alone about 1613 for Lady Elizabeth's Men, and that in 1626, after Fletcher's death, it was again revised for

---

[1] Quoted by Dyce, *The Works of Beaumont and Fletcher*, X, 109.

[2] Bullen *(D.N.B.)* and Macaulay *(C.H.E.L.*, VI, 158), who did not recognize the hand of Fletcher in the play, offered no suggestions as to the date. Thorndike dated it "1625?"; Gayley *(Beaumont, the Dramatist*, pp. 238, 378), finding no satisfactory evidence of Beaumont's verse or style, thought the play written after Beaumont's death.

performance by the King's Men.[3] Mr. Bond,[4] recognizing also
the participation of Beaumont, would date the first form before
Beaumont's death in 1616; but as he thinks some suggestion
may have been got from Shelton's translation of *Don Quixote*
(1612), he would place the first form rather than a revision
in 1613-1616.[5]

The older view, that the play was left unfinished by Fletcher
or that it was written by him in 1625, must, I think, be discarded.
As Mr. Bond noted, no fewer than eleven new plays are, on
the basis of Herbert's list, assigned by Malone to the last four
years of Fletcher's life. Moreover there is evidence that the
play was being worked on as early as 1621 or 1622, and it seems
hardly likely, from what we know of Fletcher, that he would
for four or more years have left the play in an unfinished state.
More likely he would, if for any reason he was unable to complete the play himself, have turned it over to one or more of
his many assistants.

We must, I think, also discard in all probability the view
that the play was presented in either the original or a revised
state between 1610 and 1615. For his view that the play was
revised during this period, Mr. Oliphant submitted merely his
conviction that Fletcher's verse throughout has his earlier characteristics. To this Professor Bond added what he considered
similarities between *The Noble Gentleman* and *The Two Noble
Kinsmen* (?1612), in both of which there is "insanity as the
result of unfortunate love."

An original for the love-crazed Gaoler's Daughter of the *Kinsmen*
is probably to be found in Ophelia; and it is difficult to deny suggestion for Shatillion and his love in the actual circumstances of the
perfectly sane Hamlet, his nearness to the crown, the actual royal
machinations to which he is exposed, and the lament of Ophelia
over his supposed madness (III, i, 158) as of Shatillion's mistress
here:

[3] *The Plays of Beaumont and Fletcher*, pp. 183-201.

[4] *Review of English Studies*, XI (1935), 273-75.

[5] *Ibid.*, pp. 274-75. Without mention of *Knight of the Burning Pestle's* debt to
Don Quixote, Bond thinks the date of Shelton's translation "probably" forbids our
dating *The Noble Gentleman* earlier than 1613.

> There he goes
> That was the fairest hope the French court bred,
> The worthiest and the sweetest-temper'd spirit,
> The truest, and the valiantest, the best of judgment,
> Till most unhappy I sever'd those virtues[6] . . .   [I, iii.]

The similarity to Ophelia's lament is striking, but beyond this single parallel I do not find it difficult to deny other suggestions of the influence of either *Hamlet* or *The Two Noble Kinsmen*.

The similarities which Dr. Bond sees between Shatillion and Hamlet would, I feel certain, hardly have been noticed by an audience in Jacobean England. Were *The Noble Gentleman* performed, however, between 1610 and 1615 few among the audience would have failed to recognize allusions to state policy —allusions which, whether intended or not, would certainly have aroused the King's ire and have caused the play to be closed.

The subplot of the play deals with the mad Shatillion, who imagines that the King, because his love stands "near the crown," holds her in close confinement and plots constantly to make him betray himself. "All that comes near him," says Longueville,

> He thinks are come of purpose to betray him;
> Being full of strange conceit, the wench he lov'd
> Stood very near the crown . . . .
> He is strong-opinion'd that the wench he lov'd
> Remains close prisoner by the King's command,
> Fearing her title.   [I, ii.]

Shatillion's own words explain his delusion:

> There is no jesting with a prince's title.
> Would we had both been born of common parents,
> And liv'd a private and retired life
> In homely cottage! We had then enjoy'd
> Our loves and our embraces . . . .   [I, iii.]

> But, if his majesty had suffer'd me
> To marry her, though she be after him,
> The right heir-general to the crown of France,

[6] *Ibid.*, 274.

> I would not have convey'd her into Spain,
> As it was thought, nor would I e'er have join'd
> With the reformed churches, to make them
> Stand for my cause . . . .
> If he will warrant me but public trial,
> I'll freely yield myself into his hands: . . .   [IV, iii.]
>
> Let him release my poor love from her torment,
> From her hard fare, and strict imprisonment.   [V, i.]

It is hardly conceivable that such lines would have been permitted in a play between 1610 and 1615. They would touch much too closely upon King James's treatment of his unfortunate cousin, Lady Arabella Stuart.

As the great-granddaughter of Margaret, daughter of Henry VII, the Lady Arabella (born 1575) stood in the succession to the English throne next to James, and it had indeed been argued, before Elizabeth's death, that her claim superseded her cousin's because she, unlike him, had been born on English soil.[7] King Henry IV of France, when in 1598 he began to consider what princess of Europe he should choose for his wife in case his marriage with Margaret of Valois should be dissolved, confided to the Duc de Sully that he would not "refuse the princess Arabella of England if, since it is publicly said the crown of England really belongs to her, she were only declared presumptive heiress of it"; but Henry knew Elizabeth well enough to add "but there is no reason to expect . . . [this] to happen."[8] Knowing, no doubt, that Arabella's claim to the throne had been "publicly" advanced, Elizabeth had regarded her with suspicion, had kept her closely guarded, and had regularly disapproved of marriage for her. Especially had Elizabeth disapproved of the rumored marriage of Arabella and one of the Seymours, sons of Lord Beauchamp, who "as grandson of Edward Seymour, earl of Hertford, and of Lady Catherine Grey (younger sister of Lady Jane Grey), was heir to the throne after Elizabeth according to the will of Henry VIII."[9]   To

---

[7] *D.N.B., sub* Arabella.
[8] *Memoirs of Sully,* translated from the French . . . (London, 1890), II, 70-71.
[9] *Encyclopaedia Britannica,* 11th ed., XXV, 1046.

prevent the uniting of these two strains of royal blood, Arabella had been arrested shortly before the Queen's death.

Upon James's succession to the throne he had received his cousin at court with favor, even though at the trial of Sir Walter Raleigh late in 1603 an absurd indictment was brought against Raleigh of "joining with Lord Cobham . . . to dispossess his majesty and his royal issue of this crown, and to have set up the Lady Arabella Stuart. For better accomplishing whereof, it was said they intended to have craved the assistance of the King of Spain."[10] But although James had at first treated Arabella kindly, he, just as steadfastly as Elizabeth, took every precaution to prevent her marriage. In December, 1609, she with her servants was placed in confinement because of her plan to marry —presumably the Prince of Moldavia. Less than two months later she was actually engaged to William Seymour, one of the brothers especially forbidden her by both Elizabeth and James. The two were summoned by the Privy Council, before whom they promised never to marry without the King's consent. Without securing such consent, however, they were privately married about five months later. The news of the marriage soon reached James and immediately the two lovers were imprisoned, Arabella in Lambeth and Seymour in the Tower. Both managed to escape in June, 1611, but while Seymour reached Ostend safely, Arabella's boat was overtaken and she was brought back to be lodged in the Tower until her death in 1615.

How alarmed King James was by Arabella's marriage to Seymour is suggested by a letter from John More to Sir Ralph Winwood, June 18, 1611. After observing that some thought the danger would have been slight and that the "Hott Alarm taken at the Matter will make them more *Illustrious* in the World's Eye then now they are, or (being let alone) ever would have been," More observed that "others aggravate the Offence in so strange a manner, as that it might be compared to the *Powder Treason;* and so it is said to fill his Majestye with *fearfull Imaginations,* and with him the *Prince,* who cannot easily

[10] Letter from Lord Cecil to Sir Thomas Parry, December 1, 1603. Birch, *Court and Times of James I,* I, 16.

be removed from any settled Opinion."[11] The King was deaf
to all intercessions in Arabella's behalf. A plot for her escape in
November, 1613, was frustrated, and shortly afterwards she was
reported to have become mad. "The Lady Arabella hath been
dangerously sick of convulsions, and is now said to be distracted," Chamberlain wrote Carleton in March, 1613; and he
added, glancing no doubt as James's fear because of her nearness to the crown, "which, if it be so, comes well to pass for
somebody whom they say she hath nearly touched."[12] She died
a prisoner in the Tower something over two years later—on or
about September 25, 1615.[13] Camden notes that she

died in the Tower of *London*, was interred at *Westminster*, without any Funeral Pomp, in the *Night*, in the same Vault wherein
Mary Queen of *Scots* and Prince *Henry* were buried. It is a saying
of *Charles* the Fair, in *Papir*, *Mass*. p. 382. *that those who die in
the King's Prison, are deservedly deprived of Funeral Pomp, lest
they should be thought to have been thrown into Prison wrongfully.*[14]

Wilson records indeed that the circumstances surrounding her
death "set Mens Tongues and Fears awork, that she went the
same way" as Sir Thomas Overbury—by poison; that as both
she and her husband were "at some distance ally'd to the
Crown," "a Conjunction would not be admitted in the Royal
Almanack; so dreadful is every Apparition that comes near
Princes Titles."[15]

[11] Winwood, *Memorials of Affairs of State*, III, 281. This letter furnishes another parallel between the play and the story of Arabella. As Shatillion demands
"public trial" (IV, iii), so Arabella's aunt, the Countess of Shrewsbury, when arrested
and lodged in the Tower, had cried out at her examination that she would "answer
nothing *in private*, and yf she have offended the Lawe, she will answere it *in publicke*."

[12] Letter reprinted in Birch, *op. cit.*, I, 234.

[13] The uneasiness which the Lady Arabella's nearness to the throne occasioned
King James was not stilled by that lady's distraction, or even by her death. Rumor
reported that she had left a son to inherit her right, and Lady Shrewsbury, Arabella's
aunt, spent many long months in prison for obstinately refusing to quiet the rumor
"under pretence, forsooth, of a vow formerly made, of not answering to any article
touching the said Lady Arabella." Her obstinacy was in 1618 "censured with a fine
of £20,000, and perpetual imprisonment."—Thomas Lorkin to Sir Thomas Puckering, June 30, 1618; Birch, *op. cit.*, II, 77.

[14] *Annals.* Entry under September 27, 1615.

[15] Wilson, *The Life and Reign of James I*, in Kennett, *A Complete History of
England*, II, 702.

I am not, of course, suggesting that the subplot of *The Noble Gentleman* is based upon the unhappy affair of Arabella and Seymour, or even that the two are parallel. But I do believe that the situation in the play would have been sufficiently suggestive of Lady Arabella's misfortune as to give offense, and that such lines as those already quoted, together with expressions of sympathy by other characters, would never have been tolerated upon the public stage during 1610-1615. I think it most unlikely, therefore, that the play would, if written earlier, have been revived, as Mr. Oliphant thinks, about 1613, when Arabella was in strict confinement, or that if first written about 1613-1616, as Mr. Bond thinks, it would ever have passed the censors.

At least once, however, there did reach the stage a play in which the Lady Arabella thought she recognized an allusion to herself. On February 18, 1609/10, the Venetian Ambassador in London wrote that "Lady Arabella is seldom seen outside her rooms and lives in greater dejection than ever. She complains that in a certain comedy the playwright introduced an allusion to her person and the part played by the Prince of Moldavia. The play was suppressed."[16]

Sir Edmund Chambers suggests that the play to which Arabella objected may have been Jonson's *Epicoene*, in V, i, of which appears the following dialogue:

La Foole. He [Daw] has his boxe of instruments . . . to draw maps of every place, and person, where he comes.

Clerimont. How, maps of persons!

La Foole. Yes, sir, of Nomentack, when he was here, and of the Prince of *Moldavia*, and of his mistress, mistress *Epicoene*.

Clerimont. Away! he has not found out her latitude, I hope.

But Sir Edmund notes that "if Jonson's text is really not 'changed from the simplicity of the first copy,' it is clear that Arabella misunderstood it, since Epicoene was Daw's mistress."[17]

Whatever the play to which Arabella objected, it was, the Ambassador reported, suppressed. As the texts now stand, both Arabella and King James should have found *The Noble Gentle-*

[16] *C. S. P., Venetian.*   [17] *Elizabethan Stage*, III, 371.

man much more objectionable, for only a little more than a month before the Venetian Ambassador's letter Arabella had been committed to the Tower[18] upon the discovery of her plan to escape to Scotland, "apparently with a view to arranging a marriage with Stephen Bogdan, pretender to Moldavia";[19] and she had just been restored to favor when the Ambassador wrote.[20] There is nothing in *The Noble Gentleman* which suggests an allusion to "the part played by the Prince of Moldavia," except perhaps that the one whom the Prince wished to marry was indeed closely related to the King and was by him held a strict prisoner. The only arguments I see for identifying this comedy with that suppressed upon the complaint of Arabella are that, if Beaumont had a hand in it, the play must have been composed before 1616, and that, if it did reach the stage between 1610 and 1616, it would certainly have been suppressed. But no more upon this occasion than upon the occasions when James sought to prevent her union with William Seymour, would objection have been taken to a reminder that, to safeguard his own title to the throne, the King had separated from her lover the one who "after him [was] the right heir-general to the crown," and had confined her to "hard fare, and strict imprisonment."

We may, therefore, be justified in assuming that unless it is to be identified with the comedy suppressed in 1609/10, *The Noble Gentleman* was probably not acted with its present subplot during the years 1610-1615. Yet it is in this subplot that critics have thought they recognized the touches most suggestive of Beaumont. As Beaumont died March 6, 1616, it would seem that his share, if the play was indeed written in part by him, must date prior to December, 1609.

That the play was, however, being composed or revised between 1619 and 1622, is, I think, shown by a speech by Cleri-

---

[18] Her committment is recorded in a letter by Chamberlain dated December 30, 1609. Winwood, III, 117.

[19] *Encyclopaedia Britannica*, 11th ed., XXV, 1046.

[20] Chamberlain records her restoration to favor in a letter dated February 13, 1609/10.

mont in Act I, scene i. Monsieur Marine is urging his cousin
to send his wife to court, and Clerimont replies:

> Sir, I had rather send her to *Virginia*
> To help to propagate the *English* Nation.

This reply is, I think, probably a reference to an organized
movement to transport women to the colony. Before 1626,
when the play was licensed, only one such movement is recorded. The records of the Virginia Company show that this
movement was not thought of until late 1619 and that it was
completed two years later. I quote at length from the records
of the Company so that the reader may see how exactly the purpose of the Company corresponded to that expressed by Clerimont, "to propagate the *English* Nation," may judge how much
publicity such a movement would receive and how a reference
to it might provoke laughter, and may understand more fully
my reasons for believing that the play was originally composed
or was revised in 1621 or 1622.

The advisability of transporting women to the colony was
first suggested to the Company on November 3, 1619:

As in the last Court Mr Deputy acquaynted them of mr Threas-
urer so he being now present it pleased him to relate, that although
to the time giuen him by the Companies orders he had beene absent
yet he hath not beene idle to Virginia, as he will giue Accompt of:
And therefore he had to offer to their consideracion a Proposicion
for the inlarging of the Plantation in the publique. And first touching
the Publique, he shewed how farr the Company had allready proceeded. ffirst in Ianuary last there went ffifty men wth Sr George
Yeardly to be Tenants of the Gouernors land, whereof there failed
by the way two or three, and six were now remayning to him of
Capt Argolls guarde. Afterward in Aprill next twenty men should
haue beene sent by Xofer Lawne vnto the Common Land, but
he deliuered but 15 because the Company performed not wth him,
touching the Loane of Corne and Cattle as he expected: Then 4
more were sent in the Triall according to the direccion of his Matie.
And in the begining of August Last, one hundreth more—50—to
the Colledge Land and 50 to the Common: And for one hundreth

persons or thereabout wch appeareth to haue beene sent in these 2 or 3 last yeares at the Companies charges, Sr Geo: Yeardley writeth of but three to be found remayning for the Company; So that there is by this Account vpon the Common Land 72 persons, 53 on the Gouernors, and 50 on the Colledges: 175 in the whole. Therefore he proposed now to be considered of against the Quarter Court this fortnight that there be sent next spring 130 men more, wch will make those allready sent for the Gouernor Colledge, and Common Land the full nomber of Three hundred, . . .

. . . He also thought it fitt to send 100 more to be Prentizes or Servants that the rest may goe on more cheerefully, wherein he hoped the citty would deale as worthily as heretofore. Lastly he wished that a fitt hundreth might be sent of woemen, Maids young and vncorrupt to make wifes to the Inhabitñnts and by that meanes to make the men there more setled & lesse moueable who by defect thereof (as is credibly reported) stay there but to gett something and then to returne for England, wch will breed a dissolucion, and so an ouerthrow of the Plantacion. These woemen if they marry to the Publique ffarmors, to be transported at the charges of the Company; If otherwise, then those that takes them to wife to pay the said Company ther charges of transportacion, and it was neuer ffitter time to send them then nowe.[21]

The Records show that the proposition was accordingly brought before the Quarter Court a fortnight later:

. . . And because he vnderstood that the people thither transported, though seated there in their persons for some fewe yeares, are not setled in their mindes to make it their place of rest and continuance, but hauing gotten some wealth there, to returne againe into England: ffor the remedying of that mischiefe, and establishing of a perpetuitie to the Plantation, he aduised and made it his Third Proposicion, to send them ouer One hundreth young Maides to become wifes; that wifes, children and familie might make them lesse moueable and settle them, together with their Posteritie in that Soile.[22]

There was, however, considerable delay in completing the arrangements for sending the women to Virginia. Twenty

[21] *The Records of the Virginia Company of London*, ed. Susan Myra Kingsbury, 2 vols. (Washington, 1906), I, 255-57.   [22] *Ibid.*, p. 269.

months later none had been sent, for it was not until the meeting of July 16, 1621, that the Company made plans for financing their transportation. The records of the Company under that date show that

ffower seuerall Rolls were now read and offered to such as would please to vnderwrite The ffirst being for a Magazine of Apparrell, and other necessary provisions such as the Colony stood in great need of; The Second for sendinge of 100: mayds to be made wives; . . .[23]

Although this delay in transporting the women may have been in part due to the unwillingness of those selected—as was the delay in sending the one hundred apprentices or servants—such unwillingness, I believe, can hardly explain a delay of two years. Two months after it had been first suggested that one hundred prentices and one hundred maids be sent to the colony, the one hundred prentices had been selected and the Company had petitioned the government for special authority to use force upon those unwilling to leave England.[24] Two years, however, have passed before we learn that any women had been sent. In July, 1621, as seen from the record quoted above, plans were made for financing their transportation, and at the meeting of November 21, 1621, it is noted that sixty maids had been sent.

The Third Roll was for sendinge of Mayds to Virginia to be made Wyues, wch the Planters there did verie much desire by the want of whome haue sprange the greatest hinderances of the encrease of the Plantacion, in that most of them esteeminge Virginia not as a place of Habitacion but onely of a short soiourninge haue applyed themselues and their labors wholly to the raisinge of present proffitt and vtterly neglected not only staple Commodities but euen the verie necessities of mans life, in reguard whereof and to preuent so great an inconvenience hereafter whereby the Planters minds may be the faster tyed to Virginia by the bonds of Wyues and Children, care hath bin taken to prouide them younge handsome and honestly educated maids whereof 60 are already sent to Virginia being such

[23] *Ibid.*, p. 514.
[24] See the letter of Sir E. Sandys to Secretary Robert Naunton asking for such special authority. *Domestic Correspondence, Jac. I*, Vol. CXII, No. 49, Cal. p. 118. (*C.S.P., Colonial*, January 28, 1620.)

as were specially recommended vnto the Companie for their good
bringinge vp by their parents or friends of good worth: wch mayds
are to be disposed in marriage to the most honest and industrious
Planters who are to defraye and satisfie to the Aduenturors the
charges of their passages and prouisions at such rats as they and the
Aduenturors Agents there shall agree and in case any of them faile
through mortality it is ordered that a proporcionable addicion shalbe
made vpon the rest, In the furtherance of wch Christian Accion
diuers of the said Aduenturors had vnderwritt diuers good sommes
of money none vnder 8li whereby the whole Somé of that Roll did
already amount to 800li as may appeare by the subscriptions.[25]

As I have said, this was the only organized effort to send
women to Virginia during the life of the Virginia Company.
The Company, of course, passed out of existence in 1624, a little
more than a year before *The Noble Gentleman* was licensed;
but during the interim there is no reference in the *Calendar of
State Papers, Colonial*, which suggests another shipment of
women. The crown, under which the colony passed upon the
dissolution of the Company, was indeed notoriously uninterested
in the welfare of the colonies and much less active than the Company had been in their development.

Although the efforts of the Virginia Company to transport
women to the colony must have caused much comment in 1620
and 1621, its plan had been preceded by the individual efforts
of a scoundrel named Robinson who, early in November, 1618,
"was arraigned at the King's Bench, and condemned, for counter-
feiting the great seal, and, under colour of letters patent, exacting sums of money of alehouse-keepers. . . . Another course of
his, they say, was, by virtue of this commission, to take up rich
yeomen's daughters, or drive them to compound, to serve his
majesty for breeders in Virginia."[26] For his knavery, Robinson
was on November 13, 1618, hanged, drawn, and quartered near
Charing Cross. As he undoubtedly selected his victims from
families which he knew were able and ready to pay for a release,
his efforts in behalf of Virginia would probably have attracted
little public attention before his trial and execution. When the

[25] *Kingsbury, op. cit.,* I, 566.
[26] Chamberlain to Carleton, November 14, 1618; Birch, *op. cit.,* II, 107-8.

Company soon afterwards made known its plan to transport women to Virginia, Robinson's early efforts would have been recalled and would have caused the plan to be more humorously and more bluntly commented on. Clerimont's remark about sending his wife "to *Virginia* to help to propagate the English Nation" would, therefore, if the allusion is to Robinson's knavery, have had a timeliness only during the closing days of 1618. If, however, Clerimont refers to the publicity accompanying an organized movement to transport women to Virginia, the reference must, in order to have furnished any amusement, have been written between December, 1619, and early 1622. Because of the long delay in shipping the women and because the plans for financing their transportation were not completed until the middle of 1621, I am inclined to believe that the Company did not give publicity to their efforts to secure women prior to the beginning of the year 1621. The reference in the play indicates, I think, a date very close to the actual shipping of the maids.

If *The Noble Gentleman* was being worked on during the period between December, 1619, and late 1621, it seems quite possible that there is in the play another allusion to contemporary events. In V, i, Madame Marine says of her husband:

> This gentleman, the Lord of Lorn, my husband,
> Will go down to shew his playfellows
> Where he is gay.

Although Weber suggested that there might in these lines be a punning allusion to a title held in the family of Archibald, seventh Earl of Argyle, Dyce rejected the suggestion and thought it "more probable that Madame Marine alludes to some ballad. (In the Roxburgh Collection is *A pretty ballad of the Lord of Lorn and the false steward*.)"[27] This ballad (Child, 271) was first entered on the Stationers' Register on October 6, 1580, and again, merely as the "Lord of Lorne," on December 14, 1624. Child noted that it was "apparently founded on the romance of Roswall and Lillian, which itself belongs with a well-known group of popular tales, represented by Grimm's 'Goose-girl.'" The old Lord of Lorne sends his young son to France in the care

[27] Dyce's note, X, 182.

of the Steward, who, having robbed and deserted his young master, himself assumes the title of Lord of Lorne and is affianced to the daughter of the Duke of France; but before the wedding the false Steward is unmasked and the Duke's daughter affianced to the young lord. If it was only this ballad that the dramatist had in mind, the allusion would apparently have to be to the Steward who had posed as the Lord of Lorne, with whom M. Marine has in common a counterfeit title soon to be taken away.

It is possible, however, that the dramatist had more than merely the ballad in mind. As Weber noted, a similar punning invective directed against the Earl of Argyle was written by Alexander Craig:

> Now Earl of Guile and Lord for-Lorn thou goes,
> Leaving thy native prince to serve his foes, . . .[28]

Archibald Campbell, seventh Earl of Argyle, upon pretense of ill-health, obtained permission to visit the continent in 1618. By his second wife, whom he had married in November, 1610, he had been converted to Catholicism, and upon reaching the continent he entered the service of the King of Spain in West Flanders. For deserting his country to fight in the army of a Catholic king he was on February 16, 1619, denounced as a traitor and rebel at the market-cross of Edinburgh. However, on November 22, 1621, he was again declared the King's free liege.[29] Obviously it was between February, 1619, and November, 1621, that Craig's punning invective was written, a period which corresponds quite closely with that during which the allusion to sending women to Virginia would have been most apt—December, 1619, and November, 1621. In *The Noble Gentleman* Madame Marine, in order that she might continue to enjoy the gaities of the city, has plotted with certain city friends to persuade her foolish husband that the king has created him Duke of Burgundy upon condition that he remain near the

---

[28] Dyce, *loc. cit.*, quoting from Somers' *Tracts*. In *D.N.B.*, as quoted from Scot's *Staggering State*, where the verses first appeared, the second line reads:

> Quitting thy Prince to serve his foreign foes.

[29] *D.N.B.*

court. There may, therefore, well be a playful exaggeration in likening Marine, who threatens to leave the city for the country in violation of his agreement, to the Earl of Argyle, who had shortly before deserted his "native prince to serve his foes."

At any rate it seems safe to say that *The Noble Gentleman* was being either composed or revised in the period 1619-1621. If the original composition is to be ascribed to these years, obviously Beaumont could have had no share in it. And if Beaumont did share in the play, it must have been written first not later than 1609, for between the opening of 1610 and Beaumont's death in 1616 no dramatist would have even hoped that such a theme as the play's subplot might be permitted on the stage. He would have recognized that in writing such a play he was wasting his time if not endangering his liberty. Of Beaumont's participation there would appear to be no agreement. All of the earlier critics declared against his presence, as have such recent students of Beaumont's style as Gayley and Macaulay. In his conviction that Beaumont is present Mr. Oliphant has lately been joined by Dr. Bond and Mr. Wells.[30] Although I confess that I find in the play little which insists upon Beaumont's participation, the burlesque and the mock-heroic element is strongly reminiscent of *The Knight of the Burning Pestle;* and the scenes dealing with the mad Shatillion and the faithful Lady who attends him are so much better conceived and so much more convincingly executed than the scenes of the Passionate Madman and his lady (Cupid) in *The Nice Valour* that one can hardly question that the Passionate Madman is an imitation or hardly believe that the same author conceived both situations. The other evidence which Mr. Oliphant sees for Beaumont's authorship is questionable. He assumes that the prologue which states that the play was popular twenty years

---

[30] Oliphant, *op. cit.*, p. 185. Professor R. M. Alden, in his edition of *The Knight of the Burning Pestle* (The Belles-Lettres Series, Boston, 1910), thought that "*The Noble Gentleman*, so far as verse-form goes, shows a larger number of scenes reminiscent of Beaumont than any of the plays of this group [six plays in which Beaumont's participation had been debated]; yet the style could hardly be claimed as his. The mock-heroic element, and certain details such as the parody on *Julius Caesar* (in V, i), are indeed quite in his vein. We find further suggestion, therefore, of imitators of Beaumont of inferior poetic gifts."—P. lvi.

before and which implies the joint authorship of Beaumont and
Fletcher, was written in 1625-1626—at the time the play was
licensed as by Fletcher alone. This prologue, of course, may
have been written much later, and, as it contains nothing to
identify the play to which it belongs, it is possible that it was
prepared for a revival of some play other than *The Noble
Gentleman.* With no evidence to the contrary, however, we
should assume that the prologue is properly placed in the folio.
Nor are we, then, justified in assuming that the prologue erred
in assigning part of the original composition to Beaumont. During the years immediately following his death Fletcher's fame
was so great that it was hardly necessary to call upon Beaumont's name to help fill the theater. The burden of proof,
therefore, should be on him who denies Beaumont a share.

If Beaumont did participate in the original version, then, as
I have said, the play could not have been composed after 1609.
Whether or not it was the play which the Lady Arabella caused
to be suppressed, situations in the English court would have
necessitated its being banished from the stage during the years
of Arabella's imprisonment—and no doubt for some time after
her death. If composed prior to 1609, the play would appear
to have been brought out again between 1619 and 1621 and
certain additions and, perhaps, revisions made—although it may
not even then have been approved for performance.

Although I fear the available evidence forbids its acceptance,
the suggestion presents itself that *The Noble Gentleman* may
have been performed in 1621 under a very different title. In
that year there was acted at court a play called *The Woman's
Plot,*[31] a title which fits perfectly the principal action of *The
Noble Gentleman,* in which Madame Marine, loving the gay
life of the city, elaborately and successfully plots to keep her
simple husband in Paris. No play with such a title has, of course,
survived. In 1653 the publisher Humphrey Moseley had entered to him in the Stationers' Register, together with a large
number of other plays, "A very Woman, or yᵉ Womans Plot,"

---

[31] W. W. Greg, "The Bakings of Betsy," *The Library,* 3rd Series, II (1911),
249, notes that for this performance there seems to be "no better authority than
Reed, 'Biog. Dram,' 1782." Upon what Reed based his statement I do not know.
All others have accepted the statement without question.

which he assigned to Philip Massinger. *A Very Woman* is extant and contains no woman's plot. Indeed it has long been clear from the other entries to Moseley at that time that *A Very Woman* and *The Woman's Plot* were two distinct plays, the rights to which he was apparently seeking to secure for a single fee. The former play was published in 1655, but *The Woman's Plot* remained unprinted, even though Moseley again on June 29, 1660, caused the play to be entered to him, this time without an alternate title. Many years later John Warburton claimed that *The Woman's Plot* was one of the large number of manuscript plays which he had gathered together with great difficulty and which his cook Betsy had destroyed in baking her pies. Dr. Greg has shown that Warburton's story of his cook's depredations cannot be believed and that the list of his lost manuscripts was in all probability drawn up in large part from lists of plays entered upon the Stationers' Register by Moseley in 1653 and 1660.[32]

Before Moseley's first entry of *The Woman's Plot, The Noble Gentleman* had been printed in the Beaumont and Fletcher folio of 1647. Although it would have been ironic justice upon one who sought to enter two plays for the fee for one, it would have been strange indeed if Moseley were twice subsequently to pay fees for publishing a play already in print, already in a folio in which he had himself participated. Certainly he would never have done so except in ignorance. One may well question, however, whether he actually had in his possession manuscripts of all the plays he entered in 1653. As he was attempting, by giving false alternate titles, to register twenty-four plays for the price of twelve, he obviously did not present the manuscript copies at the time the titles were entered, for to have done so would have revealed his fraud. It is possible, therefore, that he may not by that time have secured—or, indeed, ever have secured—manuscripts of some of the plays entered. He might well, without a knowledge of the play, have been misled by the change of title. Perhaps the failure to print *The Woman's Plot* after two entries in the Stationers' Register

[32] *Ibid.*, 225-59. For further evidence against Warburton's claims, see C. R. Baskervill, "A Forerunner of Warburton's Cook," *Modern Philology*, XIII (1915-16), 52.

is to be explained either by the play's no longer existing under that title or by its proving nearly identical to a play already in print.

Moseley's ascription of *The Woman's Plot* to Massinger does not forbid the possibility of the participation of Fletcher, or even that of Beaumont and Fletcher. There are errors in Moseley's ascriptions, and it will be remembered that *The Woman's Plot* is given as the alternate title of *A Very Woman*, a comedy recognized today by practically all critics as a play by Fletcher (and Massinger?) reworked by Massinger.

If *The Woman's Plot* of 1621 was a version of the play we now know as *The Noble Gentleman*, it is possible that the former was the earlier title. The title *The Noble Gentleman* is first met on February 3, 1625/26, when the play was licensed by the King's Men. Such licensing does not demand that the play was new or rewritten, but it does suggest at least revision or additions. Possibly the title was then changed, as ten years later Herbert received £1-0-0 "for allowing the [Fortune] company to add scenes to an ould play and to give it out for a new one."[33] "New titles warrant not a play for new." It is possible, too, if the two plays are the same, that the title of *The Woman's Plot* originated outside the theater and never found a place on the play manuscript. Often those referring to plays took no pains to use the author's titles. Among many instances which might be cited, the Chamber Accounts refer to payments in May, 1613, for court performances of "Hotspur, And one other called Benedicte and Betteris."[34] One recording a similar court performance in 1621 may well have recognized no greater need of accuracy. A number of the plays which in the folios have but one title each were at times known under others. Some of the 1639 quartos of *Monsieur Thomas* were printed with the title *Fathers own Son;* the 1649 quarto of *The Woman Hater* carries the subtitle *The Hungry Courtier;* the comedy which in both folios is called merely *The Humorous Lieutenant* was entered upon the Stationers' Register in 1646 as "The Noble

---

[33] Adams, *The Dramatic Records of Sir Henry Herbert,* p. 37.
[34] Chambers, *Elizabethan Stage,* IV, 180. Appendix B.

Enemie or the humerous Lieftenant," while a manuscript copy of the play, dated 1625, bears only the title "Demetrius and Enanthe."

But however tempting may be the suggestion of a relationship between *The Noble Gentleman* and *The Woman's Plot*, the available evidence argues against our acceptance of it. The only arguments which may be advanced in favor of the plays' being identical or related are (1) that the title of the lost play fits perfectly the principal action of *The Noble Gentleman*, and (2) that topical allusions indicate a performance of *The Noble Gentleman* in 1621, the year in which *The Woman's Plot* was performed at court. Neither of these arguments is strong. On the other hand, the independence of the two plays is, if not wholly established, at least strongly suggested by the list of plays belonging to the King's Men which the Earl of Essex on August 7, 1641, sent the masters and wardens of the Stationers' Company, with orders that none was to be printed without the actors' consent.[35] In this list *The Woman's Plot* is twelfth in column one, *The Noble Gentleman* ninth in column two. None of the twenty-seven (or twenty-eight?) Beaumont and Fletcher plays named is given an alternate title, though "&c" is appended to *The Woman's Prize*; none appears under other than the usual title except that *Love's Cure or The Martial Maid* is called merely *The Martial Maid*, and possibly *Nice Valour*, which does not otherwise appear, is, as Sir Edmund Chambers suggests, the play referred to as "The Bridegroome & ye Madmā." Unless *The Noble Gentleman* and *The Woman's Plot* be the exception, there is no instance of a play's being named twice. Indeed there could have been no need for such a double entry even though a play still existed in two forms, for Essex distinctly warns that

if any of those Playes shall bee offered to ye Presse vnder another name then is in the List expressed, I shall desire yo care that they may not bee defrauded by that meanes but that they may bee made acquainted with it, before they bee recorded in yr hall & soe haue Oportunity to shew their right vnto them.[36]

[35] Printed by E. K. Chambers in *Collections*, I, 5, 368-69, of the Malone Society, 1911.   [36] Printed by Chambers, *ibid.*, p. 368.

XIII

THE FALSE ONE

THE TRAGEDY of *The False One*, usually recognized as a joint composition of Fletcher and Massinger, has, in the absence of any specific evidence, been generally assigned a date "about 1620."[1] No quarto of the play was published and, although it was included in the first Beaumont and Fletcher folio of 1647, the play was not entered upon the Stationers' Register until June 29, 1660. As there is no mention of the play in Sir Henry Herbert's office book, it was presumably produced prior to May, 1622; and as the list of the principal actors appended in the Second Folio includes the names of neither Burbage nor Condell, yet does include the names of three actors not known as King's Men prior to 1619, critics have preferred a comparatively late date. Although there may be little certainty that the list of actors is necessarily a list of those who acted in the first performance, the omission of the names of two important members of the company does suggest that the stage history of the play commenced after a date when both men were active. Burbage, it will be remembered, died in March, 1619, and Condell seems to have retired from acting about 1620-1621.[2] The omission of the latter's name, however, appears hardly of great significance. Many reasons might be found for his absence from the cast. There is certainly no evidence that every member of a company acted in each play produced by his company, nor that the principal parts were always taken by the same men. It should pro-

---

[1] So dated by Oliphant *(Plays of Beaumont and Fletcher)*, Macaulay *(C.H.E.L.)*, Thorndike *(The Influence of Beaumont and Fletcher)*, Luce (Variorum Edition of *The Works of Beaumont and Fletcher*, IV).

[2] Chambers, *William Shakespeare*, II, 87. Of the eight actors named in the Second Folio list preceding *The False One*, no fewer than three are first heard of as members of the King's Men in 1619, Joseph Taylor, John Rice, and George Birch. Taylor presumably was secured to replace Burbage shortly prior to May 19, 1619; and Birch, who is not named in the Company's patent of March 27, 1619, took part in *Barnavelt* about August of that year (Nungezer, *A Dictionary of Actors*, pp. 367, 46).

voke no surprise if Condell, who was to retire about 1620 or 1621, should during the years immediately before his retirement restrict himself to very minor parts or even occasionally take no part at all.

Mr. Oliphant's efforts[3] to place the play in 1620-1621 are to me unconvincing, for his argument is based on two highly questionable assumptions: first, that Fletcher with his collaborators was turning out the same number of plays each year, and second, that, although other critics have disagreed with him, he has, with little definite evidence at hand, correctly dated to the year the other plays written between 1619 and 1622.

As there has, however, been general agreement in dating *The False One* "about 1620," I may be justified in assuming in this essay that the so-called tragedy was first acted sometime during the three years between the opening of 1619 and the close of 1621. Produced during that time, the play would have had a timeliness which has not been pointed out. The period of its composition might explain some of the incidents which the authors have added to their historical sources and, perhaps, account for the title which they selected for the play.

The main plot of *The False One* tells of Pompey's flight into Egypt before the conquering advance of Caesar, of the efforts of the Egyptian leaders to curry favor with the victorious Caesar by contriving Pompey's murder, of the struggle for power between Cleopatra and the advisers of her younger brother Ptolemy, of Caesar's love for Cleopatra, of his escape from and subsequent defeat of Ptolemy's ambitious advisers, of his subjugation of Egypt, and of his placing Cleopatra upon the throne. As far as this plot is concerned, the events of history are followed with comparative accuracy. The principal addition to the historical sources is the story of the false Septimius, of whom history records little other than that he, a Roman who had once served with Pompey and who had been left behind in Alexandria, compounded with certain Egyptian leaders to murder his former commander; that, having accomplished his dastardly deed, he received from Caesar not the expected reward

[3] *Op. cit.*, p. 234.

but only scorn. In the play, however, the story of Septimius is much more fully drawn.

In the opening scene he is rebuked and reviled by the Egyptians Achillas and Anchoreus, but with oaths and fawning flattery he offers himself to the Egyptian leader Photinus to be engaged in any base employment. In II, i, he enters bearing the head of Pompey, which Achillas, hoping to win a reward for himself, scornfully takes from him to present to Caesar. Septimius boasts that by his treachery to Pompey he has secured

> The king's love and his bounty,
> The honour of the service; which, though you rail at,
> Or a thousand envious souls fling their foams on me,
> Will dignify the cause, and make me glorious.

In the soliloquy opening the next scene, however, Septimius laments that for his deed he is now shunned by all at court:

> I pass by now
> As though I were a rascal; no man knows me,
> No eye looks after; as I were a plague,
> Their doors shut close against me.

Photinus, entering, says he may wish to employ him again "To take a rub or two out of my way," and Septimius replies:

> 'Tis most necessary;
> A mother, or a sister, or whom you please, sir.
> *Photinus.* Or to betray a noble friend.
> *Septimius.*   'Tis all one.

In III, ii, he enters "richly dressed" to Caesar's lieutenants, who revile him as "a hir'd coward," "contemptible slave," "mangy mongrel." Scaeva advises him to seek out

> some hungry desert
> Where thou can'st meet with nothing but thy conscience;
> . . . where brute beasts will abhor thee,
> And even the sun will shame to give thee light,
> Go, hide thy head! or, if thou think'st it fitter,
> Go hang thyself!

After even the wanton Eros has scorned him, Septimius gives money to three ragged and hungry soldiers, but when they learn his identity, they throw the money at his head and declare him "no company for an honest dog." In IV, iii, he appears penitent; he has given away his gold and fine clothing. The Egyptian leaders easily persuade him, however, to return to villainy, and he promises to kill Caesar (V, ii). Ever false, he instead offers (V, iii) to lead Caesar to a place where the Egyptian leaders may be surprised and taken. But Caesar scorns his offer and orders that he be hanged. As the First Soldier conducts Septimius off the stage, he exclaims in the emphatic closing couplet:

> Thou dost deserve a worser end; and may
> All such conclude so, that their friends betray.

The False One contains many verbal echoes of *Antony and Cleopatra*, and in other ways, as notably the changing moods of Cleopatra, the authors reveal their indebtedness to Shakespeare. Professor Baldwin has, indeed, suggested that the Fletcherian play was modelled upon Shakespeare's, that the rôle of Septimius was based upon that of Enobarbus: "Septimius $=$ Enobarbus, both betrayers. . . . Since Septimius takes the life of royalty [Pompey], he must be a sneaking villain unrelieved. Hence he is more darkly colored than Enobarbus. . . . In reality Enobarbus has been split in two to make Septimius and Scæva."[4]

If it be true, indeed, that the authors of *The False One* had Enobarbus in mind when portraying these characters, certainly they endowed Septimius with none of the qualities which make us sympathize with Enobarbus. The latter's hands are not stained with murder; he is a deserter rather than a betrayer, and his later remorse almost completely atones for his sin in following his judgment rather than his heart. The treachery of Septimius, on the other hand, is urged neither by his judgment nor by the dictates of his heart. From beginning to end he is presented as a false and bloody villain who is prompted only by his love of gold, as one who for pay stood ready to murder "a mother or a sister" or "to betray a noble friend."

As I have said, the principal additions which the dramatists

[4] Baldwin, *The Organization and Personnel of the Shakespearean Company*, pp. 198-99.

made to their historical sources are in the extended story of the falseness of Septimius. Lucan asks the rhetorical question, "With what infamy will posterity hand the name of Septimius down to future ages?"[5] but he nor any of the other historians tells aught of his later life, nor suggests that for his treachery he was shunned and scorned by both his enemies and allies. And surely there was nothing in *Antony and Cleopatra* to urge Fletcher and Massinger to elaborate the villain's part. They chose, however, not only to enlarge his story but to make the rôle of Septimius the title-rôle of the play. Why?

If the date usually given the play is approximately correct, if it was produced in 1619 or 1620, then it was probably being composed not earlier than the late autumn of 1618 nor much later perhaps than the early spring of 1620. Now during that period in London feeling was running very high against one who was accepted as a villain who had been bought by gold "to betray a noble friend." For the death of Sir Walter Raleigh, Englishmen could not openly vent their rage upon the King, but they could and did heap their resentment and scorn upon the King's unfortunate tool, Sir Lewis Stukeley, who had been sent by King James to arrest Raleigh and whose testimony at his cousin's trial was both hostile and damaging. After Raleigh's conviction and execution, the people, who had idolized him, turned bitter hatred upon Stukeley. Chamberlain wrote Carleton on August 20, 1618, that "though the world be not satisfied [with Raleigh's apology for himself], yet Sir Lewis Stukeley is generally decried."[6] "He tried to hold up his head at court, but not a man would condescend to speak to him."[7] Chamberlain reports that because of the snubs he was receiving,

Stukeley . . . hath been at court since, offering to his majesty, by way of his own justification, to take the sacrament upon it, that what he laid to Sir Walter Raleigh's charge was true. . . . But Sir Thomas Badger, who stood by and heard it, "Let the king," said he, "take off Stukeley's head, as he hath done the other's, and let him at his death take the sacrament, and his oath upon it, and

---

[5] *The Civil War*, viii, 608 (Loeb Classical Library, p. 483).

[6] Printed in Birch, *The Court and Times of James I*, II, 88.

[7] Gardiner, *History of England, 1603-1642*, III, 153.

I'll believe it; but otherwise I shall credit Sir Walter Raleigh's bare affirmative before a thousand of his oaths." And it is strange to see how every man at court declines that Stukeley's company, as treacherous.[8]

In a letter dated December 4, 1618, Chamberlain told Carleton that Sir Lewis "is now most commonly called and known by the name of Sir Judas Stukeley";[9] and in a letter just a month later (January 5, 1619) he describes the scornful treatment which Stukeley received from his immediate superior:

I shall conclude with my lord admiral's entertainment of Stukeley, who, being vice-admiral of the western parts, and pretending to come and give an account to his lordship of his office, came and placed himself in the dining-chamber, there expecting till his lordship passed; who taking no notice of him, he stepped to him, acquainting him with the occasion of his coming. "What," said my lord, "thou base fellow—thou! who art reputed the scorn and contempt of men—how darest thou offer thyself into my presence? Were it not in my own house, I would cudgel thee with my staff, for presuming to be so saucy."

Stukeley made his complaint unto the king, whose answer was: "What wouldst thou have me do? Wouldst thou have me hang him? Of my soul, if I should hang all that speak ill of thee, all the trees in the country would not suffice, so great is the number."[10]

There was general rejoicing when within the same month Stukeley was arrested upon the charge of clipping gold coin— the very coin with which he had been paid for his activity against Raleigh. "He had," the Rev. Thomas Lorkin wrote Sir Thomas Puckering, January 12, 1619, "received out of the Exchequer, some weeks before, £500, in recompense for the service he had done in the business of Sir Walter Raleigh; and began, as is said, to exercise the trade upon that ill-gotten money—the price of blood."[11] He was quickly condemned, largely upon the evidence of a servant who testified that Stukeley had urged him to bring false charges against Raleigh.[12] Although the King promptly pardoned him, Stukeley, finding himself "an outcast

[8] Printed by Birch, *op. cit.*, II, 102-3. [9] *Ibid.*, p. 111.
[10] *Ibid.*, p. 121. [11] *Ibid.*, p. 123.
[12] J. K. L[aughton] in *D.N.B.*; *sub*, Stucley, Lewis; Birch, *op. cit.*, II, 196.

from society in London, went down to Devonshire. The popular hatred pursued him even to Affeton, and he fled to hide his shame in the lonely island of Lundy, where he died in the course of 1620, raving mad it was said."[13]

I do not, I hasten to state, wish to imply that the dramatists modeled the character of Septimius upon that of Sir Lewis Stukeley, nor do I wish to suggest that the incidents of the play are closely paralleled in the life of that unhappy knight. If, however, allowance be granted for changes which would have to be made if the dramatists were to escape difficulty, the stories of Septimius and Stukeley are at certain points strikingly similar. If one were at that time to suggest publicly that Raleigh had been treacherously betrayed, it would have been advisable for him to overlook King James's part in that betrayal, and to place the emphasis rather upon the King's repudiation of the one who, in the hope of winning his favor, had been bought by foreign gold to betray his former friend. With this very necessary modification, the story of Raleigh's betrayer is in many particulars not unlike the story of the play. Septimius (Stukeley) a Roman (Englishman), at the instigation of Egyptians (Spaniards) and in the hope of reward from Caesar (James), treacherously causes the death of a compatriot and former friend, Pompey (Raleigh), and for this treachery is condemned and despised by all, especially by the leader of his people, Caesar (James), whom he had expected to be pleased but who, though he admitted that he "hated Pompey, and allow'd his ruin," scorned so cowardly a tool and such base ingratitude.

It is clear, I hope, that in the preceding paragraph I do not wish to imply that the story of Raleigh's betrayal is presented in an Egyptian-Roman background, with Caesar representing King James, Pompey representing Raleigh, and so on. I suggest merely that the dramatists deliberately chose a theme by which they could take advantage of a recent or current scandal —and, perhaps, give vent to their own indignation. If *The False One* was being composed during 1619 it would appear not improbable that the elaboration of the historically shadowy fig-

[13] *D.N.B.*

ure of Septimius into the title-rôle of the play was occasioned
by the wide popular resentment against one who like Septimius,
for gold and in the hope of winning favor from the King, had
betrayed a noble friend, and who for his treachery had been
"reputed the scorn and contempt of men."   An audience of
1619 or 1620 could, I feel certain, hardly have failed to think
of Sir Lewis Stukeley when the First Soldier, as he leads
Septimius off to be hanged, closes the scene with the couplet:

> Thou dost deserve a worser end; and may
> All such conclude so, that their friends betray.

I suggest that the author of this couplet intended the audience to recall Stukeley's treachery to Raleigh.   Such an intent
is presumably not unparalleled in the plays of one of the collaborators in *The False One*.

Although Fletcher seems generally to have avoided themes
which might be interpreted as having political significance, his
collaborator, Massinger (to whom all critics[14] have assigned Acts
I and V), appears not always to have restrained his inclination
to deal with contemporary politics. *The Bondman, The Ren-
egado, The Maid of Honour,* and *Believe as You List* have
been generally recognized as "obviously topical dramas," presenting political problems of Massinger's day; and a recent editor of *The Great Duke of Florence*, Miss Johanne M. Stochholm, not only insists that that play contains "topical allusions
to current English affairs," but is convinced that

Indubitably Massinger, when he "created" Cozimo and Giovanni
and Sanazarro, had in mind James and Charles and Buckingham;
and that not simply in a vague general way, but with an eye to
particular characteristics and particular events. It was probably to
check the tendency to interpret too closely and too dangerously that
Massinger devised the uncle-nephew relationship in place of the
father-son relationship of the actual contemporary situation.[15]

[14] "Like Fleay, Boyle, Bullen, and Macaulay, I award Massinger . . . the first
and last acts. Cruickshank alone dissents, giving Massinger I and 'a good deal of
IV and V.' "—Oliphant, *op. cit.,* p. 236.

[15] *The Great Duke of Florence,* edited by Johanne M. Stochholm (Baltimore,
1932), p. lxxvi.

Whether or not we are willing to accept all of the "particular characteristics" which Miss Stochholm recognizes, we can hardly question Massinger's interest in contemporary politics or the topical nature of many of his plays. Moreover, from what we know of his character and of his political views, it should not be in the least surprising either that he should share in the popular resentment against Stukeley or that he should seek to make capital upon that resentment. His chief friends, and at least his early patrons, were strongly anti-Spanish and pro-Raleigh. Whatever the mature Massinger's relations may have been with William Herbert, third Earl of Pembroke, their political views seem to have been much the same.[16] As has been recognized,[17] most inadequate were Gifford's reasons for his too often accepted suggestion that Massinger was converted to Roman Catholicism. Unless his play *Believe as You List* and the refusal of the censor to license it have been grossly misunderstood, Massinger, like the vast majority of his countrymen, was eager for English interference in the Palatinate, to succor the

[16] William Herbert, third Earl of Pembroke, shared Raleigh's hatred of Spain, and was apparently an adviser whom Raleigh trusted. When Raleigh was arrested upon James's accession, Pembroke's mother "conjured him 'as he valued her blessing, to employ his own credit and that of his friends to ensure' the pardon of Raleigh."— *D.N.B.*, *sub*, William Herbert. In 1616 Pembroke "joined with Ellesmere and Winwood in urging the despatch of Raleigh on his last expedition, undoubtedly in the expectation that Raleigh's action would compromise James's policy of peace with Spain."—*Ibid.* Some six months before his execution Raleigh wrote Winwood reminding him of "my service to my lords of Arundell and Pembroke" (21 March 1618; quoted by Harlow, *Ralegh's Last Voyage*, p. 241); and if there was any foundation for his later charge "that Pembroke and his friends had instigated the attack on the Mexico fleet, for which Raleigh suffered death," their plan was inspired not by hostility to Raleigh but by a desire to force a war with Spain.

To what extent Massinger was patronized by Pembroke is unknown. A. à Wood wrote that Pembroke had paid the poet's expenses at Oxford, and so stated Langbaine, but as Massinger left Oxford without a degree and as there is pathetic evidence of his later poverty, most writers have assumed that Pembroke, a friend to so many poets, had withdrawn all aid from the son of one who until his death in 1603 had served as house-steward both to his father, the second earl, and to him. But Massinger's loyalty to the family of Herberts is often witnessed. In the dedication of *The Bondman* to William's younger brother, Philip Earl of Montgomery, Massinger records that, although he had never been "made known to your lordship," his "duties and service to the noble family of the Herberts [had] descended to me as an inheritance from my dead father."

[17] Cruickshank, *Philip Massinger* (Oxford, 1920), p. 3; C. R. Baskervill, V. B. Heltzel, and A. H. Nethercot, *Elizabethan and Stuart Plays* (New York, 1934), p. 1355.

protestant Frederick and his English consort against Spain and the Emperor.[18] Nor is there any reason to believe that these sympathies, so strongly expressed in 1631, were in any respect different from those he would have entertained in 1619 and 1620, when the war in the Palatinate was just beginnning and when patriotic Englishmen hoped that James would come to the assistance of his daughter and her husband.

Nor, as I have said, was it unlike Massinger to capitalize upon an intense and widespread resentment against one in public disfavor—that is, unless another of his plays has again been much misinterpreted. It has been generally stated that in *A New Way to Pay Old Debts*, a play which probably dates only a few years after *The False One*,[19] Massinger has based the characters of Sir Giles Overreach and Justice Greedy upon the notorious Sir Giles Mompesson and his associate Sir Francis Michel. The flagrant abuses of these two in their commissions for controlling licenses to inn-keepers and supervising the monopoly for the manufacture of gold and silver thread, aroused such public indignation that the King was in 1621 obliged to prosecute and punish both knights.[20] The public scandal resulting from the malpractice of Mompesson and the popular hatred directed against him were very similar indeed to the scandal of Raleigh's execution and the popular hatred heaped upon Sir Lewis Stukeley. The feeling against Stukeley, indeed, may well have been the more intense, as it must have been aggravated by the people's hatred of Spain and Count Gondomar and by the recognition of the Spanish Ambassador's share in Sir Walter's execution.

That *The False One*, unlike *Believe as You List*, is not known to have met with difficulty from the censor is no argu-

[18] The argument of the play in its original form "accused Spain of usurpation and tyranny, and might be interpreted to accuse Charles of pusillanimity in his refusal to succour Frederick of Bohemia, husband of his sister Elizabeth, against Spain and the Emperor."—C. J. Sisson, *Believe as You List*, Malone Society Reprints (1928), p. xviii.   [19] Late 1625 or early 1626.

[20] See S. R. Gardiner, "The Political Element in Massinger," *Transactions of the New Shakespeare Society* (1877-1878), pp. 314 ff. Massinger's use of Mompesson has been accepted by recent editors of the play as "not unlikely" (H. Spencer), "probable" (Brooke and Paradise).

ment against the interpretation I have suggested. The latter play was objectionable apparently because it seemed to charge Charles I with cowardice and Spain with usurpation and tyranny. The Master of the Revels, Sir Henry Herbert, refused to allow it "because itt did contain dangerous matter, as the deposing of Sebastian king of Portugal, by Philip the [Second,] and ther being a peace sworen twixte the kings of England and Spayne."[21] To render *Believe as You List* acceptable to the censor the only important change made was the substitution of new names and a background of ancient Rome and Asia for the historical events of sixteenth-century Portugal and Spain. *The False One* had an ancient setting from the first. Too, in *The False One* no such allegations are made against the King or against a foreign nation. The indignation is heaped upon an English subject as in *A New Way to Pay Old Debts*. Indeed, by placing emphasis upon Stukeley's falseness and upon the scorn with which all, including the King, contemned him, the play might be said to have belittled James's own responsibility for the shameful and unpopular sacrifice of Raleigh to hopes of a Spanish alliance. James, as we have seen, had no wish or nc courage to defend Stukeley. He was quite willing that his tool should bear the full burden of public resentment.

[21] Quoted from Malone, *Variorum*, III, 229-31, by Sisson, Malone Society Reprint, p. v.

XIV

A Very Woman

THE COMEDY entitled *A Very Woman, or The Prince of Tarent*, having been licensed on June 6, 1634, was presumably first published by Humphrey Moseley in 1655 and ascribed by him to Philip Massinger. Two years earlier, when Moseley entered the play along with a number of others upon the Stationers' Register, he had used a different subtitle, calling it "A Very Woman, or ye Womans Plot." Since in the play as he printed it there is nothing even faintly resembling a woman's plot, it has been generally assumed that in substituting this alternate title he was seeking to enter two distinct plays for the price of one.[1] As the prologue, which must have been written by Massinger in 1634, states that the play is a revision of one "long since acted," efforts naturally have been made to identify *A Very Woman* as a revision of some play whose title alone has come down. None of these theories, however, seems altogether tenable.

The most unlikely suggestion is that *A Very Woman* should be identified with *The History of Cardenio*, which was acted at court by the King's Men in 1612 and 1613, and then more than forty years later entered by Moseley upon the Stationers' Register as the work of Fletcher and Shakespeare. There seems to be no reason at all for this identification save that Fletcher's hand is recognized in *A Very Woman* and that in this extant

---

[1] Presumably a play bearing the title of *The Woman's Plot* was acted at court in 1621. W. W. Greg, "The Bakings of Betsy," *The Library*, 3rd Series, II (1911), 249, has noted, however, that for this performance there seems now to be "no better authority than Reed, 'Biog. Dram.,' 1782." Warburton claimed that the manuscript of *The Woman's Plot* was among those which were destroyed by his economical cook in the baking of her pies, but it is most doubtful whether Warburton is to be believed.—See *ibid.*, pp. 225-59, and C. R. Baskervill, *Modern Philology*, XIII (1915-16), 52. I have suggested the possibility that *The Woman's Plot* may have been a title used to identify *The Noble Gentleman*, which I think was on the stage in 1621. (See pp. 162 ff.) The title is, of course, one which would suit equally well scores of Elizabethan and Jacobean comedies.

comedy one of the principal characters bears a name somewhat like Cardenio. The name is Don Martino Cardenes. This slight similarity is given a false emphasis by Oliphant, who, although he does not accept the identification, calls Cardenes "Cardenio,"[2] and by Macaulay, who writes of the lost play as "Cardenes, Cardema or Cardano."[3] (In the records as reprinted by Chambers the variant spellings are Cardenna and Cardenno.)[4] Against the identification is, as Oliphant noted, the fact that Moseley entered both plays upon the same date, ascribing one to Fletcher and Shakespeare and the other to Massinger. Moreover, as I shall attempt to show later, it is unlikely that the Cardenes-plot of *A Very Woman* would have been written prior to 1616, and not unlikely that Cardenes was in the earlier version of the play called merely Don Martino. Finally, *The History of Cardenio* seems most likely to have been based upon the story of Cardenio and Lucinda, as told in Thomas Shelton's translation of *Don Quixote*[5] (1612), which appeared just a few months before the play was presented.

Much less unsatisfactory is Fleay's suggestion[6] that *A Very Woman* be identified with *The Spanish Viceroy*, for which the King's Men, having acted it without license in December, 1624, were forced to make most humble apology.[7] A Spanish viceroy does appear in *A Very Woman*, but his part is small. There is, too, although I believe it has not been noted, matter in *A Very Woman* which might well have been objectionable to the licenser in 1624, and which might, therefore, explaining why the play was acted without license, be advanced to urge the identification. Don John Antonio, Prince of Tarent, has come to Palermo to seek the hand of the Viceroy's daughter, and though her brother urges her to be polite to him and to remember

[2] Oliphant, *The Plays of Beaumont and Fletcher*, p. 252.

[3] *Cambridge History of English Literature*, VI, 159. In his brief introduction to *A Very Woman* Gifford also spoke of the lost play as "*Cardenes* or *Cardenio*."

[4] *The Elizabethan Stage*, IV, 180. Appendix B.

[5] Part 1, chapters XXIII-XXXVII.

[6] *Biographical Chronicle of the English Drama*, I, 227-28.

[7] Murray, *English Dramatic Companies*, I, 160-61.

> How this prince came hither,
> How bravely furnished, how attended on,
> How he hath borne himself here, with what charge
> He hath continued; his magnificence
> In costly banquets, curious masks, rare presents,   [I, i.]

she continues to scorn and despise him, giving his presents to his rival's servant and refusing even to see him when he is ready to give over his suit and return home. Although the Prince later in the play, unrecognized in his disguise of a slave, does win the lady's love, the treatment accorded him during the earlier scenes might well be thought too reminiscent of the treatment which Prince Charles had received from the Infanta Maria when he had gone to press his suit in Madrid during the preceding year. December, 1624, the month in which Prince Charles signed a marriage treaty with Henrietta Maria of France, would have seemed hardly the month to permit a play which brought to mind the Prince's unsuccessful efforts to win the hostile Spanish princess. Beyond the facts that *A Very Woman* has a Spanish viceroy among its characters and perhaps contains matter to which a licenser might well object in 1624—and we do not know that the actors had been refused a license—there appear no arguments for the identification. Like *Cardenio, The Spanish Viceroy* was entered upon the Stationers' Register by Moseley at the time he entered *A Very Woman* and given the alternate title *The Honor of Women*—apparently another effort of a tricky publisher to enter two plays for the price of one; and, as Mr. Oliphant observed, when Moseley "was so bent on economizing, he was hardly likely to pay twice for entering [on the same day] differing versions of the one play."[8]

To a less degree this same argument may be effective against the view that *A Very Woman* is one and the same as *A Right Woman*,[9] which Moseley entered in June, 1660, as "by Beaumont and Fletcher." Unless he was confused, as of course he

[8] *Op. cit.*, p. 251.

[9] Dyce, *Memoir*, p. xlvii: "May we not conjecture that it is a rifacimento of *A Right Woman.* . . ."

may have been, he would certainly not have paid a new fee to
enter a play which he had not only entered earlier but had even
printed five years before. *A Right Woman* by Beaumont
and Fletcher was one of the dramatic manuscripts which Warburton claimed to have possessed, but even the acceptance of his
story would not help us determine the relationship—if any—
between the two plays.

Quite suggestive, however, is Moseley's ascription of *A
Right Woman* to Beaumont and Fletcher. Although he had,
both in the Stationers' Register and on the title-page of the
printed play, assigned *A Very Woman* to Massinger alone, "all
modern critics (with the exception of Swinburne, who considered it wholly Massinger's) regard it as an alteration from
Fletcher."[10] The passages in the play which seem unmistakably Fletcher's are few, but seem nonetheless unmistakably
from his pen. I am not so sure, however, that the present form
of the play represents Massinger's "alteration from Fletcher."
It is certain that the play has been altered, but to me the evidence of the text indicates that Massinger was altering not from
Fletcher, but from Massinger and Fletcher. I can see no reason to suppose that Fletcher's share in the play was ever extensive. Mr. Oliphant has called attention to the difference
in tone in the prologue to *A Very Woman* from that of *Lover's
Progress,* a prologue written by Massinger to his alteration from
Fletcher. In the latter he expresses confidence that the audience
will hear some good scenes, but with

> becoming modesty—
> (For in this kind he ne'er was bold),

he gives all credit to another and adds that "What's good was
Fletcher's, and what's ill his own." This is the modesty which
appears in the prologues to most revisions and revivals of
Fletcher, many of which were probably by Massinger. The
audience is almost regularly reminded that the original was
by Fletcher. But in the prologue to *A Very Woman,* Fletcher's
name is not invoked to assure a good reception. Here Massinger boldly declares himself ready to

[10] Oliphant, *op. cit.,* p. 251.

Maintain to any man that did allow
'Twas good before, it is much bettered now.

In view of Massinger's accustomed modesty and of the defer-
ence he habitually showed toward Fletcher, it is probable that
he regarded the original which he has much bettered not as
Fletcher's but rather as his own. That such was the case is,
I think, the evidence of the text. In the list of the dramatis
personae the son of the Duke of Messina appears as Don Martino Cardenes. Nowhere in the play is he addressed or spoken
of by both names. Save in Act I he is invariably called Martino.
Among other scenes, Massinger is today always assigned the
whole of Act I and the first two and a half scenes of Act II.
In the dialogue of Act I "Cardenes" appears twelve times,
"Martino" not at all; in Massinger's portion of Act II "Cardenes" is not used at all while "Martino" is used eight times.
Only once is he spoken of in scenes attributed to Fletcher, and
then (IV, iii) he is called, of course, "Martino." As "Martino"
is the name used by Fletcher and everywhere save in Act I by
Massinger, it was presumably the earlier name. It would seem
that Massinger for some reason later wished to substitute "Cardenes," but the substitution was made only in Act I.

Presumably, therefore, Massinger's contributions to the comedy were made at two distinct times; and, as there is no reason
to suppose that the play was twice revised, the natural assumption would be that his original contribution was made in collaboration with Fletcher. The theory of original collaboration
is supported not only by the tone of the prologue and by the
confusion of the name Martino Cardenes but also by the striking similarities which *A Very Woman* bears to plays in which
Massinger and Fletcher are known to have collaborated late in
Fletcher's life. The comedy owes a great deal more to—or at
least has a great deal more in common with—certain of these
plays than could possibly have been suggested by the novel of
Cervantes which has been customarily cited as its source.

Without dissent being voiced, *A Very Woman* has been per-
sistently stated to have been "based upon" or "derived from"

Cervantes' story *El Amante liberal*. So state, among others, Fitzmaurice-Kelly (twice),[11] Schelling (twice),[12] Underhill,[13] and Chelli.[14] Oliphant has no mention of a source in his discussion of the play, and for this omission we should credit him with an independence which the others have not shown and possibly a recognition that *El Amante liberal* was not the source. None of the others give any indication of having read both the play and the story. Indeed their references often indicate that they have not. Schelling, for instance, as authority for his statement that "the source of this play is *El Amante Liberal*" cites Fitzmaurice-Kelly's introduction to the *Exemplary Novels*, where we find no discussion whatever but the mere statement that Fletcher and Massinger "drew *A Very Woman or The Prince of Tarent* from El Amante liberal," and a reference to Ward's *History of English Dramatic Literature* and to Koeppel's *Quellen-Studien*. Ward, likewise, has no discussion; he refers to Koeppel in a footnote, stating that he has shown it probable that "the dramatists *made use of El Amante Liberal*."[15] Aside from brief summaries of certain situations in the play and the novel, Koeppel[16] adds little to the original comment by Moriz Rapp in 1862: "Classische Erinnerungen sind unverkennbar, Cervantes orientalische Scenen schimmern deutlich hervor, sowohl aus dem Don Quixote als auch einige Hauptmotive aus der Novelle *El amante liberal*."[17] Koeppel, however, concluded that the novel, "although handled in the greatest freedom," was the source of the play. He even follows

[11] "Cervantes in England," *Proceedings of the British Academy*, II (1905-1906), 23, and his Introduction to the English translation of the *Exemplary Novels*, 2 vols. (Glasgow, 1902), I, xxxvi.

[12] *Elizabethan Drama*, II, 233, and *Foreign Influences in Elizabethan Plays* (New York and London, 1923), p. 121.

[13] J. G. Underhill, *Spanish Influences on English Literature* (New York, 1899), p. 277.

[14] *Étude sur la collaboration de Massinger avec Fletcher et son groupe* (Paris, 1926), p. 295.

[15] *History of English Dramatic Literature*, 3 vols. (London and New York, 1899), II, 39, n. 2.

[16] Emil Koeppel, *Quellen-Studien zu den Dramen George Chapman's, Philip Massinger's und John Ford's*. Strassburg, 1897. (*Quellen und Forschungen zur Sprach- und Culturgeschichte der germanischen Völker*, vol. LXXXII.) *A Very Woman* is discussed on pp. 144-46.

[17] *Studien über das englische Theater* (Tübingen, 1862), pp. 246-47.

Rapp's fantastic suggestion that "sodann ist der krank auftretende Cardenes eine fast plumpe Erinnerung an Hamlet."[18]

That the similarities and differences between the novel and the play may easily be recognized, I shall give a full summary of the action of each.

El Amante liberal

Without the ruins of Nicosia the unhappy Ricardo tells his friend Mahamut, a renegade Christian slave, how he and the beautiful Leonisa had been carried off by pirates. Leonisa had refused his love and had instead given her affection to Cornelio, "a young gallant, neat and spruce, with white hands and curled hairs, having a mellifluous voice, and amorous words at will, and in a word, being all made of amber, musk, and civet, clad in tissue, adorned with rich embroideries." Finding them in her garden, Ricardo first upbraided her for her cruelty and then addressed many "disgraceful speeches" to Cornelio, as "Go, get thee gone, and sport thyself among thy mother's maids, and there have a care of kembing and curling thy locks, and keeping thy hands clean and white; thou art fitter to handle soft silks than a hardhilted sword." Only after many of his kinsmen, attracted by Ricardo's loud voice, had surrounded them did Cornelio even make a show of rising from his seat. Ricardo, drawing his sword, set upon them all, wounding seven or eight of them, while "Cornelio betook himself to his heels, and by his swift flight escaped my hands." Before Ricardo could be overcome by numbers, Turkish pirates entered; the kinsmen fled, and Ricardo was taken captive along with Leonisa, who had swooned at the first sight of his glittering sword. Returned to their ships, the pirates were on the point of hanging Ricardo because in the fight he had killed several of their best men. Moved by compassion, Leonisa did him her "first and last kindness": she informed the Turks that by hanging him they would forfeit a great ransom. Ricardo's steward arranged to ransom both his master and Leonisa, but asked three days in which

---

[18] No objection, however, may be made to Rapp's observation, in which he was followed by Koeppel, that Plautus' *Curculio* furnished the dramatists the drunken Borachia.

to raise the sum necessary. Before these arrangements were completed, however, the pirates, frightened by the approach of six Italian galleys, hastily weighed anchor and sailed away. At the island of Pantanalea, the captains of the two pirate galleys divided their captives, Leonisa being taken by one and Ricardo by the other. As Leonisa was being led into the other ship, she turned her eyes to look upon Ricardo and both swooned. A fierce storm then broke upon the two galleys, and that in which Leonisa had been placed Ricardo saw shattered upon the rocks.

Upon the death of the captain soon afterwards Ricardo passed into the hands of Bashaw Hazen, newly named Viceroy of Cyprus. As Hazen and Ali, the new and the old viceroys, met outside the walls, a Jew brought to them for sale a most beautiful and richly dressed young Christian woman. Both fell at once in love with her and sought to buy her, claiming that they wished to present her to the Grand Signior. It was finally agreed that each bashaw would pay half of the Jew's price and that Leonisa, for Ricardo recognized that it was she, should be entrusted to the care of the Cadi, Mahamut's master, who was to conduct her to the Sultan. The Cadi, however, has also fallen in love with Leonisa, and plans to outwit his rivals and secure her for himself; whereas his wife, Halima, becomes enamoured of Ricardo, who, through the aid of Mahamut, had been purchased by the Cadi.

When the group set sail for Constantinople, many different plots had been laid. The Cadi had no intention of giving Leonisa to the Grand Signior, but hoped on the voyage to get rid of his wife so that he might have Leonisa. Halima, likewise, hoped that with the aid of Ricardo and Mahamut she might get control of the ship, dispose of the Cadi, return to her native Christian faith and marry Ricardo. He and Mahamut, familiar with the plans of both their master and their mistress, hoped, of course, to become masters of the vessel and to escape with Leonisa. Before any of these plans could be put into effect, however, two vessels were descried coming from opposite directions. The first proved to be the soldiers

of Hazen, sent to abduct Leonisa. The second vessel, which
arrived almost immediately, was commanded by Ali Bashaw,
who had disguised his soldiers as Christians so that his theft
of Leonisa might not become known. The confused battle continued until only a few of the Turks remained alive, and them
Ricardo, Mahamut, certain kinsmen of Halima and other Christian slaves, were able easily to overpower. Giving the wounded
Cadi his ship, the Christians sailed for Sicily in the better of
the captured vessels. As they neared the port Ricardo requested
Leonisa to dress herself in the rich costume and veil in which
the Jew had brought her to Nicosia, and all others likewise
attired themselves in Turkish dress. The ship was adorned
with flags and streamers, and cannon discharged to attract attention of those on shore. A great crowd was there to watch
them land and was much puzzled as the seeming Turks saluted
their homeland with their kisses. There had come the kinsmen
of both Leonisa and Ricardo, together with Cornelio and the
Governor. Having been recognized and embraced by the Governor, Ricardo took Leonisa by one hand and Cornelio by the
other, "who as soon as he knew him and found that he held
him fast, his colour began to change, and began to shake and
tremble for fear." But Ricardo, joining the hands of the two,
declared that, although he loved Leonisa better than life, he
knew that she loved Cornelio, and upon the two of them he
would bestow all of his share in the rich spoils they had brought
home. But the "discreet Leonisa" having first obtained her
parents' permission that she dispose of herself as she wished,
answered: "O valiant Ricardo, my goodwill and affection
hitherto so reserved, so perplexed and doubtful, shall now declare itself in your favour, to the end that you men may know
that all women are not ungrateful, . . . I desire nothing more
than to have thee to be my husband." They are promptly married, as are Mahamut and Halima.

A Very Woman

[I, 1] The Prince of Tarent, Don John Antonio, who has
spent some time in Palermo in a vain hope of winning the love

of Almira, daughter of the Viceroy, finding that her love has been given to Don Martino Cardenes, son of the Duke of Messina, and that her choice is approved by their parents, prepares to return home. His friend, Don Pedro, Almira's brother, requests his sister that the Prince may

> Take his leave of you, and receive the favour
> Of kissing of your hands.

Almira refuses even to see him, and ostentatiously bestows a jewel the Prince had sent her upon Cardenes' page. Cardenes, entering, applauds her decision. When all but Cardenes have retired, the Prince comes to take his leave. After he has been insulted and struck by the insolent Cardenes, they fight and Cardenes falls severely wounded. Cardenes is carried off, the Prince is placed under guard, and Almira and the Duke join in demanding that the Viceroy instantly condemn the Prince.

[II, 1] The Captain to whose care the Prince has been given owes his life to Don Pedro. Together they seek to persuade the Prince to save himself by flight. After many speeches on friendship, the Captain and the Prince leave to board a vessel.

[II, 3] Almira, overcome by her grief, vows not to outlive her beloved Cardenes and upbraids her father and brother for allowing "the false prince" to escape.

[III, 1] The Prince and the Captain, dressed as Turks, are offered for sale in the slave-market, their ship having been captured and they sold into slavery. The former is bought by Cuculo, whose wife Borachia serves as duenna to Almira, and the latter by the doctor attending Cardenes.

[III, 2] Cuculo warns his slave, the disguised Prince, to keep wine away from Borachia.

[III, 3] Cardenes, his melancholy observed by his physicians, laments his unmannerly behavior to the Prince of Tarent.

[III, 4] Almira is urged by her friend Leonora to abandon her melancholy and sullen grief—unsuccessfully.

[III, 5] Almira for the first time sees Borachia's slave, the Prince, who brings Leonora a message from Pedro. Her interest in him is at once manifest. In rapid succession she observes

"A handsome man!" "A very handsome fellow—And well demean'd!" "And speaks well, too!" "I would I'd heard him, friend. Comes he again?" "'Tis no matter. Come, let's walk in."

[IV, 2] His physician presents several masks before Cardenes to relieve the melancholy from which he still suffers because of his wrongs to the Prince.

[IV, 3] Almira now is completely enamoured of the supposed slave. She can talk of nothing else. "How strangely this fellow runs in her mind. . . . Her sadness clean forsaken." She sends for Borachia and persuades her to call the slave. She then questions the disguised Prince, demands his story, and is much moved when, without disclosing his identity, he says that his name is Don John Antonio and that he had loved one much like her but had met only disdain. "Never conscience Touch'd me till now," she observes aside; "nor true love: let me keep it."

[V, 2] The Prince, still as a slave, enters with a letter, thrown him by Almira, in which she expresses her love for him and orders him to meet her that night in the garden. The Prince then ponders the giddiness of women:

> . . . when I was
> Myself, set off with all the grace of greatness,
> Pomp, bravery, circumstance, she hated me,
> And did profess it openly; yet now,
> Being a slave, a thing she should in reason
> Disdain to look upon; in this base shape, . . .
> To dote thus fondly.

[V, 3] As they await in the garden, Almira and Leonora are seized by pirates, but Don John Antonio, rushing in, wrests a sword from one and holds the group at bay until Pedro and the guard come to the rescue.

[V, 4] All meet at the Viceroy's palace. Cardenes and Almira greet each other coolly, Cardenes explaining that he has been cured of love. Almira announces that her love is now given the slave who has rescued her. The Viceroy orders the slave broken upon the wheel and Almira promises to inflict upon herself whatever he is made to suffer.

[V, 5] The Prince, now appareled like himself, leaves with Pedro for the Viceroy's palace.

[V, 6] Word of his identity has preceded the Prince. As he enters, Cardenes creates a stir by crying

> Sir, 'tis best known to you, on what strict terms
> The reputation of men's fame and honours
> Depends in this so punctual age, in which
> A word that may receive a harsh construction
> Is answer'd and defended by the sword: . . .
> I have received from your hands wounds, and deep ones,
> My honour in the general report
> Tainted and soil'd, for which I will demand
> This satisfaction—that you would forgive
> My contumelious words and blow, my rash
> And unadvised wildness first threw on you.

And as further proof that he is a different person from what he was, he gives up all his interest in Almira to the Prince.

Some similarities there undoubtedly are between the novel and the play; but to me they do not seem particularly striking. In both there is the theme of the unpromising but finally successful suit of the hero—a common enough theme. Both heroes are sold into slavery but the conditions under which they serve are totally unlike. The heroines are alike only in that they transfer their affections from one suitor to another; the reasons for the transfer are quite different. Cardenes' tardy renouncing of all claim upon Almira may hardly be called similar to the offer of Ricardo, the liberal lover, for the offers are prompted by entirely different situations. In characterization the novel and the play have nothing in common. Cardenes is the exact opposite of Cornelio, Almira the exact opposite of Leonisa. The "discreet" Leonisa does not love below her rank; she gives her love to one who had rescued her and served her long that "men may know that all women are not ungrateful." On the other hand Almira, a very woman, mutable and unreasonable,[19]

---

[19] The earliest instance of the proverbial phrase "a very woman" cited by *A New English Dictionary* is: " 'She had one poynt of a very woman, . . . she was . . . mutable, and turnyng' *a* 1548. Hall, *Chron., Hen. VI.*" There is no doubt that the title of the play has this same sense, although the phrase seems to have been used

having scorned Prince John Antonio when he was "set off with all the grace of greatness," dotes fondly on him when she thinks him a slave, "a thing she should in reason Disdain to look upon."

If *El Amante liberal* was indeed the inspiration—it certainly cannot be called the source—of *A Very Woman*, then Massinger and Fletcher here used their borrowed material in a way which they did not ordinarily employ in their other borrowings from the *Novelas Ejemplares*. The settings are quite different, no names are common to both play and story; no situation and no character is taken over. If the dramatists wrote with the novel in mind, they wrote certainly not "to the end that you may know all women are not ungrateful" but rather to illustrate playfully the conventional view of the fickleness and unreasonableness of woman's affections. In this attitude, as well as in the characters and situations, *A Very Woman* is much closer to other plays in the Beaumont and Fletcher canon than it is to *El Amante liberal*.

Although it can hardly be said without a knowledge of their dates that *A Very Woman* draws upon other plays in the Beaumont and Fletcher canon, it is in many respects strikingly similar to some of those written between 1619 and 1622. In *The Island Princess* (1620-1621), usually ascribed to Fletcher alone, the scorned suitor, Armusia, supported unsuccessfully by the Princess' brother, is finally accepted; his rival, Ruy Dias, like Cardenes, overweening and bellicose, becomes his friend only after being overcome in a duel he has forced upon Armusia. In *The Laws of Candy* (concerning the authorship and date of which there is wide disagreement) Prince Philander of Cyprus is a suitor of Princess Erota, by whom he is scorned and made to woo Antinous for her, but in the end he is accepted by her. In *The Mad Lover, Nice Valour,* and *The Noble Gentleman* (1621?) there is the same treatment of melancholy which is so successful in *A Very Woman*. For the purpose of satire upon the English, in *A Very Woman* an English slave is introduced

---

with a somewhat different meaning in Fletcher's *Rule a Wife and Have a Wife*, II, iv, 48-49.

and ridiculed and in *The Pilgrim* (1621) appears an English madman in the madhouse at Segovia.

But the most striking parallels are to be found in *Custom of the Country* and *Lover's Progress*. The latter play is closest to *A Very Woman* in its many speeches condemning the practice of duelling, but one plot of *Custom of the Country* is strikingly like *A Very Woman* both in its action and in its theme. As was seen in the summary of the latter play, Don Cardenes is an arrogant and quarrelsome gallant, who, forcing a fight upon Don John Antonio, is severely wounded. It is announced that he is dead, but by the skill of a physician he is not only restored in body but so changed in character that at the end of the play he demands the right to restore his tainted honor not by resorting to the sword, a practice he bitterly condemns, but by apologizing to the one whom he had wronged. In *The Custom of the Country* the "proud distempered" Duarte forces a fight upon Rutilio and is by him apparently killed. But by a skillful doctor Duarte, too, is cured both in body and in mind. Before he seeks out Rutilio, pays his debts, gives him money, and assists in arranging his marriage, Duarte says to the doctor who has cured him:

> You have bestow'd on me a second life,
> For which I live your creature: and have better'd
> What nature framed unperfect: my first being
> Insolent pride made monstrous; but this later,
> In learning me to know myself, hath taught me
> Not to wrong others.   [IV, i, 1-6.]

Without seeming in any way intrusive this whole passage could have been inserted among the speeches of Cardenes. Indeed Cardenes speaks of his first and second life:

> My first life,
> Loaded with all the follies of a man, . . .
> Was by my headstrong passions, which o'er-ruled
> My understanding, forfeited to death:
> But this my new being, this my second life,
> Begun in serious contemplation of

What best becomes a perfect man, shall never
Sink under such weak frailties.   [V, iv.]

The two speeches are so similar in both their provocation and
their wording that it is impossible to believe that one was not
written with the other in mind.

Which of the two passages was written earlier, however, it
is not so easy to determine. While for the story of Cardenes'
reformation no source is known, the story of Duarte is to some
extent told in Cervantes' *Persiles y Sigismunda,* from which
Fletcher and Massinger drew most of *The Custom of the Country.* In the novel, however, Duarte, who is given no name,
is indeed killed by Rutilio; he does not live, through the aid
of a wise physician, to condemn quarreling and expatiate upon
the perfect man. It is in this latter regard, of course, that
Duarte most nearly parallels Cardenes. Although no definite
conclusion may be reached, the slight evidence available points,
I believe, to the Duarte plot as the earlier. First, it is, as I
have said, found in the source of the play, and the changes
made in the dramatization are no more than were necessary to
provide for a happy ending. The mental and physical reformation is only roughly sketched in a single scene (IV, i), the doctor
making only eight speeches (six of less than two lines) and
none of the treatments he used being presented upon the stage.
The cure of Cardenes, on the other hand, is elaborately presented in no fewer than three scenes (II, ii; III, iii; IV, ii),
one of them containing several masks which are to banish his
melancholy. It would seem, therefore, especially since Duarte's
story is in part suggested by Cervantes, that that of Cardenes
is a later and more elaborate development, written perhaps soon
after *The Custom of the Country.*

This latter play may be dated within comparatively narrow
limits. As it is mentioned by Herbert only as "an old play,"
it must have been presented prior to May 14, 1622, the date
of the earliest entry in his office-book. *Persiles y Sigismunda*
appeared in 1616, a French translation of it was printed in
1618, and on February 22, 1618/19, an English translation was

entered upon the Stationers' Register, "the claim of which, rather than of the original, to be the source of our play," Professor Bond states, "does not admit of a doubt."[20]

Whether *A Very Woman* preceded or followed *The Custom of the Country*, the limits of its composition would seem to be much the same. As it is not mentioned by Sir Henry Herbert, it was presumably prior to May, 1622. I am not convinced that it owes anything to *El Amante liberal*, published first in Spain in 1613, in a French translation in 1615, and in an English translation not until 1640; but the many speeches in the play attacking quarreling and duelling, especially the whole story of the reformation of Cardenes, are, as I have shown in an earlier essay,[21] expressive of an attitude not found in the plays of the Beaumont and Fletcher canon prior to 1616. From that time on, however, the plays pay increasing attention to that growing vice, and *A Very Woman* is in this regard most like *The Custom of the Country*, *The Pilgrim*, and *Lover's Progress*, all of which come between 1619 and 1623. Although many of the eloquent speeches attacking the duello may well have been late additions, the condemnation of duelling could hardly have been inserted only at the time of revision, for the whole story of Cardenes is an attack upon the idea that honor must be won and defended by the sword, and the confusion of his name, already pointed out, would indicate that his part had been much the same in the original draft.

Although the evidence seems too slight for any but purely tentative conclusions, we are, I think, justified in the following beliefs:

1) That *A Very Woman* bore no relationship to *The Woman's Plot* or to *Cardenio*, and probably none to *The Spanish Viceroy*. Whether it is related to *A Right Woman* must remain a question.

2) That as Massinger's contributions to the play seem to have been made at two distinct times, and as no hand save his and Fletcher's is recognizable, the comedy as we have it prob-

---

[20] R. Warwick Bond in Variorum Edition of Beaumont and Fletcher, I, 477.

[21] Essay VIII, "The Attitude toward the Duello in the Beaumont and Fletcher Plays."

ably represents a later reworking by Massinger of a play in which he and Fletcher had originally collaborated.

3) That *El Amante liberal* cannot correctly be called "the source" of the play; that the dramatists borrowed little if anything from Cervantes' novelle.

4) That *A Very Woman* was written sometime between 1616 and 1622—probably between 1619 and 1922.

XV

Notes toward Dating
WIT WITHOUT MONEY

AMONG STUDENTS of the Beaumont and Fletcher plays there has
been general agreement that the comedy *Wit without Money*
was composed entirely by Fletcher and that it was written in
or soon after the year 1614. For this date very little evidence,
however, has been advanced. In editing the play for the interrupted Variorum Edition, Mr. R. B. McKerrow briefly sum-
marizes the reasons for the accepted date:

> That this play was completed after August, 1614, is shown
> by the reference to the dragon which appeared in Sussex during
> that month (II. iv. 53), while, on the other hand, the allusion to
> the New River, opened in 1613 (IV. v. 61), forbids us to place it
> much later than this date. We shall, I think, not be far wrong if
> we attribute it to the autumn or winter of 1614.[1]

As Mr. Oliphant has observed, there is no specific reference
to the New River; it is to "rumours of New Rivers," which
"may imply a date either before 1613 or some considerable time
later."[2] The reference to the dragon in Sussex,[3] however, unless it be a later insertion, remains to forbid the assignment of
the play to a date earlier than the autumn of 1614. In addition,
there are within the play what I take to be several topical allusions which indicate that the comedy was composed or underwent revision at a considerably later date, probably the summer
of 1620.

In Act II, scene iv, Valentine urges his younger brother to
earn his living by writing:

> . . . . . . write, write, write anything;
> The world's a fine believing world; write news . . . .

---

[1] *The Works of Beaumont and Fletcher*, Variorum Edition, II, 231.
[2] *The Plays of Beaumont and Fletcher*, p. 150.
[3] See *The Harleian Miscellany* (London, 1809), III, 227-31.

> Predictions of sea-breaches, wars, and want
> Of herrings on our coast, with bloody noses;

and Lance interjects:

> Whirlwinds, that shall take off the top of Grantham steeple,
> And clap it on Paul's.

In Lance's addition we have, I believe, a waggish allusion to the highly organized, but nonetheless futile, efforts which were made during the spring and summer of 1620 to raise funds for the repair of St. Paul's Cathedral and the erection of a steeple to replace that destroyed by lightning in 1561. Shortly after the destruction of the steeple Elizabeth had ordered that steps be taken toward its reparation, but nothing had been done, and as the years passed the absence of the steeple aroused little interest.

Late in his reign, however, King James, characteristically, became passionately desirous to see the steeple rebuilt. On March 20, 1620, Chamberlain wrote Carleton that the King was expected at St. Paul's Cross to hear the Bishop of London preach, and to enquire into the repair of the cathedral, which was in a very ruinous state.[4] Accordingly, six days later,

. . . upon the 26th of *March*, being *Sunday*, the King, attended by several Noblemen, rode to St. *Pauls* in great State, on Horseback; where he was met by the Lord Maior and Aldermen, in their Formalities, at the West Door of St. *Pauls*. Here the King alighting, went to the Brazen Pillar, where he kneeled down, and prayed for the good Success of his pious Intention. Afterwards he went to the Quire, and there heard an Anthem; and from thence went to the Cross, where the Bishop of *London*, Dr. *John King*, preached a Sermon upon a Text given him by the King, which was *Psalm* cii, ver. 13, 14. *Thou shalt arise and have mercy upon Zion, for the time to favour her, yea, the set time is come. For thy Servants take pleasure in her stones*, &c. And when the Sermon was ended, he repaired to the Bishop's Palace, where Consultations were taken what was most fit to be done, in order to the beginning and carrying on of so pious a Work.[5]

---

[4] *C. S. P., Domestic*, CXIII.

[5] Stowe-Strype, *Survey*, 1720, Bk. iii, pp. 150-51.

To such an extent was the King moved by the sermon, or by the thought of the text which he had selected, that he is reported to have said that he would fast on bread and water but the repairs should be made.[6] He offered generous contributions, £2000 annually, and although circumstances prevented the repairs, when he knighted the Lord Mayor more than two years later, he reminded him that one of the most urgent affairs to which he should attend was the repair of the cathedral.[7]

In writing of James's visit to the cathedral Nichols called attention to "three very curious pictures, now in the possession of the Society of Antiquaries," which "represent the King's present Visit to St. Paul's; but *by anticipation* three years before it took place, being painted in 1616." He continues, describing one of the pictures in more detail:

Round the black frame of this leaf is written in gold capitals: AND WHEN IT CAME INTO THE KING'S MINDE TO RENEWE THE HOVSE OF THE LORD, HEE ASSEMBLED THE PRIESTS AND THE LEVITES, AND SAID VNTO THEM, 'GOE OVT VNTO THE CITIES OF JVDAH, AND GATHER OF ALL ISRAELL MONEY TO REPAIRE THE HOVSE OF GOD FROM YEERE TO YEERE, AND HASTE THE THINGE; AND THEY MADE A PROCLAMATION THROVGHOVT JVDAH AND JERVSALEM, &c. 2 CHRON. c. 24, v. 4, 5, 6. On the inside of the same leaf is depicted the old Church of St. Paul, without its spire, which had been destroyed by lightning in 1561.[8]

Nichols does not give his reasons for assigning two of the pictures to 1616. It would seem rather remarkable certainly that three pictures of the event should have been painted "by anticipation," but as one of the three carries the memorandum "So INVENTED AND AT MY COST MADE FOR ME, H. FARLEY, 1616," Nichols suggested that it was "one of many efforts made by H. Farley, a private individual, to prompt his Sovereign to this good and necessary work." There is no evidence that the

---

[6] *C. S. P., Domestic*, Chamberlain to Carleton, April 1, 1620.

[7] Chamberlain to Carleton, June 22, 1622. Birch, *Court and Times of James I*, II, 316.

[8] *Progresses of James I*, III, 592.

King had for long anticipated such a visit or that any general interest was earlier being shown in the repairing of St. Paul's. So elaborately organized, however, was the campaign of the King and the Bishop in the spring of 1620 that it may be compared only to the loudest efforts of a twentieth-century promoter.

In the best approved manner of today a commission was appointed and feasted by the Lord Mayor. Chamberlain was on the commission, but from the first betrayed a rather cynical interest. On April 29, 1620, he wrote Carleton:

> We have here a great commission come forth for the business of Paul's, comprehending all the council therein, divers bishops, . . . divers aldermen, and other citizens. . . . The whole number is sixty-six; and the first day of sitting was this day sennight. . . . The King is very earnest to set it forward, and they begin hotly; but I doubt, when all is done, it will prove, as they say, Paul's work.[9]

Beginning hotly, the commissioners on July 22, 1620, ordered that the houses at the east and west ends of the cathedral be pulled down before the first of August.[10] Those living in the condemned houses refused to move, made jests, indeed, that the order was "not meant in earnest";[11] the owners resorted to petitions and legal suits, and "the Collection of Monies went so slowly forward, as, that though a good proportion of Stone was brought in by the Bishop, yet the prosecution of the Work became quite neglected. Neither was there anything more done, until Dr. *Laud* became Bishop of this See, which was in the year 1628."[12] If within a month of the King's visit to the cathedral one was saying that the repairs of the cathedral were likely to prove "Paul's work," there would during the months which followed have been real and timely significance to the waggish reference of Lance to "Whirlwinds, that shall take off the top of Grantham steeple," famous for its great height, "And clap it on Pauls."[13]

[9] Birch, *op. cit.*, II, 203.   [10] Camden's *Annals.*

[11] Chamberlain to Carleton in Birch, *op. cit.*, II, 209.

[12] Stowe-Strype, *op. cit.*, p. 151.

[13] Although I hesitate to refer to it in the text, for fear of being thought too eager to find allusions, it may be noted here that Camden under September 2 records in his *Annals* that "A South-Wind blows furiously." I know of no damage done by it.

The aptness of other references in the passage I have quoted from Act II, scene iv, is less easily dated, but as allusions to topics on the tongues of Londoners they would come aptly in 1620—one of them, certainly, more aptly than at any other time. The first subjects suggested for Francisco's pamphlets are predictions of sea-breaches and war. Sea-breaches, of course, England suffered almost annually; to them I shall return later.

Since 1619, when war had broken out in Germany, many subjects of the pacific James had hoped that he would abandon his desire for an alliance with Spain and boldly take the part of his Protestant son-in-law. James, of course, had not declared war, but some of his more impatient subjects had raised troops at their own expense. A placard inviting volunteers to enlist had, on the morning after his arrival in England, been found nailed to the door of the Spanish Ambassador's house.[14] Camden records that on June 11, 1620, "Voluntiers are pick'd up in the City, by Beat of Drum, to the *Bohemian War*, under the command of the Earls of *Oxford, Essex, Jo. Wentworth, &c.*"[15] Indeed, Chamberlain seemed to think that war could hardly be averted when he wrote to Sir Dudley Carleton on July 8, 1620, that the English Ambassador to Spain,

Sir Henry Wooton is as confident of himself, and his dexterity in managing the business he goes about, that he told divers of our captains he was in hope to effect that they should keep their swords in their scabbards. In the mean time, our new levies go on but heavily; and whereas they thought they should have been oppressed with followers, they are fain to send far and near into the country to make up their numbers; which, if they were more full, they would be gone presently this next week.[16]

To those less familiar with James's attitude, such public enlisting of troops would undoubtedly have suggested that the next news would be an open declaration of war. Essex, indeed, at this time seems to have expected some active support from the King, but when he returned to England for reinforcements late in the year and "to solicit the King to send those Regiments

---

[14] Gardiner, *History of England, 1603-1642*, III, 336.
[15] *Annals*.   [16] Birch, *op. cit.*, II, 204.

promised," he was, Wilson tells us, disappointed to find "the *Court Air* of another temper, and not as he left it, for it was much more inclined to the *Spanish* Meridian."[17] It would appear, therefore, that during the summer of 1620 there was more reason than either before or afterwards to expect England to enter the war. A pamphlet predicting early war would doubtless, as Valentine said, have sold well.

The "predictions of Sea-breaches," like the "rumours of New Rivers," it is quite impossible to allocate to any definite time—if indeed it really be an allusion to any disastrous sea-breach of the immediate past. For centuries, of course, a great portion of England had periodically suffered severe losses when high tides had broken through the dikes and flooded the lowlands. If there was a version of *Wit without Money* written in 1614, doubtless to many among the audience, if not to the dramatist himself, the "prediction" of further sea-breaches would have recalled the costly ravages of the sea within a goodly portion of Norfolk in November of the preceding year, when, according to an abstract presented by the Jurors at the Session of Sewers held in December, 1613, the damage within and without the ring of marshland was estimated at £37,862.[18] And these losses were aggravated by mighty floods which followed the heavy snows of the ensuing January and February.[19] But breaches in the dikes and the consequent flooding of marshland continued annually; such an allusion as "prediction of sea-breaches" offers, therefore, no aid in the dating.[20]

In the hope of preventing these frequent and costly depredations of the sea, James and his government devoted considerable energy toward encouraging the draining of the marsh-

---

[17] Arthur Wilson, *History of Great Britain* (London, 1653), p. 153.

[18] William Dugdale, *The History of Imbanking and Draining of Divers Fens and Marshes* (2nd ed., 1772), p. 280. [19] *Ibid.*, p. 281.

[20] Certainly there is nothing more than a humorous fancy in the prediction of a want of herring. Much to the annoyance of certain Englishmen, the Dutch had for a long time all but monopolized the herring industry off the British coast. Although their right seems to have been first questioned seriously about 1613, an agreement was not reached until December, 1619. Several times during the interval Dutch missions were in England to discuss the herring fishing. Even if in the passage quoted from the play there be an allusion to these disputes, the period during which it would have point is too great for the allusion to assist in dating the play.

land. The draining was to be accomplished, of course, by the digging of new sluices and the deepening of existing rivers. Nothing came during his lifetime of James's ambitious scheme of draining the Great Level, but during the years from 1619 to 1621 there was frequent exchange of letters among James, the undertakers, and the Commission of Sewers. Under April 13, 1620, the undertakers pledged themselves to effect the draining within three years from the date an agreement should be reached as to their share in the land reclaimed, to "open the outfalls of Nene and Weland, and make those rivers navigable as high as Wisbeche and Spalding,"[21] as well as to better the navigation of the Grant and the Ouse. Because many marsh-dwellers, accustomed[22] to eke out a livelihood on the swamps, were reluctant to see the land drained and many landowners unwilling to grant to the undertakers so large a share as they demanded, the discontent and the resorts to the courts would attract wide interest in the scheme which the King at that time was eagerly prosecuting. It is clearly to rumors of new rivers such as these rather than to such as New River that Valentine refers in the lines,

> Till water-works, and rumours of New Rivers,
> Rid you again, and run you into questions
> Who built the Thames.   [IV, v, 61-63.]

This passage has been generally misunderstood. Quarto 1 reads *built Theamea;* Quarto 2 and the folio, where the passage is printed as prose, read *built Thames.* In his note on these lines Dyce was guilty of a stupidity as great as any for which he condemned poor Weber. "If *built the Thames* be the right reading," he wrote, "(which I greatly doubt), it perhaps may mean—built bridges over the Thames." In his edition of the play, Dr. McKerrow reprints Dyce's suggestion without comment, without exclamation points or any indication of merriment or disapproval. Indeed, from his capitalizing "New Rivers" and seeing an allusion to the New River, 1613, one may suspect that he misunderstands the passage and quotes

---

[21] Dugdale, *op. cit.,* p. 405.   [22] *Ibid.,* p. 402.

Dyce approvingly; for he reduces to the lower case the remaining capitals of the speech which in the folio reads:

. . . till Water works, and rumours of New Rivers rid you again and run you into questions who built Thames, till you run mad for Lotteries, and stand there with your Tables to glean the golden Sentences, and cite 'em secre[t]ly to Servingmen for sound Essayes, till Taverns allow you but a Towel room to Tipple Wine in. . . .

There is no more reason for capitalizing "New Rivers" than there is for capitalizing "Tipple Wine." As the reference to the Thames shows, there is no reason to suspect an allusion to the New River. The new rivers reported by rumor are not to be, like New River, conduits of fresh water carried through hills and in wooden troughs high over vales; they are to be rivers like the Thames. The obvious meaning of the passage is that there are so many rumors of rivers to be constructed by man that one is led to wonder who it was that built the Thames. Such man-made rivers were the means whereby the marshes were to be transformed into arable and pasture lands; and during the summer and autumn of 1620 there could not but have been many rumors of the rivers to be constructed in effecting this transformation.[23]

In an earlier scene (II, iii) there is an allusion to the sports of London which again, I think, fits most naturally into the summer of 1620. Lamenting their threatened departure for the country, the servants of the Widow recall the various sources of excitement furnished by the city, of which their removal will deprive them. Isabella joins them and laments that in the country there will be

> No plays nor galley-foists; no strange ambassadors
> To run and wonder at. . . .

[23] The draining of the Great Level was not the only work of the sort which was undertaken about this time. In 1620 Sir Hugh Middleton, the builder of New River, "began the work of reclaiming from the sea a flood district at the eastern extremity of the Isle of Wight, called Brading Harbour (*Cal. State Papers, Dom.*, 1619-23, p. 172)."—*D. N. B. sub*, Sir Hugh Middleton. The Dutchman, Cornelius Vermuyden, who was to play the most important part in the draining of marshes throughout England, although the date of his arrival is unknown, may already have been summoned, for he was in England when in September, 1621, the Thames broke down its banks near Havering and Dagenham in Essex.

While upon occasions too numerous to reckon the citizens of London had crowded to stare at strange visitors, it is interesting that in the very month in which James made his pilgrimage to St. Paul's there returned to England, after an absence of two years, the foreign ambassador who not only was the most cordially hated by patriotic Englishmen but was wherever he went eagerly followed by the curious multitude. The Spanish Ambassador, Diego Sarmiento de Acuña, Count of Gondomar, landed at Dover on March 5, 1620, and a splendid reception was prepared for him. He entered London on the eighth, "before an exceptional concourse of people, and was met, honoured, and lodged by the king's order, receiving a remarkable welcome."[24] But there was also a reception of another sort given him by the London populace. Having obtained permission to raise by the beat of the drum volunteers to protect the Protestant Palatinate, Gray "began to beat the drum on the very day and almost at the very hour when the Spanish ambassador entered London, and in the direction of his house at the moment of his arrival there."[25] "The next morning a placard, inviting volunteers to enlist, was found nailed to his [the Ambassador's] door."[26] Within the week of his arrival he had his first audience with the King. The crowd that gathered to witness him was so great that, as Camden records:

Count *Gundomar*, the *Spanish* Ambassador, going to the King in *Whitehall*, the Rails near the Door of the Great Chamber being broken by the Multitude of People, fell down, and with them the Earl of *Arundell*, Lord *Grey*, Lord *Gerard*; but received no Hurt.[27]

Gondomar's personal unpopularity and the Londoner's hostility to his master caused James no little difficulty. A few days before Gondomar had left for Spain in 1618 his house had been stormed by a mob of four or five thousand Londoners, irate because the carriage of one of his attendants had injured a child.[28] Nor did the populace confine their violence to the Ambassador's servants. In October, 1620, the Venetian Am-

---

[24] *C. S. P., Domestic*, CXIII, 15. Chamberlain to Carleton, March 11, 1620; *C. S. P., Venetian*, XVI, 204. Lando to the Doge and Senate, March 19, 1620.

[25] *Ibid.*, p. 206.   [26] Gardiner, *op. cit.*, III, 336.

[27] *Annals*, March 10, 1620.   [28] Gardiner, *op. cit.*, III, 135.

bassador in England wrote to the Doge and Senate that, annoyed by Gondomar's conduct of affairs in the proposed marriage of the Prince and the Infanta, "The King and many of the ministers have some idea of printing a manifesto as a justification to the world and to show that his Majesty has been deceived. But perhaps they will not do so for many reasons, but chiefly because it will be difficult to restrain the people from committing some notable outrage upon the Spanish Ambassador."[29] Their fear, it would seem, was well founded, for Camden records that on March 29, 1621, "Some *London* Apprentices, who had rudely handled the *Spanish* Ambassador, were whipped through the City," and that the next week James paid a personal visit to the Guildhall to reprove "the Magistrate for the insolence of the Vulgar against Ambassadors."[30]

Although the best known and the most cordially hated of the foreign ambassadors in London, Gondomar was not the only one whom Londoners in 1620 "ran and wondered at." He was, however, to some extent directly responsible for the crowds which followed and paid honor to the Ambassador of Bohemia, whose principal mission in England was to persuade James to give aid to his son-in-law, Frederick, recently elected King of Bohemia. Naturally as a Spaniard, whose master was intent on dethroning Frederick, Gondomar could not recognize the Bohemian ambassador as the representative of a crowned head. Not only had he snubbed the Bohemian, but he had been and continued successful in dissuading James from giving assistance to his son-in-law. Hating Gondomar as a Spaniard, the crowds of London which stared at him with curious and hostile eyes were elated by any show of favor to his rival, whose cause many had identified as their own. In the same letter in which he had referred to the King's fear of some "notable outrage upon the Spanish Ambassador," Girolamo Lando wrote the Doge and Senate of Venice that

The other day the prince fetched the Ambassador of Bohemia in his own carriage. Whereas only a little while ago he was practically

[29] *C. S. P., Venetian*, XVI, 434, October 11, 1620.
[30] *Annals*, April 6, 1621.

abandoned even by those of his own party, who were alarmed and scarcely dared to visit him any more, he now enjoys the attentions of the nobles and of men of every condition, who hasten to his house to show him honour. This morning when he went to Church thousands followed praising and blessing him.[31]

During the summer or early autumn of 1620 a London audience could fully appreciate Isabella's unhappiness in the threatened departure for the country, where there would be "no strange ambassadors to run and wonder at."

During Act I, scene i, lines 149 and following, Valentine, who, of course, prefers to live by his wits rather than by the income from lands, explains that his estate is

> . . . gone, and I am glad on't. . . .
> I tell you, sir, I am more fearful of it,
> (I mean of thinking of more lands or livings,)
> Than sickly men are travelling o' Sundays,
> For being quell'd with carriers.

That men should be more afraid of being attacked while travelling on Sundays than on other days of the week seems clearly a reference to the dispute concerning the rightful observance of Sunday. According to Gardiner,[32] it was first in Lancashire in 1617 that any public or ecclesiastical attention was focused upon the Puritan interpretation of Sunday as the true representative of the Jewish Sabbath, and hence as a day to be observed by a "complete abstention, not only from all work, but from every kind of amusement." When the King was returning from Scotland he was, as he passed through Lancashire, petitioned by those whom the Puritan magistrates had deprived of their traditional Sunday sports. It was this petition which led James, upon his return to London, to write his *Declaration concerning Lawful Sports*, 1618. "If he had," wrote Gardiner, "contented himself with leaving it behind him for the use of the Lancashire magistrates, it is probable that little more would have been heard about the matter."[33] But James ordered his *Declaration* publicly

---

[31] *C. S. P., Venetian*, XVI, 434, October 11, 1620.
[32] *Op. cit.*, III, 247.   [33] *Ibid.*, p. 251.

read in the pulpits of all churches, and overnight what had been an almost wholly local issue became one of national interest and violent feelings. And so it continued for several years. Many of the priests refused to read the King's message from their pulpits; others complied with the command, and then proceeded in their sermons to maintain that the King's order was contrary to God's law. That the quarrel continued hot through 1620 is shown by the articles brought against the Vicar of Branham in March (the same month in which the Spanish Ambassador arrived in England and James made his visit to St. Paul's) and his trial before the Ecclesiastical Commission in October of that year;[34] and by the expulsion of Mr. Shepherd from the House of Commons on February 16, 1620/21, for his remarks the day before upon the second reading of the bill dealing with the observance of the Sabbath.[35] No fewer than thirty-three members spoke upon the proper punishment to be given the offender.

Wilson records an instance of the ill-feeling engendered by the King's *Declaration* which, indeed, suggests that there may have been some particular incident alluded to in the passage I have quoted from the play:

This new incroachment upon the *Sabbath* gave both King and people more liberty to *prophane* the Day with *authority:* For if the *Court* were to remove on *Monday*, the Kings Carriages must go out the day before. All times were alike; and the Court being to remove to *Theobalds* the next day, the Carriages went through the City of *London* on the Sabbath, with a great deal of clatter and noise in the time of *Divine service*. The Lord Mayor hearing of it, commanded them to be stopt, and this carried the *Officers* of the Carriages with a great deal of *violence* to the Court, and the business being presented to the King with as much asperity as men in authority (crossed in their *humours*) could express it; It put the King into a great *Rage, swearing, he thought there had been no more Kings in* England *but himself*; yet after he was a little cooled, he sent a *warrant* to the Lord Mayor, commanding him to let them pass, which he obey'd, with this *Answer, while it was in my power, I did my duty; but that being taken away by a higher power, it*

---

[34] *C. S. P., Domestic*, CXIII, 128-29, 188.

[35] Gardiner, *op. cit.*, IV, 33.

is my duty to obey. Which the King upon second thoughts took well, and thanked him for it.[36]

If the various passages to which I have called attention be accepted as timely topical allusions, we seem safe in assuming that *Wit without Money* was being worked upon at some time after the spring of 1620. The reference to the dangers to carriers on Sunday would be apt only after 1618, that to the missing steeple of St. Paul's only after March, 1620. In the latter year also were rumors of war most current, although, of course, the anti-Spanish party had advocated it since the outbreak of the trouble in Germany nearly two years before. As there might well have been, in view of the great activity in draining commenced in 1621, many "rumours of new rivers" circulated in 1620, so after Gondomar's return in March of that year had there been in him and in the Bohemian Ambassador, more noticeably than ever before, ambassadors whom the populace of London delighted "to run and wonder at." Finally, there is another passage in the play which may indicate that the play was composed before March, 1621. In a speech from which I have already quoted (in the discussion of "rumours of new rivers"), Valentine tells the suitors of the Widow that they may continue to think that they have undone him

> till you run mad for lotteries
> And stand there with your tables to glean
> The golden sentences, and cite 'em secretly
> To serving men for sound essays. . . .   [IV, v, 63-66.]

The connection between the "lotteries" and the "sentences" may be somewhat doubtful, but as the King on March 8, 1621, issued a proclamation suppressing lotteries,[37] there may well be here an allusion to the abuse which led to their suppression.

During the first decade of the seventeenth century there seem to have been several private lotteries,[38] and the term "lot-

---

[36] Wilson, *op. cit.*, p. 106.

[37] Pollard and Redgrave, *Short Title Catalogue*, No. 8660.

[38] C. L'Estrange Ewen, *Lotteries and Sweepstakes* (London, 1932), pp. 68-69, records one in Westminster in 1604, another by an Italian merchant, Julian Miccottie, in 1606-1607, and a petition for a license by one Cornelius Drebbel sometime before 1612. "Whether Drebbel secured his license is unrecorded."

tery" may well have been used for wheels of chance and other gambling devices. But during the second decade of the century there were, by special royal permission, a series of lotteries conducted by the Virginia Company of London to raise funds for its plantation in Virginia. Everyone was urged to buy chances and thereby "advance so worthie an enterprise tending so greatly to the enlargement of the Cristian truth, the honor of our nation, and benefit of English people. . . ."[39]

The first of these lotteries, the First Great Virginia Standing Lottery, was, as E. Howes records,[40] "drawne and finished" by July 20, 1612. Although the liveried companies and even churches voted sums for chances, the income to the company was much less than had been expected; and so a new lottery, known as the Little Virginia Standing Lottery, was at once prepared, with the price of a chance reduced from 2*s.* 6*d.* to 1*s.* Tickets, however, sold so slowly that the drawing had to be postponed until 1614. In the meantime tickets were being sold for the Second Great Standing Lottery, sometimes known as the Five Shilling Lottery. Pamphlets were published declaring this to be the last lottery and describing the 9,743 prizes—the range from 4,500 crowns to 2—and the generous "welcomes" and "awards" which were added to attract new purchasers.[41] But tickets again sold so slowly that the drawing did not begin until November, 1615, and some of the fortunate adventurers had to wait more than four years longer—until 1620—before receiving the prizes they had won.[42]

These three lotteries, as "standing" lotteries, had been held only in London. The Virginia Company, seeking further revenue, instituted now what were known as "running" or "ring"

[39] Letter from Sir Edwin Sandys to the Mayor and Jurates of Sandwich, April 8, 1612. Printed by Ewen (p. 72) after E. D. Neill, *Early Settlement of Virginia and Virginiola* (Minneapolis, 1878), p. 44.

[40] *The Annales of England* (John Stow) by E. Howes (1615), p. 913*a* (Ewen, *op. cit.*, p. 74).

[41] One reprinted by Ewen (pp. 79-83) refers to "many former Publications."

[42] At a court of the Company on April 8, 1620, the Treasurer reported that "there remayneth some thinge still to pay which cheifly is prizes due to Adventurors vppon the great standing Lottery."—*Records of the Virginia Company of London*, ed. by S. M. Kingsbury, I, 235. Quoted by Ewen, p. 84.

lotteries, which, traveling from one town to another, operated until the end of 1620.[43]

That these lotteries were the object of much criticism is shown by the recommendation of Sir Edwin Sandys, November 4, 1620, that his colleagues in the Virginia Company publish a justification "of the Lottarie now of late very much disgraced[,] that itt may be deliuered of many fowle aspersions vniustly cast vppon itt by malignna' tounges: notwithstanding itt is evident that the monney thereof arisinge hath sent allredie to Virginia 800 Persouns to the great advancement of that Plantation."[44] In the following February King James sent word to the House of Commons that he "never liked the Ring Lottery; ever suspected it; Yielded, because he was informed, the Plantation of Virginia could not subsist without it; Will now suspend it and revoke it quite, if shall be found here a grievance."[45] Apparently it was found a grievance, for on March 8, 1621, there was published the King's Proclamation against Lotteries, in which he explained that he had permitted the lotteries "for the inlarging of Our Gouernment, increase of Nauigation and Trade, and especially for the reducing of the sauage and barbarous people of those parts to the Christian faith"; that "the sayd Lotteries . . . do dayly decline to more and more inconuenience, to the hinderance of multitudes of Our Subjects";[46] and that therefore all lotteries were from thenceforth forbidden.

It seems most probable, I think, that the allusion to lotteries in *Wit without Money* antedates March, 1621. It might, of course, have had point during any of the preceding fifteen years; but if there is, as I feel there is, a tone of contempt in Fletcher's reference, it would well suit the summer and autumn of 1620 when Sir Edwin Sandys complained that the lottery was "now of late very much disgraced" and "many fowle aspersions vniustly cast vppon itt by malignna' tounges"—shortly before King James was to declare that the lotteries "do dayly decline

[43] Ewen, *op. cit.*, pp. 84-86.
[44] Kingsbury, *op. cit.*, I, 279 (Ewen, p. 86).
[45] *Journal of the House of Commons*, I, 582b (Ewen, p. 86).
[46] Reprinted by Ewen, pp. 86-87.

to more and more inconuenience, to the hinderance of multitudes of Our Subjects."

To be sure, if, as has been generally assumed, there was a
version of *Wit without Money* as early as 1614, no such reference can be used to indicate the latest possible date for a revision, for the reference might have been in the original version.
No one, however, has ever suggested that the play as it has
come down to us, first printed in a quarto of 1639, has undergone revision; nor have I been able to detect any evidence to
indicate that it has—other, of course, than the allusion to the
dragon of Sussex. Perhaps the manner in which the allusions to
topics and events of 1620 are grouped in two or three places
within the play may suggest that they were later insertions. But
whether the play was being composed or merely being ren-
ovated, it was, I believe, certainly being worked upon during
the summer or early autumn of 1620.

XVI

The Date of THE PILGRIM

JOHN FLETCHER's tragi-comedy *The Pilgrim* was presented at the court during the Christmas season of 1621-1622.[1] It has been usually accepted that its source was in part Lope de Vega's *El Peregrino en su Patria* (1604); and as in 1621 there appeared an English translation of Lope's story,[2] made from an earlier French translation, most scholars have assumed that Fletcher's comedy was based upon the English translation and have accordingly ascribed it to the year 1621. The list of actors who in the Second Folio are stated to have taken part in the play would also fit 1621; but as these lists need not always constitute the original casts, and as there is already evidence that the play was presented in 1621-1622, the list offers little additional evidence for the date of composition. Neither is it, without supporting evidence, safe to assume that Fletcher used the English translation, for whether or not Fletcher knew Spanish, there is every reason to believe that he knew French and that in writing several of his plays he made use of the French translations of the tales of Cervantes.[3]

Macaulay has observed that the resemblance between *The Pilgrim* and *El Peregrino* "is only in trifling details, and there may be no connection."[4] As will, I think, be made clear before the end of this essay, there is reason to believe that Fletcher was indebted to Lope for these "trifling details," but unless other evidence can be advanced, we are hardly justified in assigning the play to a date more definite than the six-year period

[1] Adams, *The Dramatic Records of Sir Henry Herbert*, p. 49.

[2] Entered upon the Stationers' Register as "A booke called *the pilgrim of Casteell or The Fortunes of Llamphilus and Nisa*" (Arber, *Transcript*, IV, 21) and based upon the French translation by d'Audiguier, *Les diverses fortunes de Pamphile et de Nise* (1614).

[3] It is, for instance, reasonably certain that Fletcher used the 1615 French translation of Cervantes for *Love's Pilgrimage* and for *The Chances*.

[4] *Cambridge History of English Literature*, VI, 157.

from 1615 to 1621. Fortunately other evidence is not lacking. *The Pilgrim* contains several topical allusions which, I think, clearly indicate that the play was composed in the summer or autumn of 1621.

In I, i, Alinda, with true Fletcherian gusto, exclaims:

> And, o' my Conscience,
> If once I grow to breeding, a whole Kingdom
> Will not contain my stock;

and her maid, Juletta, observes:

> The more the merrier:
> 'Tis brave to be a mother of new Nations.

As the other topical allusions I shall note seem to support the dating of the play in 1621, it seems likely that we have in the quoted lines a reference to the efforts which during that year the Virginia Company was making to transport to the colony an "hundredth . . . woemen, Maids young and vncorrupt to make wifes . . ."[5] "that wifes, children and familie might make them [the colonists] lesse moueable and settle them, together with their Posteritie in that Soile."[6] As I have pointed out in writing of *The Noble Gentleman*,[7] where one of the characters replies, when urged to send his wife to court,

> Sir, I had rather send her to *Virginia*
> To help to propagate the *English* Nation,

although the suggestion of transporting women was first made at the meeting of November 3, 1619, none had been sent twenty months later, and it was not until the meeting of July 16, 1621, that provisions were made for financing their transportation.[8] Soon after this date the plan was carried through, for from the records of the meeting of November 21, 1621, we learn that in order that "the Planters minds may be the faster tyed to Virginia by the bonds of Wyues and Children, care hath bin taken to prouide them younge handsome and honestly educated mayds whereof 60 are already sent to Virginia. . . ."[9] As this was the

---

[5] Kingsbury, *The Records of the Virginia Company of London*, I, 256.
[6] *Ibid.*, p. 269.　　[7] Essay XII.
[8] Kingsbury, *op. cit.*, I, 514.　　[9] *Ibid.*, p. 566.

only organized effort to transport women during the life of the
Virginia Company and as it must have excited a good bit of
interest during the summer and autumn of 1621, there can be
no doubt as to the allusion in *The Noble Gentleman*; and the
certainty of that allusion increases the likelihood that Fletcher
is again glancing toward the Virginia brides when he has Juletta
exclaim

> 'Tis brave to be a mother of new Nations.

As the Company had presumably made little effort to secure
women colonists until the plan for transporting them had been
arranged, it is probable that little publicity was given the scheme
before the middle of July. The reference would continue timely
until some months after the maids had sailed, but would be most
apt during the weeks preceding and following their departure—
the autumn of 1621.

In I, ii, Seberto, reproving Alphonso's gruffness toward the
wandering beggars who infest his house, observes that

> A comely and sweet usage becomes strangers,

and Alphonso hotly replies,

> We shall have half the Kingdom strangers shortly,
> An this fond prodigality be suffer'd.

Feeling against foreigners was running high during 1621, and
such a retort would have provoked delight and applause in any
London theater. Although the foreign tradesmen in England
had always been unpopular, the "extraordinary influx of strangers" and the intensity of the feeling against them in 1621 are
shown by there being listed under June of that year in the
Calendar of State Papers, Domestic twenty-four different items
relative to the serious dangers resulting from this influx. In the
preceding April the Rev. Joseph Mead had written Sir Martin
Stuteville that "On Sunday comes forth a terrible and strict
proclamation. In this proclamation, as I understand it, the city
government is much taxed; and it is strictly commanded that no
man, so much as by countenance or look, abuse or express any
irreverence for strangers. . . ."[10] Such a proclamation, however,

[10] April 9, 1621. Birch, *The Court and Times of James I*, II, 248-49.

could not quiet the indignant citizenry. From the twenty-four items listed in *C.S.P., Domestic,* under the following June, I quote three which indicate the rapid increase in the foreign residents and suggest the reasons for their unpopularity.

146. Statement of the inconveniences arising from the extraordinary influx of strangers, and proposal to appoint an officer to register and swear them.

148. Petition of the City of London to the King, complaining of the loss incurred by aliens living under more favourable conditions than natural subjects; praying him to institute a commission to inquire into the laws and constitutions respecting them, and to suggest regulations for their future government.

163. Statement [by Sir Robt. Heath], that the strangers in London embrace 100 professions, in all of which the English complain of losing their work. Proposal to meet the case by a general yearly registration of strangers, by exacting a certain quarterage from them, in proportion to their station, and by forbidding them retail trades, or going to fairs or markets. . . .[11]

In response to the continued ill-feeling and the insistent demands that the status of the English tradesman be improved by the abolition of special privileges to the foreigner, a commission was on July 30, 1621, at length issued to

the Lord Keeper, Lord High Treasurer, Attorney and Solicitor General, and others, to consider of the Statutes concerning aliens, and either to induce them to conformity with the laws already in force, especially regarding not selling by retail and the use of handicraft trades, or to modify the laws, for the better convenience of strangers and good of the subject, under such directions as His Majesty shall from time to time prescribe.[12]

On the same day "directions were given by the king to the Commissioners to take a yearly account of all aliens resident in England, to permit all wholesale merchants to continue their trade, but to restrain all retailers, unless they would submit to restrictions as to servants and apprentices, and pay quarterage as

[11] CXXI, 270-72.
[12] *C. S. P., Domestic,* CXXII, 280. July 30, 1621.

the English in their several companies did."[13] A satisfactory solution was not, however, to be soon reached.

In January, 1622, the Goldsmiths' Company complained of 183 alien Goldsmiths for making counterfeit jewels and engrossing trade, so that the goldsmiths were impoverished. . . . The Coopers' Company complained on the number of aliens employed as coopers by foreign brewers. The Clockmakers pressed upon the Council the number and deceitful tricks of foreigners practising their trade, and prayed that they not be allowed to work except for English masters.[14]

Other trades made similar complaints.

It will be noticed that the months which saw the most frequent protests against aliens and against James's kindly treatment of them, saw also the perfecting of the Virginia Company's plan to transport women to Virginia. The feeling did not, of course, evaporate upon the creation of the commission. Throughout the next year the commission received memoranda from representatives of various trades setting forth the dangers threatening them because of the competition of the alien residents.

Of the remaining allusions to which I shall call attention, one deserves only brief treatment and should perhaps have been relegated to a footnote. In III, vii, the scene of which is a mad-house, a "malt-mad" Englishman is introduced, and the First Keeper explains that

> When they have a fruitful year of Barly there,
> All the whole Island's thus.

That a "fruitful year" was anticipated during the summer of 1621 is attested by Chamberlain. "We have as much cause to complain of the weather," he wrote Carleton on July 21, "for such a summer, I think, was never seen . . . yet there is great show of corn and grape upon the ground, if it please God to send it well in."[15]

The English Madman, having first called for drink, offers a toast "To the great Turk"—a toast to which many Englishmen

[13] W. D. Cooper, *Lists of Foreign Protestants and Aliens Resident in England, 1618-1688*, Camden Society, LXXXII (1862), ix.

[14] *Ibid.*, pp. ix-x.   [15] Birch, *op. cit.*, II, 270.

would have been willing to drink in the summer of 1621. That there is here a timely allusion is shown by the last line of Roderigo's speech in IV, ii, when he says in reply to Pedro's question whether men should not defend the honor of their mistresses:

> If they be vertuous,
> And then the Sword adds nothing to their lustre,
> But rather calls in question what's not doubted;
> If they be not, the best Swords, and best valours
> Can never fight 'em up to fame again;
> No, not a Christian War, and that's held pious.

This last line can, I believe, be definitely dated within narrow limits. War between Poland and the Turks had been threatening for some time when in March, 1621, "The waiwood of *Sandomar's* Son, the Ambassador from the King of *Poland*, goes to the king at *Whitehall*, and signifies to him in Latine how great Wars were depending over *Christendom* by the common Enemy the *Turk*, occasioned by the Troubles in *Germany*."[16] It is clear that for the war which was declared within the next month Poland was seeking aid from the other Christian nations.

James, who had inherited the title Defender of the Faith and who was, whatever his faults, a sincere Christian, sided at once against the Turks. "The King," wrote the Venetian Ambassador in England, "goes about saying that he will always be zealous against the Turk, and he would never regard as a good Christian prince any one who did not do the same. . . ."[17] By such speeches and by the publication of documents King James sought to mold public opinion. As the Polish Ambassador's oration, in both Latin and English, had been entered in April, so on June 7, 1621, there was entered upon the Stationers' Register "vnder the hands of Sir George Caluert knight, principall secretarie to his Majestie," etc., "A Book called, *True*

[16] Camden, *Annals*, March 18, 1621. Kennet, p. 657. This Latin oration, together with an English translation, was entered upon the Stationers' Register, April 5, 1621, "vnder the handes of Sir George Caluert, knight, principall Secretary to his Maiestie," etc.

[17] *C. S. P., Venetian*, XVII, 30-31. Girolama Lando to the Doge and Senate, April 23, 1621.

Copys of the insolent, cruell, barbarous, and Blasphemous letter, written by the great Turke, for Denouncing of Warre against the King of Poland, And of the Magnanimous and most Christian answere made by the said King thereto."[18] Clearly James regarded the war as a Christian war, a position in which he was encouraged by the Spanish Ambassador, Gondomar, and perhaps by his own desire to win favor with the new Pope, Gregory XV, who was giving aid to Poland, and so advance the scheme he held nearest to his heart, of effecting the marriage of Prince Charles to the Spanish Infanta. He granted Poland a levy of 10,000 soldiers in England.[19] "It is not thought, however," wrote the Venetian Ambassador, "that they will be able to raise even 3000, since the captains named are of slight standing and less following."[20] As King James had been so outspoken concerning the duty of a Christian to oppose the Turk, it can not be doubted that the captains and others interested in the levy argued that the war was a pious one. But the difficulty in raising the troops allotted was not due solely to the slight standing of the captains. As the Ambassador had learned when on July 30, 1621, he reported to his government an English loan to Poland, most patriotic Englishmen would have preferred to have the Sultan not an enemy, but rather an ally in restoring the Elector Frederick:

After much reflection upon the movements of the Turks . . . they have at length assigned 10,000 *l.* to the Polish ambassador upon the levies . . . it would seem almost impossible to raise it, especially as all those of the Palatine's party have opposed it, strongly alleging the danger that English merchants in Constantinople will incur on this account, and the great prejudice it will cause to any intention to make representations to the Sultan if he should incline to send help to Germany. But the Spanish ambassador has supported it with great zeal. . . .

Sir Thomas Roe, chosen as ambassador for Constantinople, greatly deplores and exclaims against the assistance in money and levies granted to Poland.[21]

[18] Arber, *Transcript*, IV, 17.
[20] *Ibid.*
[19] *C. S. P., Venetian*, XVII, 30.
[21] *Ibid.*, pp. 92-94.

With the King and the captains urging as a pious duty a war against the common enemy of Christendom[22] and with the majority of the people disinterested or stoutly opposed to it, there would, during the summer of 1621, have been timely significance in the line,

> No, not a Christian War, and that's held pious.

There would, however, be little significance in such a line after November of the same year. The English troops which had been raised with difficulty, never saw action against the Turk. Girolamo Lando wrote Venice, October 15, 1621, that the King of Denmark had refused them permission to pass through his kingdom.[23] Four weeks later Lando again wrote that "The troops levied here for the Polish war and turned back, as I reported, will make no further attempts to go, and many have already proceeded to Flanders, as Denmark has again declared that he will not let them pass on any account."[24] Three days later a report from the Low Countries states that many of the British soldiers had returned to England.[25] As far as England was concerned, the pious Christian war was over.

Evidence of another sort—similarities which *The Pilgrim* bears to other Beaumont and Fletcher plays—although less specific than topical allusions, would likewise support a date after 1619. There is in several of the speeches of the reformed bully and outlaw, Roderigo, eloquent condemnation of the fashionable practice of duelling. As I have shown in an earlier chapter, not before 1616 did the authors of these plays cease to

---

[22] That the Turk also considered the war one in which the alignment might be Christian *versus* non-Christian is shown by his action when the English Ambassador sought to return home before the arrival of his successor. As related by Zorgi Giustinian, Venetian ambassador at Constantinople, "The English ambassador, having completed the period of his embassy, has obtained leave from his king to return home. . . . As the ambassador wished to leave he asked the Caimecam for an order to go to Adrianople to kiss hands and take leave, and although the Caimecam said he could not do this, the ambassador prepared horses and coaches to proceed to that town. The Caimecam interfered and stopped him. He explained this by saying that peace with Poland was not yet absolutely certain, and the Turks might suspect assistance would be given by Christian princes if the war was renewed, and think that his removal before the arrival of his successor might be done by this king with that object."— C. S. P., *Venetian*, XVII, 183. December 21, 1621.

[23] *Ibid.*, 148.

[24] *Ibid.*, p. 160. November 12, 1621. [25] *Ibid.*, p. 165.

echo the popular view that a gentleman should maintain his reputation by his sword; and not before 1619 or 1620 is there to be found with equal eloquence the expression of the view that in fighting to support the honor of a virtuous mistress one adds nothing to her lustre, "But rather calls in question what's not doubted," that only a fool would fight simply to show he dared to (IV, iii).

There seems, too, to be in *The Pilgrim* a situation borrowed from *Women Pleased*, which, if the list of actors given in the Second Folio be correct, was acted if not composed between 1619 and 1621. In *Women Pleased* (IV, ii) the heroine Belvidere, after a song off-stage, enters disguised as an old beldam to encourage, advise, and direct the man she loves. Her disguise is both an important element in the plot and thoroughly in keeping with the characters and story as borrowed from Chaucer's Wife of Bath's Tale. In *The Pilgrim* (V, iv), however, the action is not furthered by the appearance, immediately following music off-stage, of Alinda and Juletta disguised as bearded old women. Speaking in the same tetrameter used by the disguised Belvidere in directing Silvio, they exhort Roderigo to a repentance already well demonstrated and direct him and Pedro to go "to Segovia for their fortunes" (V, vi). As there is no suggestion of such a scene in *El Peregrino*, I suspect that Fletcher is in *The Pilgrim* doing what he seems to have done quite often—using for a second time a situation which he thought had proved successful.

But at certain other times in *The Pilgrim* Fletcher clearly borrowed from *El Peregrino* or from one of the translations of it. Mr. Macaulay is hardly justified in saying that "the resemblance is only in trifling details, and there may be no connection."[26] In view of a close resemblance which I shall note later, it is reasonable to assume that Fletcher was indebted to Lope, first of all, for his title. Although he takes over no names and no characters—if the figures of Lope's tale may be said to be characters—he does borrow several situations. The two stories are alike in being a confused round of lovers' separation, search, meeting, further separation, etc. In both the heroine is in male

---

[26] *Cambridge History of English Literature*, VI, 157.

attire during the greater part of the time; in both there is the gentleman-outlaw robber, to whom the lovers are captives at the same time, who is a suitor for the heroine's love, and who gives orders—not obeyed—that the hero be hanged. That these details, trifling and conventional though they are, were suggested by *El Peregrino* is shown by the strikingly similar use of the mad-house in the two stories. Pedro *(The Pilgrim)* like Pamphilius *(El Peregrino)*, arriving in a strange city and eager to see the "sights," is taken to visit a mad-house. There he discovers Alinda, as Pamphilius does Nisa, the two girls in male attire having been picked up in the city in a dazed condition. In both stories the lovers recognize one another but are torn apart when their kissing and embracing are interpreted as confirming the madness of what the keepers think to be boys. Both Pedro and Pamphilius urge that such indulgence may ameliorate the madness, but the girls are dragged away to their cells. There are, in addition, a number of other minor resemblances. In both mad-houses there is a mad scholar, who speaks learnedly and civilly. As Pamphilius is beaten and thrown into chains as a madman when, after Nisa's release, he angrily insists that she was no boy, so is the anger of Alinda's father mistaken for madness and he thrown into chains when he comes to the mad-house seeking his daughter after her departure.

The debt to *El Peregrino* and the similarities to other of Fletcher's plays suggest for *The Pilgrim* a date much the same as that urged by the allusions which I noted earlier. If these allusions are to be recognized, as I believe they must, as topical allusions, and if they were not later insertions but allusions contained in the original draft of the play, they would indicate as the outside limits of the composition of *The Pilgrim* the end of April and the middle of November, 1621, for before April the Christian war had not begun and by the end of November it was over. The reference to the Virginia brides urges the preference of the last few months of this period. As the English translation of *El Peregrino* was entered upon the Stationers' Register on September 18, 1621, there can be little doubt that it was from it that Fletcher borrowed and that *The Pilgrim* was written in the last three months of 1621.

XVII

The Prologues and Epilogues

In the Booksellers' address to the reader, which was appended as a preface to the 1679 Beaumont and Fletcher folio, it is claimed that "an ingenious and worthy Gentleman" had furnished "several Prologues and Epilogues, . . . which were not in the former Edition [of 1647], but are now inserted in their proper places." This promise was one of the many promises which these booksellers failed to fulfill. Not one prologue or epilogue is in the Second Folio added to the plays which had been published in the First Folio. Of the fifty-one plays in the later folio only twenty are equipped with both prologue and epilogue. Four others are equipped with prologues only,[1] and one with epilogue only.[2] Less than one half of the plays, therefore, have both or either. Only a slightly better proportion existed in the folio of 1647. Of its thirty-three plays, sixteen have both, and four others have only the one or the other. The omissions were not due to lack of space. In every instance where the prologues and epilogues do not appear, there was abundant space for them to be included; often when they are included additional pages are devoted to them. We may justly assume, therefore, that the publishers of both folios printed all the prologues and epilogues which they had. Others, if they ever existed, had been lost.

Of the prologues and epilogues printed in the two folios many obviously had been prepared for revivals. Eight of the prologues, indeed, refer to Fletcher as dead, and two others state that the plays are being revived after many years absence

---

[1] The four include *Wit at Several Weapons*, where what was most certainly a prologue is appended with the heading Epilogue. See below.

[2] In the Second Folio, as in earlier quartos, four and a half lines are printed at the end of *Cupid's Revenge* and headed "Cupid's *Speech*." Clearly, however, this is not an epilogue and belongs where editors have placed it—before the last scene of the tragedy.

from the stage.[3] An eleventh prologue which must be discarded
is that of *The Coronation,* included among the fifty-one plays of
the Second Folio, but previously claimed by Shirley. There
remain, therefore, only thirteen extant prologues which may
conceivably have been composed when the plays were first presented.[4] I doubt if all of these were indeed so nearly contemporary. Nor do I see any reason for assuming that others were
written and lost. Not only did the vogue of the prologue come
and go, but Beaumont, Fletcher, and Massinger seem to have
disliked writing them—probably because the form had become
so conventionalized that it was most difficult to secure anything
resembling freshness or originality. Less than one third of
Massinger's plays are equipped with prologues, and in several
of them it is stated that they were written for revivals. Massinger's dislike of the prologue and epilogue is shown in the
dedication of *The Unnatural Combat* in 1639. "I present you
this old tragedy," he wrote Anthony Sentleger, "without prologue or epilogue, it being composed in a time (and that too,
peradventure, as knowing as this) when such by-ornaments were
not advanced above the fabric of the whole work." And in the
opening lines of the Blackfriar's prologue to *The Emperor of
the East* (lic. 1631), he confesses:

> But that imperious custom warrants it,
> Our author with much willingness would omit
> This preface to his new work.

Similar dislike of these appendages is shown by the authors of
the prologues to *Nice Valour,* written for a revival, and to *The
Humorous Lieutenant,* which has been thought to have been
written by Fletcher at the time when the play was first acted.

The first of the Beaumont and Fletcher plays to be printed
was *The Woman Hater,* which appeared in 1607 with no epi-

---

[3] These are *The Elder Brother, The Loyal Subject, The Chances, Lover's Progress,
Woman's Prize, Love's Cure, The Noble Gentleman, Wit at Several Weapons, Nice
Valour, The Coxcomb.*

[4] *Captain, Custom of the Country, Fair Maid of the Inn, The False One, Humorous Lieutenant, Little French Lawyer, Love's Pilgrimage, Mad Lover, Rule a
Wife, Spanish Curate, Two Noble Kinsmen, Wife for a Month, Woman Hater.* As
noted later, some of these may well have been written for revivals.

logue, but with a prologue written in prose, because, it is explained, "Inductions are out of date, and a Prologue in Verse, is as stale as a black Velvet Cloak, and a Bay Garland: therefore you shall have it in plain Prose." Not until twenty-seven years later, when *Two Noble Kinsmen* was published in 1634, was a prologue printed with another Beaumont and Fletcher play, although during that time there had appeared twenty-one quartos of eight plays. All eight of these plays had been first published before Fletcher's death in 1625, although the only one for the publication of which he was responsible would appear to be *The Faithful Shepherdess* (1609), without prologue or epilogue until the 1633 revival.

Of the nine plays, then, printed before *Two Noble Kinsmen* (1634), only one, *The Woman Hater*, has prologue or epilogue. In all seventeen plays printed first in quarto and hence omitted from the First Folio, only two others are accompanied by these "by-ornaments," and the prologue of one of the two (*The Elder Brother*, 1635), as it refers to Fletcher as dead, was obviously prepared for a late revival.

It would appear, therefore, that by 1607 the usual type of prologue was recognized, at least by the authors, as stale and flat, and that until after Fletcher's death "such by-ornaments" as the prologue and epilogue were not—at least so far as the printed plays were concerned—"advanced above the fabric of the whole work." That they were indeed not considered necessary adjuncts is suggested by their omission from the play manuscripts. Seven of the Beaumont and Fletcher plays are preserved in contemporary manuscripts.[5] In none of them is there either prologue or epilogue, although when the plays were printed two were accompanied by prologues frankly prepared for revival,[6] and a third by one which declares the play new.[7]

---

[5] *Beggars' Bush* (Folger Shakespeare Library, MS. 1487.2), *Bonduca* (B.M., Add. MS. 36758), *Elder Brother* (B.M., Egerton MS. 1994), *Faithful Friends* (Victoria and Albert Mus., Dyce MS. 10), *Honest Man's Fortune* (*ibid.*, Dyce MS. 9), *Woman's Prize* (Folger Shakespeare Library, MS. 1487.2), and *Humorous Lieutenant* (printed by Dyce in 1830 under the title which the MS. bears, *Demetrius and Enanthe*).

[6] *The Elder Brother* and *Woman's Prize*.   [7] *The Humorous Lieutenant*.

If, however, the thirteen prologues which are not patently prepared for revivals were written when the plays were new, and if they are correctly placed in the First Folio, then it is difficult to determine any extended period during which the prologue may be said to have been definitely abandoned.   In only six of the prologues is the claim made that the play is new, and three of these are among the six which contain references rendering them peculiarly suitable to the play following.   Allusions to Middleton's *Game at Chess* indicate that the prologue to *Rule a Wife* was written in 1624, the same year in which the play was licensed.   There are, therefore, five prologues which we may be certain were originally penned for the first production of the particular play with which they are now associated: (1) *Woman Hater* (1607)—as the prologue was printed in the quarto of that year; (2) *The Two Noble Kinsmen* (1613); (3) *Love's Pilgrimage* (1616); (4) *The False One* (1620); and (5) *Rule a Wife* (1624).   As all of these plays may be definitely dated, these prologues indicate that throughout Fletcher's career his plays were at least from time to time accompanied by prologues especially prepared when the plays were completed. The evidence does not indicate, nor indeed does Massinger suggest, that there was a period during which the prologue was abandoned.   Massinger merely testifies that many plays before *The Unnatural Combat* (presumably prior to 1622 as it was not entered by Herbert) possessed neither prologue nor epilogue— "by-ornaments" required by "imperious custom" in 1631.

The prologue to *The Humorous Lieutenant,* if it belong to that play, suggests that the dramatists were about 1619 still or again complaining of the prologue, "usual to a Play," as stereotyped:

> Would some man would instruct me what to say:
> For this same Prologue, usual to a Play,
> Is tied to such an old form of Petition;
> Men must say nothing new beyond commission:
> The Cloaks we wear, the Leggs we make, the place
> We stand in, must be one; and one the face.
> Not alter'd nor exceeded; if it be,
> A general hisse hangs on our levitie: . . .

This play has been dated 1619, because that year fits the cast of actors as given in the folio of 1679. If the actors named took part, the play could not be later than 1619, although I think it unsafe to assume that the list of actors must necessarily be a list of those who participated in the play's first presentation. The extant manuscript made by Ralph Crane and dated November 27, 1625, does not contain the prologue, nor does the prologue itself, as does the epilogue, contain anything which renders it suitable only for this comedy. It does, however, claim that the play is new, and, although the actors at times certainly palmed off old plays as new, no such fraudulent claim could probably have been made of so successful a comedy as this deserved to be. There is throughout most of the prologues much repetition and similarity of expression, but this particular prologue closes with a request strikingly like that at the end of the prologue to *Rule a Wife*, definitely dated 1624 by its allusion to Middleton's *Game at Chess*. In the prologue to *Rule a Wife* the speaker closes with "sit noble then, and see," whereas at the end of the present prologue the audience is urged to "sit nobly then, and see." The parallel suggests (but hardly proves) that one author wrote both prologues, but it perhaps argues no more for proximity of date than it does for remoteness. The prologue does, however, clearly show that the poet was weary of the restrictions demanded by convention.

This dislike on the part of the dramatists and, perhaps, the shifting fashions may at times have led to prologues and epilogues being used with plays other than those for which they were originally written. The insertion into the 1635 quarto of *The Knight of the Burning Pestle* of the prologue to Lyly's *Sappho and Phao* has been interpreted as a *jeu d'esprit* of the publisher, and Professor Alden hazarded the guess that it "was probably never used on the stage."[8] As *The Knight* was revived "by her Majesties Servants at the Private house in Drury lane" in 1635, and as the previously cited comments by Massinger show that in 1631 and in 1639 "imperious custom" de-

---

[8] R. M. Alden, *The Knight of the Burning Pestle* and *A King and No King* (Belles Lettres Series), 1910, p. 138.

manded the recital of a prologue, the chances are at least even that Lyly's euphuistic prologue was in that year spoken before Beaumont's burlesque. In its first two quartos *Thierry and Theodoret* has no prologue, but when it was republished in 1649 it was accompanied by the prologue which in the folios goes with *The Noble Gentleman*. This substitution suggests how a prologue might be made to serve more than one play, as does also the inclusion in a 1661 quarto of *The Beggars' Bush* of the prologue and epilogue assigned in the First Folio to *The Captain*. Indeed, few of the prologues or epilogues contain such specific references as make them suitable only for particular plays. Usually they are phrased in most general terms. In only six of the twenty-three is there a definite allusion to the theme which is to follow.[9]

Although it seems never to have been noticed, in one instance the epilogue is at such variance with the play that precedes it as to make it seem improbable not only that it could have been especially written for that play but that it could ever have been recited at a performance of it. With the ravishing of Lucina, with the treacherous murder of Aecius, with the drawn-out agony of the Emperor's death by poisoning, and with the subsequent death of Maximus immediately after he is crowned with a wreath by the senators, there is in *Valentinian* to an extent rare in the Beaumont and Fletcher tragedies an effort to arouse pity and horror. It is something of a shock, therefore, when in the epilogue the tragedy is spoken of as though it were a comedy. After expressing the hope that the audience will feel that the play was worth the admission charged, the epilogue closes with the lines:

> The price is easie, and so light the Play
> That ye may new digest it every day.
> Then noble friends, as ye would choose a Miss,
> Only to please the eye a while and kiss,
> Till a good Wife be got: So let this Play
> Hold ye a while until a better may.

[9] *The False One, Love's Pilgrimage, Fair Maid of the Inn, Two Noble Kinsmen, Rule a Wife,* and *Woman's Prize.*

The statement "so light the Play," etc., and the comparison to a Miss "to please the eye a while and kiss" suggest not the deliberate building of horror but rather farcical comedy—such comedy as that of *Woman's Prize*, in which the prologue warns the audience not to expect

> Set speeches, high expressions, and, what's worse
> In a true comedy, politic discourse

(all of which appear in *Valentinian*), then calls attention to the small admission charge, and invites the audience to see the play often:

> The end we aim at is to make you sport; . . .
> Hear, and observe his comic strain, and when
> Ye're sick of melancholy, see't again:
> 'Tis no dear physic, since 'twill quit the cost,
> Or his intentions, with our pains, are lost.

Such a misassignment would have been an error natural to make, and is one easily explained. It has already been noted that these ornaments did not form an integral part of the manuscript play; that they were written and preserved on separate sheets is borne out by the evidence of the First Folio, where during the first part of the volume the prologues and epilogues, when they appear, are both appended at the end of the play, generally on separate sheets, whereas in the latter part of the volume they are regularly placed properly one at the beginning of the play and one at the end. Written and kept on separate sheets, prologues and epilogues might easily lose their proper place.

Another error among the prologues and epilogues occurs, I believe, with *Wit at Several Weapons*. In both folios this play is treated as though it had no prologue and at the end is printed what purports to be "The Epilogue at the reviving of this Play." The error seems almost too obvious to note, but Oliphant writes of it as an "epilogue" and all editors seem to have thought of it as such. But clearly it is not an epilogue but a prologue. It begins, as do many of the other prologues, by reminding the audience of Fletcher's achievements in wit and closes with,

We'll not appeal unto those Gentlemen
Judge by their Cloaths, if they sit right, nor when
The Ladies smile, and with their Fanns delight
To whisk a clinch aside, then all goes right:
'Twas well receiv'd before, and we dare say,
You now are welcome to no vulgar play.

"When the Ladies smile" suggests anticipation, and the closing couplet makes it obvious that the lines were to be spoken before and not after the play was presented.

Several of the prologues contain estimates of the time to be required in acting the plays which follow, but unless the acting versions were considerably different from the texts we have, the authors seem to have given slight consideration to their estimates. *Two Noble Kinsmen* (85½ pages in the Cambridge edition) and *Love's Pilgrimage* (86½ pages) are each said to take two hours, while the much shorter *Lover's Progress* (77 pages) is said to require three hours—the same time as *The Loyal Subject* (92 pages), one fifth again as long. The explanation, however, may be that the first two prologues were written by the authors of the plays while the last two were prepared for revivals.

The ideas and the language of the prologues and epilogues, as I have already noted, are for the most part so alike as to render hazardous any effort to distinguish authorship by tracing verbal and mental similarities. Authors repeated both themselves and each other. Prologues written for revivals are phrased often in language paralleling closely that of original prologues one or two decades earlier. It seems, therefore, quite impossible to determine convincingly the history of most of the prologues which either do not definitely claim to have been composed when their plays were new or do not frankly admit that they were prepared for revivals. I wish, however, to question the usual ascription of one epilogue and two prologues. *The Mad Lover* with its prologue and epilogue is generally assigned wholly to Fletcher;[10] *The Spanish Curate* is divided between Fletcher and Massinger, the prologue ascribed to Fletcher and

[10] See Oliphant, *The Plays of Beaumont and Fletcher*, p. 142.

the epilogue to Massinger.[11]   But the ideas and phrasing of all
four seem to me so like Massinger's that I hesitatingly ask that
his claim be considered.   It is not necessary to assume that he
had a share in the composition of *The Mad Lover;* its prologue
and epilogue he may have penned for a revival as he must have
done for revivals of several other plays.   In neither is there a
statement that the play is new.   The epilogue to *The Spanish
Curate,* ascribed to Massinger, closes with the lines:

> Those are fair,
> And worthy love, that may destroy, but spare;

that of *The Mad Lover* with

> You may frown still,
> But 'tis the nobler way, to check the will.

It is quite possible that this idea is to be found in many authors.
It is, for instance, found in the closing lines of the song sung
in *The Chances* (II, ii):

> 'Tis god-like to have power, but not to kill;

but as this song was not in the play as printed in the First Folio,
it cannot be unquestionably given to Fletcher.   There are certainly few ideas which Massinger so frequently repeated.   In
The Maid of Honour (III, i), is given the Latin:

> in great minds
> *Posse et nolle, nobile;*

in *The Duke of Milan,* III, i:

> what a worthy thing it is
> To have power, and not to use it;

in *The Unnatural Combat:*

> To revenge
> An injury is proper to the wishes
> Of feeble women, that want strength to act it,
> But to have power to punish, and yet pardon,
> Peculiar to princes.

[11] See *ibid.,* p. 250.

In the prologue to *The Spanish Curate* and in both the prologue and epilogue to *The Mad Lover* there is another suggestion of Massinger in the extended metaphor from sailing—the only such metaphor in any of the prologues: the play is a bark, the approval of the audience the wind that, the poet hopes, will fill its sails. In the former play the prologue declares:

> Therefore I leave it [the play] to it self, and pray
> Like a good Bark, it may work out to day
> And stem all doubts; 'twas built for such a proof,
> And we hope highly: if she lye aloof
> For her own vantage, to give wind at will,
> Why let her work. . . .

And in *The Mad Lover:*

> . . . now to Sea we goe,
> Faire fortune with us, give us room, and blow;
> Remember ye 're all venturers; and in this Play
> How many twelve-pence ye have 'stow'd this day:
> Remember for return of your delight,
> We launch, and plough through storms of fear, and spight;
> Give us your fore-winds fairly, fill our wings,
> And steer us right, and as the Saylor sings,
> Loaden with Wealth, on wanton seas, so we
> Shall make our home-bound voyage chearfully.

Both of these prologues have been generally assigned to Fletcher, but that the figure is more characteristic of the style of Massinger is attested by Dr. Makkink's study, *Philip Massinger and John Fletcher, A Comparison.* Dr. Makkink observed:

Similes drawn from the observation of the sea, or the life of sailors are numerous in almost all *Massinger's* plays. . . . In several cases the word "bark" occurs. . . .

Similes drawn from the contemplation of the sea do not occur in *Fletcher's* works; those derived from the life of sailors are very insignificant in number; I have not been able to find more than four in all his plays.[12]

[12] H. J. Makkink (Rotterdam, 1927), p. 182. The four instances, which he cites in a footnote, are *Loyal Subject*, III, ii; *Women Pleased*, II, vi; *Wild-Goose Chase*, IV, i; *Chances*, I, x. As he cites neither of these prologues, Dr. Makkink apparently limited his examination to the plays proper.

Index